AMERICAN FANATICS

NORTH AMERICAN RELIGIONS

Series Editors: Tracy Fessenden (Arizona State University), Laura Levitt (Temple University), and Anthony Petro (Boston University)
Founding Editor: David Harrington Watt (Haverford College)

Since its inception, the North American Religions book series has steadily disseminated gracefully written, pathbreaking explorations of religion in North America. Books in the series move among the discourses of ethnographic, textual, and historical analysis and across a range of topics, including sound, story, food, nature, healing, crime, and pilgrimage. In so doing they bring religion into view as a style and form of belonging, a set of tools for living with and in relations of power, a mode of cultural production and reproduction, and a vast repertory of the imagination. Whatever their focus, books in the series remain attentive to the shifting and contingent ways in which religious phenomena are named, organized, and contested. They bring fluency in the best of contemporary theoretical and historical scholarship to bear on the study of religion in North America. The series focuses primarily, but not exclusively, on religion in the United States in the twentieth and twenty-first centuries.

Books in the Series

Ava Chamberlain, *The Notorious Elizabeth Tuttle: Marriage, Murder, and Madness in the Family of Jonathan Edwards*

Terry Rey and Alex Stepick, *Crossing the Water and Keeping the Faith: Haitian Religion in Miami*

Isaac Weiner, *Religion Out Loud: Religious Sound, Public Space, and American Pluralism*

Hillary Kaell, *Walking Where Jesus Walked: American Christians and Holy Land Pilgrimage*

Brett Hendrickson, *Border Medicine: A Transcultural History of Mexican American Curanderismo*

Jodi Eichler-Levine, *Suffer the Little Children: Uses of the Past in Jewish and African American Children's Literature*

Annie Blazer, *Playing for God: Evangelical Women and the Unintended Consequences of Sports Ministry*

Elizabeth Pérez, *Religion in the Kitchen: Cooking, Talking, and the Making of Black Atlantic Traditions*

Kerry Mitchell, *Spirituality and the State: Managing Nature and Experience in America's National Parks*

Finbarr Curtis, *The Production of American Religious Freedom*

M. Cooper Harriss, *Ralph Ellison's Invisible Theology*

Ari Y. Kelman, *Shout to the Lord: Making Worship Music in Evangelical America*

Joshua Dubler and Isaac Weiner, *Religion, Law, USA*

Shari Rabin, *Jews on the Frontier: Religion and Mobility in Nineteenth Century America*

Elizabeth Fenton, *Old Canaan in a New World: Native Americans and the Lost Tribes of Israel*

Alyssa Maldonado-Estrada, *Lifeblood of the Parish: Masculinity and Catholic Devotion in Williamsburg, Brooklyn*

Caleb Iyer Elfenbein, *Fear in Our Hearts: What Islamophobia Tells Us About America*

Rachel B. Gross, *Beyond the Synagogue: Jewish Nostalgia as Religious Practice*

Jenna Supp-Montgomerie, *When the Medium Was the Mission: The Religious Origins of Network Culture*

Philippa Koch, *The Course of God's Providence: Religion, Health, and the Body in Early America*

Jennifer Scheper Hughes, *The Church of the Dead: The Epidemic of 1576 and the Birth of Christianity in the Americas*

Sylvester Johnson and Tisa Wenger, *On Imperial Grounds: New Histories of Religion and US Empire*

Deborah Dash Moore, *Vernacular Religion: Collected Essays of Leonard Primiano*

Katrina Daly Thompson, *Muslims on the Margins: Creating Queer Religious Community in North America*

Jonathan H. Ebel, *From Dust They Came: Government Camps and the Religion of Reform in New Deal California*

Gale L. Kenny, *Christian Imperial Feminism: White Protestant Women and the Consecration of Empire*

Leslie Beth Ribovich, *Without a Prayer: Religion and Race in New York City Public Schools*

Amanda J. Baugh, *Falling in Love with Nature: The Values of Latinx Catholic Environmentalism*

George González, *The Church of Stop Shopping and Religious Activism: Combatting Consumerism and Climate Change through Performance*

Candace Lukasik, *Martyrs and Migrants: Coptic Christians and the Persecution Politics of US Empire*

Aram G. Sarkisian, *Orthodoxy on the Line: Russian Orthodox Christians and Labor Migration in the Progressive Era*

Jeffrey Wheatley, *American Fanatics: Religion, Rebellion, and Empire in the Nineteenth Century*

American Fanatics

*Religion, Rebellion, and Empire
in the Nineteenth Century*

Jeffrey Wheatley

New York University Press

New York

NEW YORK UNIVERSITY PRESS
New York
www.nyupress.org

© 2026 by New York University
All rights reserved

Library of Congress Cataloging-in-Publication Data
Names: Wheatley, Jeffrey author
Title: American fanatics : religion, rebellion, and empire in the nineteenth century / Jeffrey Wheatley.
Other titles: Policing fanaticism, religion, & race in the American empire, 1830 1930
Description: New York : New York University Press, [2026] | Series: North American religions | Enhanced and updated version of the author's thesis (doctoral)—Northwestern University, 2020. | Includes bibliographical references and index.
Identifiers: LCCN 2025028435 (print) | LCCN 2025028436 (ebook) | ISBN 9781479825448 hardback | ISBN 9781479825455 paperback | ISBN 9781479825462 ebook | ISBN 9781479825479 ebook other
Subjects: LCSH: Religion and sociology—United States—History—19th century | Religious fanaticism—United States—History—19th century
Classification: LCC BL60 .W486 2026 (print) | LCC BL60 (ebook)
LC record available at https://lccn.loc.gov/2025028435
LC ebook record available at https://lccn.loc.gov/2025028436

This book is printed on acid-free paper, and its binding materials are chosen for strength and durability. We strive to use environmentally responsible suppliers and materials to the greatest extent possible in publishing our books.

The manufacturer's authorized representative in the EU for product safety is Mare Nostrum Group B.V., Doelen 72, 4831 GR Breda, The Netherlands. Email: gpsr@mare-nostrum.co.uk.

Manufactured in the United States of America

10 9 8 7 6 5 4 3 2 1

Also available as an ebook

For my parents, Janeen and Jack Wheatley

For colonialism, this vast continent was a den of savages, infested with superstitions and fanaticism, destined to be despised, cursed by God, a land of cannibals.
—Frantz Fanon, *The Wretched of the Earth*

Much Madness is divinest Sense—
To a discerning Eye—
Much Sense—the starkest Madness—
'Tis the Majority
In this, as all, prevail—
Assent—and you are sane—
Demur—you're straightway dangerous—
And handled with a Chain—
—Emily Dickinson, "Much Madness is divinest Sense"

CONTENTS

Introduction: The Politics of Fanaticism ... 1

1. Evangelical Enthusiasm: Revivals and Early Theories of Fanaticism ... 25

2. The Figure of the Fanatic: Nat Turner and Black Religion ... 49

3. The Feminine Fanatic: Love and Betrayal in Anti-Abolitionist Literature ... 72

4. The Fanatic Mind: Psychiatry, Law, and the Case of Charles Guiteau ... 91

5. Policing Fanaticism Abroad: Militant Prophets in US-Occupied Philippines ... 116

6. Enthusiasm Against Fanaticism: The US Empire and Its Critics ... 155

Conclusion ... 169

Acknowledgments ... 175

Notes ... 177

Bibliography ... 195

Index ... 207

About the Author ... 219

Introduction

The Politics of Fanaticism

The story goes like this. In the early 1900s, a spiritual being radiating a bright light descended upon the city of Tayabas in the Philippines. Amid the crowd that formed to witness the spectacle was Ruperto Rios, a local military chief. The spirit pointed to Rios and bestowed upon him supernatural power and significance. In the wake of this revelation, Rios began to talk of building in the Philippines a "New Jerusalem," a reference to Revelation 21. He would help lead the way to this utopia, claiming himself as the rightful Pope and the Son of God. Some citizens of the Tayabas region, and especially those facing economic distress, found his vision compelling. "Rios," according to one of his followers, "was a direct descendant of God and nothing earthly could harm him."[1] Over time, he was able to establish himself as a militant messianic authority figure.

Rios's religious and political mission emerged within the context of Filipino resistance to colonialism and Euro-American racial governance. Filipinos, including Rios, fought for independence against Spain in the 1890s. Many continued to resist as the United States claimed and occupied the Philippines in the wake of the Spanish-American War. Rios, as part of an ongoing guerrilla warfare campaign against the United States, situated himself within Christian narratives and circulated sacred Indigenous objects, called *anting anting*, that provided powers to his followers. These objects, which were often small charms, provided a variety of abilities, including protection from bullets. Rios himself possessed an especially powerful anting anting that served as a ritualistic and symbolic testament to his power: a wooden chest with the word *independencia* carved into it. Rios told his followers that he would soon open the chest. At that moment, one report from the US Secretary of War stated, "'Independence' would jump out, they could catch her and be ever afterwards happy."² The spirit would bring about a new reign in the Philippines. If Rios's soldiers kept fighting, then eventually the time would come to open the chest. Just around the corner, Rios envisioned a Philippines that had no US military presence, no taxes, no private property, and no jails.

US government agents, military officials, and the press categorized Rios as a religious fanatic. His independencia chest was "fanatical paraphernalia" that he used to manipulate the "dense ignorance and credulity" of his followers.³ Papa Rios was not the only Filipino called a fanatic. He was one among several militant messianic figures actively resisting US rule in the early 1900s. Others included men such as Papa Isio, Felipe Salvador, and Santa Iglesia. Women, too, played an important role in these movements, often creating and circulating anting anting. Americans reductively explained resistance to be a result of an undeveloped, superstitious form of religion constituted by a mix of Catholicism, Indigenous traditions, and, in the south of the archipelago, Islam. Going further, many US officials argued that the presence of such politicized and prophetic religion was a sign of the racial inferiority of Filipinos, whom white US soldiers often referred to using anti-Black slurs.⁴ Such categorizations transmuted a colonial occupation into a race war on religious fanaticism.⁵

The alleged fanaticism of Filipinos produced awe and disgust among Americans. Consider the language used by Vic Hurley, a military officer who chronicled US conflicts in the Philippines in the early twentieth century. "The fanatic," Hurley described as he relayed an account of Rios's captured fighters, "rolled his glistening eyes as he drank in the thought of the approach of the millennium."⁶ Such sensationalist representations of the fanatical enemy that circulated in US media had a blunt political purpose to legitimate US rule and superiority. However, this went beyond rhetoric. Concern about religious fanaticism also influenced military strategies. US forces confiscated Rios's independencia chest on March 8, 1903. They captured and executed Rios that June. The *Chicago Daily Tribune* headline phrased the news in a peculiar and telling way: "Rios Sentenced to Hang: Fanatical Filipino Leader Must Suffer Death Penalty."⁷ Not "will" suffer—"must" suffer. For US authorities, these figures cultivated religious movements that did not deserve freedom or recognition as true religion. Instead, Rios's supernatural claims were a racial problem in need of governmental policing as part of a project of pacification.

This book began as a research project on US representations of superstitions in the Philippines. I quickly discovered the prominence of the language of fanaticism, often coupled with the language of superstition, in US War Department reports, newspapers, sermons, and anthropological studies of Filipino religion and culture. The term was everywhere. I could not help but see parallels to my teenage years when the War on Terror ushered in a new wave of anti-Islamic sentiment. Even though "fanatics" like Rios were few and far between, US officials treated these religious figures as emblematic of Filipinos as a people, a perilous presumption considering the diversity of the archipelago. I began to discern that all of this "fanaticism talk," to adapt Tisa Wenger's phrasing of "religious freedom talk," was a way of racializing Filipinos *through* a particular fixation on Filipino religion, here rendered as irrational, primitive, radicalizing, and violent.[8] This framing conveniently left out the political aims of Rios and downplayed other, less fantastical anticolonial movements.[9] It also belied the fact that Filipino religious resistance movements emerged as responses to Spanish and US imperialism, both of which had their supernatural rationales to legitimate violence and motivate soldiers to fight. Turn-of-the-century US imperialism was fueled by a variety of factors. One of these factors was a white Protestantism enthusiastic in its divine duty to Christianize and civilize, through violence if necessary. Rios's marshaling of religion for combat and to imagine a new political order mirrored US colonial officials' use of religion to assert superiority and expand US power.

I began to research the history, rationales, and effects of the concept of fanaticism in US history. When did this term become popular? What other religious communities had been categorized as fanatics? What historical theories of fanaticism were Americans drawing on? Some historians and religious studies scholars of the United States have studied fanaticism by focusing on isolated uses against marginalized religious groups, such as the Church of Jesus Christ of Latter-day Saints and Black religious movements.[10] Scholars have given the term's use in the colonial era more sustained attention. In her history of the psychology of religion, for example, Ann Taves examines the apologetics of Protestant ministers during the First Great Awakening over the theological merit and propriety of revivals. Some, like Charles Chauncy, argued that revivals relied too much upon excessive rituals, the manipulation of passionate feelings, and dubious claims about the effects of the Holy Spirit. Others, like Jonathan Edwards, offered moderate defenses of revivals. Both sides wielded the language of fanaticism and enthusiasm. Fanaticism, in this early era, was a subcategory to the more common charge of enthusiasm, and writers rarely provided clarity on the difference between them. The earliest concerns about fanaticism in the United States, then, revolved around white Protestants, and specifically an early form of what scholars now call evangelicalism. This seems a far cry from how Americans, especially the white Protestant men who held political and religious power, confidently contrasted Filipino fanaticism with the rationality, freedom, and modernity of US religion. However, these two scenes share a complex history.

This book tells this history by analyzing, comparing, and connecting select moments of fanaticism talk in the United States. The story begins in the early 1800s as Protestant evangelicals began to differentiate fanaticism and enthusiasm in terms of definition and moral evaluation. It ends in an era of evangelical and imperial enthusiasm directed, in part, against fanaticism as a global problem. This story features a wide range of people with diverse social positions and agendas. The cast of characters consists of many well-known figures, including the antislavery rebel Nat Turner, the revivalist Charles Finney, the novelist Harriet Beecher Stowe, and the social gospeler Josiah Strong. It also features figures whose relevance to US religion and the concept of fanaticism is not so obvious. These include the English theologian Isaac Taylor, the Iowan poet Rebecca Harrington Smith, the psychiatrist John Gray, and the anthropologist Dean Worcester. It does not give extensive attention to European philosophers such as Hume, Locke, Kant, Hegel, and Marx. Their brief writings on fanaticism have received due attention, and I do not see substantial evidence of their direct influence on nineteenth-century US theories of fanaticism.

This book's aim is not to provide a better, more objective theory of fanaticism, nor is its goal to make a pronouncement about who the "real" fanatics are. That said, following in the work of Talal Asad, I do point out how alarmism over fanatical violence has perpetuated *and* obscured the violence of the secular state by rendering it as legitimate and normal.¹¹ The same obscuring function applies to Christian-legitimated violence against fanatics (many of whom, such as Rios, were Christian themselves). This book is an inquiry into the applications and trajectory of fanaticism as a political term whose import emerged in the context of social conflicts, projects of governance, and lived religious realities.

This book makes two related arguments, the first historical, the second theoretical. The historical argument is that Americans in the nineteenth century transformed fanaticism from a concept rooted in Protestant theological apologetics to one used in service of religio-racial governance, a concept I will expand on below. Protestant evangelicals increasingly worked to shed the accusation of fanaticism by emphasizing a fine difference between fanaticism and enthusiasm. This rejected an Enlightenment-style understanding of religion as properly and essentially about belief or a moral code. Instead, intellectuals and religious authority figures argued that religion was based in sentiment. The question of what counted as fanatical became the specific sentiments (love, hate, fear, joy) and their intensity. Enthusiasm, of the Protestant variety, was necessary for the morality and vitality of the United States, including, at times, its imperialism and racial hierarchies. Theologians and secular authorities in this era heralded the sentiment of universal Christian love and contrasted it with the sentiments of hate and exclusion attributed to other traditions. Consider the harmful stereotypes of the self-hating Catholic, the angry Muslim, the greedy Jew, and the provincial heathen. Novel claims about the US nation and empire as a force for combatting religious fanaticism became a powerful legitimation and a strategic goal across diverse fields of US theology, literature, law, military, and psychiatry. Influential figures in these fields envisioned a US nation driven by Christian enthusiasm to govern populations at home and to civilize the hordes of fanatics abroad.

This way of imagining social order and the problem of fanaticism emerged, in part and not reducibly, from the parallel projects of slavery and imperialism. This way of imagining social order was also tied to the growth of evangelicalism, a religion of heart and sentiment that has done much in service of justice and peace and much in service of injustice and violence. To be clear from the beginning, my argument is not that evangelicalism or Protestant Christianity is inherently racist or imperialist. And I am not arguing that evangelicalism was the only force driving white supremacy or imperialism. Both claims are simplistic and veer into the dangerous territory of essentializing evangelicalism, a transcultural movement that has had diverse relationships to the US nation and imperialism. My argument, to put it another way, is that there emerged a style of talking about religion and talking about race that relied upon the threat of the fanatic to bolster projects of religious and racial governance within which white Protestant evangelicalism was represented as the measure and destiny of humanity.

Secularism and the Modern Reinvention of Fanaticism

This book's theoretical argument is that fanaticism came to serve a key role in the repertoire of secularism, allowing Americans to claim the ideal of religious freedom while targeting select religious beliefs and practices as existentially threatening to that freedom. Secularism is a messy word because people use it in diverse ways. Despite this messiness, secularism is an indispensable concept for scholarship on religion in modernity. I do not mean secularism as an ideology that is wholly hostile to religion but secularism as the narrative and ideology that modern societies are different from premodern societies because they appropriately separate and define the religious from the secular, governing each into their proper roles. Religion, in the secular frame, is supposed to be relatively private, voluntary, tolerant, and amicable with the existing social order. The secular—the space of reason, liberal deliberation, and neutrality regarding religious issues—is the domain of the state, the public sphere, and scientific inquiry. A critical approach to secularism helps reveal how religion is a modern concept whose use is shaped by political (that is, normative) considerations. Historically, fanatical religion is *like* but not quite religion, at least the kind of religion that deserves social legitimation and government protection.

As a number of scholars who study secularism critically have argued, this very distinction and corresponding definitions of the religious and the secular emerged within the Christian West. They gained much of their power because Westerners used them to justify and guide projects of colonialism and slavery. It is within a secular framework that the problem of fanaticism has become intelligible and given moral urgency. This book is one of the many works of scholarship that respond, directly or indirectly, to a question asked by Ann Pellegrini and Janet R. Jakobsen: "If what gives secularism its moral import is its promise of universality and reasonableness as distinct from the narrowness and fanaticism of religion, what does it mean that this universalism and the rationality it embodies are actually particular (to European history) and religious (Protestant) in form?"[12] The figure of the fanatic, with their unmediated revelations, their radical challenges to the existing social order, and their putative certitude, breaks from the expected secular governance of religion and the separation of secular reasoning and religious faith. A brief survey of fanaticism's etymology will help explain this argument and set the stage for my focus on the nineteenth century.

When using the words "fanatic," "fanatical," and "fanaticism," we are participating in a long history of these concepts that predates modern secularism and dates to ancient Rome. The Latin *fanum* simply described a sacred place. A *fanaticus* was a person possessed or inspired by a god or goddess. A fanaticus could be portrayed positively or negatively. Some ancient uses of fanaticus referred to religious phenomena that the writer viewed as reasonable. Fanatics could be real or fake, good or bad. In contrast, the modern concepts of fanatic, fanatical, and fanaticism are politically and morally charged. Further, many commentators view fanaticism as a perennial social problem that existentially threatens the modern secular ideals of civil society, democracy, liberalism, and freedom. David Brooks, for example, has called the twenty-first century an "age of fanaticism."[13] Though I have all sorts of personal concerns about religion and politics today, I am not convinced that we are in an age of fanaticism, at least in any way that is exceptional within human history. Human history is full of the diverse forms of passion, supernaturalism, and conviction that get packaged and pressed together into a totalizing, pathologizing accusation of fanaticism. But we are, certainly, in an age of alarm over fanaticism. To call someone a fanatic is to prevent further inquiry, nuance, and contextualization. It is a conversation stopper. To be called a fanatic is damning.

The first step in a robust critical analysis of fanaticism is to question representations of fanatics as, simply and reducibly, delusional or bloodthirsty. The concept of fanaticism can *seem* like it explains behavior, but it is trapped in its own circular logic. Fanatics are fanatical because of their fanaticism. Shallow uses of the term are present in news media, government agency reports, and scholarship. Consider this fictional anecdote that opens up the 2009 article "Pluralism: An Antidote for Fanaticism, the Delusion of Our Age" by psychologists George S. Howard and Cody D. Christopherson:

> A suicide bomber on a bus sweats as he passes the last seconds of the lives of everyone on that bus. All will die because of a lack of pluralism. The bomber can only think of his hatred for the west or the paradise that awaits him. If he were a pluralist he would think (along with William James), "How goes it for the rest of the universe if I end our lives in this manner?" Concretely, he might ask, "What if God's name is Jesus not Allah?" "What if the concept of God is a delusion?" . . . And with that the bomber pulls out the wire which disarms the bomb. The group of fellow travelers does not know how close they came to death. Except he will not disarm the bomb because he is a fanatic and not a pluralist.[14]

This is all too easy and comforting for the authors of the article. Even as a piece of fiction, this anecdote is part of a troubling pattern. The fanatic here has no personal background, no social context, no politics, and no motivation besides hate, certitude, and a *lack* of rationality and tolerance. They have no name. Further, the passage implies that the bomber is Muslim (consider the language of "paradise") and that their Islamic faith obstructs a pluralistic ethics. Their Islamic faith is explicitly contrasted with Christianity (the possibility of thinking that "God's name is Jesus") and with atheism ("What if the concept of God is a delusion?"). Instead of imagining a robust, substantial pluralism, this article re-creates hackneyed anti-Islamic stereotypes and implicitly links Christianity with liberal views. This is exactly what I urge we avoid: representing "fanatics" as abstracted figures engulfed in unthinking delusions as a way to bolster one's preferred ideology—William James's pluralism and pragmatism, I suppose.

Before we dive more into the question of *how* to analyze accusations of fanaticism, some history is in order to explain why the Howard and Christopherson anecdote may feel like common sense. To begin broadly, when did the semantic shift from relative neutrality to near certain denunciation occur? In the sixteenth and seventeenth centuries, variations of the term "fanatic" spread through German (*schwärmer*),

French (*fanatique, phanatique*), and English (*fanatic, fanatick*, or *phanatick*). The first recorded use of fanatic in English was in 1525. Fanatical popped up in in 1550, fanaticism in 1652.[15] The Protestant Reformation and its effects contributed to this revival of the concept. Europeans used the term as Protestants and Catholics battled over the nature of salvation and as Protestant groups argued over the content and scope of true Christian reform. Martin Luther used the term *schwärmer*, which English writers have largely translated as enthusiast or fanatic, in theological attacks on the papacy, the Anabaptists in Münster, and the German Peasants' Revolt. He based schwärmer on the metaphor of a swarming of bees—an irrational swirl of theological ideas disconnected from biblical truth. When Luther used this term against his opponents, he was arguing that their inspiration was demonic. The fanatics' beliefs constituted a false form of Christianity, and their actions were dangerous to the early modern social order. As such, schwärmer signaled the outer boundary of tolerance and necessitated princely authorities to use their powers—including state violence—to defend true Christianity.[16]

In the wake of the Reformation, a host of Western philosophers raised new questions about religious tolerance, discerning truth in a fractured Western Christendom, and the ideal relationship between church and state. Fanaticism became an important term for political theory and the Enlightenment value of reason. As Dominique Colas argues, denunciations of fanaticism are at "the very heart of modern conceptions of the political."[17] The philosopher of classical liberalism John Locke, for example, believed that fanaticism was defined by an overconfident certitude of one's beliefs and a lack of rational judgment. As Douglas John Casson has summarized, Locke's imagined fanatic figure was an "unregulated self" who failed "to govern themselves according to a criterion that lies outside of their beliefs and desires."[18] The fanatic figure served as a foil for Locke's vision of the proper self-governing liberal subject.

In his 1764 essay "Essay on the Maladies of the Head," philosopher Immanuel Kant began to describe fanaticism as a corruption of human nature and reason. He highlighted it as a dire problem:

> Things stand quite differently with the fanatic (visionary, enthusiast). The latter is properly a deranged person with presumed immediate inspira-

tion and a great familiarity with the powers of the heavens. Human nature knows no more dangerous illusion. If its outbreak is new, if the deceived human being has talents and the masses are prepared to diligently accept this leaven, then even the state occasionally suffers raptures. Enthusiasm leads the exalted person to extremes, Muhammad to the prince's throne and John of Leyden to the scaffold.[19]

Locke and Kant were invested, philosophically, in the rationalization of religion and marking the proper limits of religion in a modern society. One could view this trajectory from Luther to Enlightenment figures like Locke and Kant as a secularization narrative, wherein philosophers shifted the method of combatting fanaticism from heralding true Christianity to heralding a universal secular reason. Fanaticism was not caused by the devil so much as distinct psychological and sociological phenomena that could be studied, and perhaps remedied, through scientific methods and proper secular governance. Spread the gospel of reason. Subordinate the supernatural to the natural. Define religion as a set of beliefs or a moral code that could play nice with given social norms. The will must triumph over the passions. There is something to this secularization narrative, but it neglects the contingency of what counts as religious and what counts as secular. This is where the concept of secularism comes in.

Reviewing the state of critical secularism studies, Charles McCrary and I have surveyed two key insights: the "Protestant secular" and secularism as a strategy of governance.[20] Critical analyses of the Protestant secular, or how Protestant norms and authorities have wielded power over what counts as religious and what counts as secular, have become a common framework for secularism studies, at least those that focus on historically Protestant-majority societies, such as the United States. Tracy Fessenden, for example, examines how specific forms of Protestantism came to be overrepresented as the model of proper "Christianity" and "religion." Further, she examines how the Protestant emphasis on individualism, self-governance, and agency came to be the norm for protecting not just "true religion" but the ability of a people to live within a secular modern political order. The effects of this are worth quoting at length:

The co-implication of secularism and Reformed Christianity has meant, for example, that Christian religious polemic could remain compatible with America's vaunted history of religious liberty and toleration by being cast in strictly secular terms. Thus at various points in American history, Muslims, Catholics, or Mormons could be construed as enemies of republican institutions, Jews as a racial or economic threat, and Native American ritual practice as an affront to environmental or drug policy, all without apparent violence to cherished notions of religious freedom.[21]

The language of fanaticism facilitates a particular Protestant hegemony in representing fanatics as a threat simultaneously to true religion (of voluntary faith, the Bible, or spiritual evolution) and to true secular values (of individuality, reason, or mental health). This is a profound irony considering that the origins of US concern over fanaticism fixated on evangelical styles of belief (individualistic faith) and ritual (revivalism with its confidence to effect born again conversions).

If examining the enduring relevance of Protestant concerns in conceptualizations of fanaticism is one part of critical secularism studies, the other is how secularism operates as a strategy of governance. The concept of fanaticism is not just defined by a universal template of secularism. It is rather constantly being deployed and adjusted in efforts to govern communities that are rightly or wrongly viewed as "unruly," that is, resistant to such governance. As Jason Josephson-Storm puts it, secularism is part of a modern discursive framework that governs through distinctions, subjecting beliefs and practices to legitimation (the secular), toleration (religion), or banishment (things that are "not-quite-religion," as I have put it, like fanaticism).[22] Generally speaking, this tripartite way of dividing human beliefs and practices serves the interests of dominant groups of people, religious institutions, and the secular state. What is "not-quite-religion"? In addition to fanaticism, specific terms that fit into this category and have received scholarly attention include superstitions, cults, heathenism, fetishism, scams, and animism.[23]

All of these terms share "building blocks" commonly associated with "religion." They entail supernatural beings and forces. Rituals.

Authority figures. Sacred time, objects, and space. Myths. Ethics. Symbolism. These building blocks are the data of the academic study of religion, as I teach in my classes. Despite so much overlap, the secular frame insists on our capacity and duty to sunder religious fanaticism from religion proper. Fanaticism violates the conceptual boundaries of religion, at times through embracing violence, at times through its confidence in direct, contemporary revelations, and at times through a sense of undue means of recruiting followers ("brainwashing" of "cults" in today's parlance). Fanatics, having lost themselves in a delusional religious mission, have forfeited their individual willpower and use of reason. Religious fanaticism operates as simultaneously too much religion and the antithesis of religion. The secular political rationality pressures and at times demands that religions (selectively chosen) rein in their passions, minimize supernaturalism, sniff out insincerity, break apart any political use of religion. Scholars of religion, of course, can and should blur the lines between religion proper and its negatives. But for many agents of modern states and secular knowledge, these are, or at least should be, mutually exclusive realms, each accorded a different political valuation and form of governance, from granting freedom to military intervention.

Part of the horror and fascination with Ruperto Rio's independencia chest is that, in the colonial secular frame, he seemed to confuse the secular political ideal of independence with supernatural power. For Rios and many of his followers, operating with a Christian messianic and supernatural worldview, this made good sense and served as a powerful motivation. For the United States, the chest and spiritual sense of independence constituted an irrational categorical confusion, despite the many supernatural notions underpinning American understandings of freedom. States work to ensure such secularist separation through various apparatuses that have different goals and rationales. The state, which includes agencies of education, law, zoning, taxation, immigration, is not monolithic. Further, as this book shows, the forms of governance believed to be needed to prevent or combat fanaticism are not limited to states. Individuals, religious communities, and secular sciences such as psychiatry all have ideas and practices of governance that are part of a secular imaginary within which religion is a discrete phenomenon in need of careful management for the sake of modern liberal society. State agencies exist alongside a web of other institutions, communities, and media that, in often contested ways, have shaped the meanings of fanaticism and deployed it in efforts to govern behavior, identities, and practices of people at home and abroad.

Religion, Race, and Affectability

It is probably obvious by now that I do not think that Americans in the nineteenth century or today have used the concept of fanaticism in neutral, fair, or consistent ways. Humans use words not merely to describe the world around us but to extend our own preconceived worldviews and power. Novel uses and theories of fanaticism emerged at the intersection of writings by intellectuals and the prerogatives of projects of governance, especially the slave regime and Anglo-American imperialism. Because of the demands of legitimation and governance, writings about fanaticism increasingly emphasized fanatical religion as a marker of essential, racial difference. Fanatics may be individual figures leading a small community, but, in this secular and colonial framework, their presence implied a dire affectability—the gross generalization that there are whole groupings of humans who are unable to self-govern, reason, or develop civilization due to excessive supernatural delusions, passions, or sacred violence. Fanatical religion, here, stands in opposition to "true religion," a key concept for the Protestant secular. John Modern has summarized the essence of Protestant "true religion" as belief that is "conceived of as a choice rather than an obligation, the cause of practice rather than the effect."[24] Though some Americans wondered if Rios was a confidence man, most believed that even if he started as one he had become psychologically absorbed in his own delusions. Fanatics do not choose fanaticization. I refer to the emphasis on fanaticism as an affective phenomenon as "religio-racial affectability." Fanatics as affectable subjects—at times with a focus on fanatical leaders who receive revelations and at times with a focus on fanatical followers and their credulity—is a recurring theme in the chapters that follow.

Throughout the nineteenth century, public concern over fanatical Protestant revivalism shifted to an emphasis on the fanaticism of nonwhite and non-Protestant groups, including Black Americans, Jews, Catholics, Muslims, and Filipinos. Consider the scene of the

Filipino rebel rolling his "glistening eyes" as he was affected by Rios's vision of the coming millennium. Or consider the fictional anecdote of the suicide bomber driven purely by hate. The "problem" of these rebels was not just cognitive. It was not about choices made. The problem was affective. Their religious sentiments had overwhelmed their sense of reasoning agency and thus signaled a weak constitution to begin with. The sign of Filipino or Islamic racial inferiority for many white people, was not just skin color, but religious beliefs, practices, and affects. The idea of fanatics as having corrupted forms of agency was one powerful way that Americans constructed religious and racial hierarchies. Such constructions, of course, always came with debate and contestation, especially among those targeted as inferior in such rubrics.

This book's primary argument, as I have stated, is that fanaticism came to be a key term of "religio-racial governance." This requires elaboration. First, recent scholarship has complicated the understanding of religion as belief and race as identity based on skin color. Judith Weisenfeld has popularized the concept of "religio-racial," which I adopt and adapt in this book in a number of ways. Her focus in the impeccably researched book *New World A-Coming* is the self-identifications of groups such as the Nation of Islam and Father Divine's Peace Mission, both of which defy any neat separation between religious identity and racial identity. Weisenfeld gestures toward a broader power structure within which these Black communities are operating: "All religious groups in the United States could be characterized as religio-racial ones, given the deeply powerful, if sometimes veiled, ways the American system of racial hierarchy has structured religious beliefs, practices, and institutions for all people."[25] My use of religio-racial is less about self-identification, which is Weisenfeld's focus, and more about projects of governance and corresponding imaginaries that, through the language of fanaticism, measure racial supremacy/inferiority through the capacity of religious self-governance and moderation. I find it telling that many of the so-called fanatics in the chapters that follow received that label because of claims of divine revelation that foretold and sanctified an alternative social order and that they did so precisely in contexts where alternatives to the categorical and structural norms felt impossible.

As Weisenfeld informs my use of "religio-racial," Sylvester Johnson informs my use of governance. In *African American Religions, 1500–2000: Colonialism, Democracy, and Freedom,* Johnson situates the production of religious and racial identities within practices of colonial governance. "As a political formation," Johnson writes, "race is made through granting to some people the privilege of membership in the political community (the body politic) of the ruling polity while ruling others as a dominated population *perpetually* and *ineluctably* alien to that governing polity."²⁶ By focusing on who governs and whom is governed by state power, Johnson opens up analyses of race to consider the wide variety of markers of difference used to justify racial governance. Taking a broad view of history, skin color has been one increasingly important marker of race, but it has existed alongside, and sometimes competed with, religion, language, culture, nationality, and civilization. The idea that some groups of people are more susceptible to radicalization through religious affects is also an important method of race-making in the modern world. This is more than just discourse, or at least discourse as it is sometimes considered (errantly) as merely language games. As Vincent Lloyd has called for, "secularism should be addressed not just as the management of discourse but also as the management of practices and bodies."²⁷ Because of limits of the archives and the necessary media to tell a broad story of fanaticism as a concept, this book does not always live up to this call. Still, the chapters, together, show the utility of situating discourse within broader aims and problems of governance and on-the-ground effects.

Asserting that fanaticism is part of the repertoire of secular racial governance means that scholars should approach the figure of the fanatic not as a fact but as a tool Americans—and those subject to American power—used within specific conflicts. This use most often entailed demonizing rhetoric, but could also entail cultivating powerful feelings, or affects, of hatred, disgust, love, anger, or fear. American representations of fanatics aimed to create an affective response of disgust and otherness. The term's history and the way it pathologizes one's opponents without regard to nuance or context serves as a warning sign to not take deployments of it at face value. This is not to say that every use of "fanaticism" is inherently about race or racist, or even necessarily purely contrived. But I do contend that, increasingly throughout the nineteenth century, Americans conceptualized fanaticism as not just about irrational beliefs in the supernatural, but as signifying one's racial constitution—essential, inherited properties of mind and body used to create hierarchies of political and social legitimation.

To capture the logic, or illogic, of fanaticism-talk, I use and develop the idea of "affectability." Fanatics in the nineteenth century were often described as "affected," meaning that their individual agency or willpower has been compromised by passionate feelings, supernatural delusions, or undue submission to rebel religious authority figures. As was the case in US discourse about Filipinos, the presence of fanaticism suggested an excessive affectability signified a compromised ability govern, or moderate, themselves appropriately.[28] White Americans contrasted the affectability of Filipino religions, and many other marginalized religions examined in this book, with their own sincere religious beliefs, which they imagined to have individually and rationally chose. Consider also the imagined fanatic figure in Christopherson and Howard's article. The suicide bomber on the bus "can only think of hatred for the west or the paradise that awaits him."[29] The fanatic *can only* think or feel the all-consuming their hatred and delusional worldview. The figure of the fanatic is an inverse of the figure of the free person. Political theorist Wendy Brown succinctly framed a similar dichotomy as "who has religion" and "who is religion."[30] More specifically, the construction of the racialized fanatic is also the construction of the modern, often white, sincere believer, which, as Charles McCrary has examined, has a privileged position in American culture and law as the essence of true religion.[31]

I see my attention to affectability as a way that scholars may continue to study the co-constituted nature of religion and race in novel ways. I first encountered the concept of affectability through Denise Ferreira da Silva, who describes it as a way in which modern racial distinctions hinge on who is affectable and who is affective.[32] Adapting da Silva's conceptualization, this project suggests that affectability is as much a concept of religion-making as it is of race-making. Further, the analytic of affectability might help scholars of religion better show the intersection of religion-making and race-making. Scholar of religion Robert Orsi has argued that modern distinctions between good and bad religion often pivot on ideas of supernatural presence and how humans relate to supernatural presence. "To be a modern person," Orsi writes, "meant precisely to free oneself from superstitious and infantile subservience to, and dependence upon, supernatural figures, those really present in bread and wine, as well as those in plaster, paint, water, and rock."[33] This progression of humans out of the enthrallment of premodern religion into Protestantism and/or secular subjectivity is part of what anthropologist Webb Keane has called the "moral narrative of modernity."[34] We have, or must, disenchant ourselves. Fanatics have not just been unmodern figures but figures who defy, at times rhetorically and at times violently, the expectations of modern religion and modern race. I worry about the modern secular demands placed, selectively, on religious communities and traditions that present strong critiques, grounded in their own rationales, against modern norms of knowledge and social order.

For all of my critiques of the concept of fanaticism, I do not always view it, reducibly, as a mere rhetoric of power that manufactures reality. Sometimes it is! But this book balances the critique of the politics of religious fanaticism as a concept with the reality that rebellious, and even violent, movements have historically drawn on ideas both religious (related to sacred powers) and political (related to the order of state and society). Scholar of religion Dana Logan has persuasively argued for a similar nuance to "cults" and the reality of coercion.[35] Some groups studied in this book were even open to the charge of fanaticism. They adopted and performed being fanatical. They claimed divine revelations, cultivated heated affects, and legitimated sacred violence. Crucially, they had their own goals, reasons, and strategies. Calls for radical action based on divine revelations have been a powerful force in history, especially, though certainly not exclusively, for marginalized communities. Among the contributions I hope for this book, one is that it can be a model of how to study contested terms (e.g., "fanaticism," "cults," "fetishism") with attention to their political uses and attention to the actual political and religious beliefs and practices of those subject to such terms. Admittedly, accessing these beliefs and practices can be difficult in some cases due to limited and biased archives. For example, the majority of primary sources for chapter 5 on the US occupation of the Philippines are filtered through the US colonial government. My point, however, remains that the concept of fanaticism is deployed within webs of multiple agents, though not with equal power or effect.

Another limit of this book is that it is not a comprehensive account of every usage or group accused of being fanatical. Most religions in the United States have been accused of fanaticism at one time or another, meaning a comprehensive account would require multiple volumes. With greater time and space, this book could include attention to many other communities: Joseph Smith and the LDS Church, Catholics, and Native Americans, especially during the Plains Indian Wars. The term's ease of application—how easy it is to hurl it at an opposing religious group—is a reason we should approach the language of fanaticism with a degree of skepticism. Though not comprehensive, each chapter in this book examines a selective episode in American history, presented in roughly chronological order. Each exemplifies distinct media (e.g., essays, governmental reports, court cases, novels) and violent or rhetorical conflicts that shaped the meaning of fanaticism over time.

My archives and cast of characters are admittedly eclectic. The sources do not fit neatly into an intellectual history or a lived religion analysis. They cut across social domains, media, theories, and experiences. But as my mother, an interior designer, taught me, you can make an eclectic style work through attention to balance and recurring patterns. I hope my frames and citational furnishings fulfill this goal. All the figures examined in this book, and many more beyond its scope, helped shape the meanings, theories, and judgments entailed in fanaticism, making it a foundational concept for the stories that Americans tell about themselves and the wider world. There is always more to be said in depth and in breadth. My aim here is to analyze and connect select influential cases to foster a new critical method of researching contested terms like "fanaticism" and to give a sense of the general development of the term in the United States. I see "fanaticism" not as an empty signifier—something that people throw around with ease with no real connection to reality—as much as an overflowing signifier. The problem of the term is not its emptiness. The problem is that it has too many associations, connotations, and judgments that, if the goal is understanding and clarity, require a "discerning Eye," to quote my epigraph from Emily Dickinson. The project is to disentangle fact from rhetoric from lie within the social conflicts each chapter explores.

Plan of the Book

The book begins examining early American debates over and theories of fanaticism. In the eighteenth and early nineteenth centuries, English texts were likely to use the language of "fanatical" alongside "enthusiastic" as adjectives describing discrete rituals and behaviors believed to be impious, performative, and overly reliant on passionate feelings. Chapter 1 situates the popularization of fanaticism, and its distinction from enthusiasm, in the context of waves of Protestant innovation, revivalism, and energy in the early nineteenth century. While skeptics like Thomas Jefferson, in the 1820s, fretted about the unruly and energetic spirit of American religion, ministers like Charles Finney defended the use of passionate feelings and rejected accusations of fanaticism. Amid these debates, Anglican evangelical Isaac Taylor wrote the book *Fanaticism* in 1833 and published it in the United States in 1834. Taylor developed an evangelical theory of fanaticism, arguing that religions are systems of feeling that shape human imaginations and direct action in the world. Revivals, he claimed, were sources of Christian enthusiasm, a necessary tool for the sake of missions and Anglo-American imperialism. Fanaticism, in contrast, was a product of "inferior" religions and races. The problem of the modern world was the taming of religious passions. This could happen only through white Protestant stewardship and globalization, in which the United States had a special role to play.

While theories of fanaticism sought to capture and manage religious passions and energies, popular fascination and terror of fanaticism came mostly through representations of individual fanatics who, taken together, culminate in the stock figure of the fanatic. The 1830s witnessed a wave of religious figures who spoke of novel divine revelations. Prophetic figures such as Joseph Smith, William Miller, and John Humphrey Noyes developed new religious movements and, as a result, often got labeled as fanatics in popular representations. One of the most important of these in shaping the American imagination of the fanatic figure was Nat Turner, who helped mobilize the 1831 Southampton Rebellion, wherein enslaved Black Americans rose up and executed white slave-owning families. Chapter 2 argues that Turner, once captured and destined to be executed, performed the figure of the fanatic as a strategic decision that enabled his claims of divine revelation about the evils of the slave regime to spread throughout the public sphere, inspiring fear in defenders of the slave regime and hope among abolitionists. In response, the slave regime, including state governments, increased their efforts to police Black religion, viewing it as a latent form of fanaticism that, if unchecked by white Protestant surveillance and the threat of state violence, could lead to similar prophetic rebellions.

In the 1850s, allegations of fanaticism focused increasingly on American regions as cultivators of fanatical affects. Responding to Harriet Beecher Stowe's *Uncle Tom's Cabin* and its appeal to moral sympathy, defenders of the slave regime and southern culture wrote anti-Tom novels that accused Stowe and abolitionism of a perversion of Christianity and religious freedom. Mostly written by women such as the Iowan Rebecca Harrington Smith, these novels presented a distinctly feminine theory of fanaticism, as chapter 3 examines. The evil of abolition, these novels dramatized, was too much white love for Black people and their freedom. This theory shifted the focus from masculine hate and violence toward an excess of feminine sentimentality that served as a betrayal of white Christian families. The problem of fanaticism, in this logic, was intimate and familial, constituting a failure of the proper governance of the white Protestant family.

In the 1870s and 1880s, fanaticism talk returned to the scale of the individual, with the nascent field of psychiatry and emerging legal ideas of "religious insanity" shaping the figure of the fanatic as a puzzle to be solved. Chapter 4 examines the case of Charles Guiteau, who assassinated President James Garfield in 1881 on the idea that God appointed Guiteau to save the nation from another civil war. Like Nat Turner, Guiteau became a lightning rod for public debate in the court case *United States v. Charles Guiteau* and embodied the figure of the fanatic in the 1880s. Unlike with Turner, however, the discursive parameters of the criminal legal case and public debate took place within the nascent field of psychiatry. Fanaticism, in such rare instances, could be a shield as much as a sword. Chapter 4 situates psychological debates over Guiteau within broader shifts of expert thinking on the role of the brain, nervous system, and race on religious insanity. Guiteau's defense team argued an insanity defense based on religious delusions. Guiteau, for his part, proudly proclaimed his sanity and explained his religious mission to the court. In the courtroom, in newspapers, and in publications to come, American legal experts and psychiatrists debated the relationship of insanity to legal culpability, punishment, and religious fanaticism.

In the late nineteenth century, the US empire spread across oceans to claim Hawaii, Cuba, Puerto Rico, and the Philippines. To provide a case study of this new global era of imperialism, chapter 5 examines practices of colonial governance in the US-occupied Philippines from 1898 to 1910. US Americans once again turned to the language of religious fanaticism to describe unruliness directed against American powers. This was especially the case in the Philippines, where the diversity and mixing of Catholicism, Islam, and Indigenous traditions perplexed American officials. What followed was a wave of government reports and studies on the cultures and religions of the archipelago. These studies were part of a project to assess the religious and racial landscape of the Philippines for the purposes of pacification and colonial governance.

Chapter 6 takes stock of the general discourse of fanaticism and enthusiasm in the early twentieth century. It begins by examining reference works and their changing definitions. It proceeds to look at late nineteenth-century Protestants who, drawing on Taylor, distinguished the good of white imperial enthusiasm with the bad of fanaticism, often racialized. Of course, there were also American voices that critiqued American imperialism and racism through the language of fanaticism. The conclusion relates this history to contemporary cults, radicalism, extremism, and terrorism and provides theoretical and methodological recommendations for studying contested terms.

By the dawn of the US overseas empire in the early 1900s, many Americans believed that the United States had a sacred and global mission to target and reform religious fanaticism, extremism, and terrorism. President William McKinley reflected this mentality. McKinley was an evangelical Methodist who talked openly about the United States as an instrument of God's will to civilize and Christianize the world. At least in his own narration after the fact, McKinley made the decision to occupy the Philippines after restless nights in the White House when he got "down on my knees and prayed Almighty God for light and guidance." The guidance he received was a series of economic benefits and the idea that Filipinos were "unfit for self-government" and thus there was "nothing left for us to do but to take them all."[36]

The idea of the moderate and enlightened nature of American religion, of course, always had its critics, both within the United States and beyond. That said, the increasingly global nature of the US empire in the early twentieth century set a precedent of Americans viewing foreign peoples and their religions as problems in need of an American civilizing and religious freedom project. This project entailed the targeting of fanaticism.

This model has continued throughout the United States' twentieth- and twenty-first-century global conflicts and occupations. These eras are beyond the scope of this book, but a few cases deserve mention as examples. In Haiti in the 1930s, the problem religion preventing proper freedom and civilization was vodou. In postwar Japan, the problem religion was state Shinto. In the Cold War era, it was communism, which influential evangelical preacher Billy Graham referred to as "a fanatical religion that has declared war upon the Christian God." During the War on Terror, the era that I grew up in and that shaped my interest in studying religion academically, the problem has been Islam.[37] Select domestic communities, too, have been policed as fanatical, at times with tragic consequences. The Nation of Islam, the Black communal movement MOVE in Philadelphia, the Branch Davidians in Waco, and many others.[38]

Each of these contexts, of course, is distinct in so many ways, and I do not want to flatten them or ignore concerns over actual harmful conduct within some of these groups. That said, these examples share a pattern of representing dangerous, fanatical religions that call for agents of the state and a Protestant-inflected civil society to govern, reform, or eliminate such religions. Again, this is not to blame evangelical-style Protestantism for state and racist violence, as if such an argument would make sense, but to question the norms, frameworks, and models that we feel necessary to discern and defend proper religion from its antagonists. This is a plea to avoid rushing in headfirst with the language of fanaticism on the tip of our tongues when there is an individual or community we deeply disagree with and believe to be a threat to modern society. Surely there are better ways to understand and to critique. I would add that to understand, with all the perils of transgressing our own worldviews, is the first and necessary step before effective critique. My aim is historical, but I believe that such a plea is relevant for today as well.

To scrutinize the origins—or, more accurately, one of the origins—of this pattern of representation, chapter 1 turns to early nineteenth-century debates over the propriety of emerging evangelical revivalism. If William McKinley, with his imperial evangelical faith, closes this book, Thomas Jefferson, a skeptic who also did much to grow the US empire, opens it with a concern over what he saw as the fanaticism of the evangelical spirit. The chapter proceeds to examine how evangelicals, reacting to skeptics and moderate Protestants, argued against the charge of fanaticism and helped pave the way for greater social legitimation of evangelical styles. Isaac Taylor's *Fanaticism* outlined an imperial evangelical vision through his critique of the fanatical religions and races of the world. As the following chapters reveal, Americans using the language of fanaticism were more likely to draw on Taylor's evangelical theory than the theories of enlightenment skeptics like Jefferson.[39] This was the beginning of how evangelical Protestants began to disassociate themselves from accusations of fanaticism and begin redirecting such accusations toward other groups, other rituals, other investments in the sacred. My hope is that the chapters that follow provide insights into the logic of fanaticism as a contested term and guidance on how to study and evaluate contested concepts within webs of meaning, conflict, and governance.

1

Evangelical Enthusiasm

Revivals and Early Theories of Fanaticism

In an 1822 letter to the philosopher Thomas Cooper, Thomas Jefferson wrote that "the atmosphere of our country is unquestionably charged with a threatening cloud of fanaticism."[1] Nearing the end of his life, the American architect of religious freedom had grown concerned about the state of religion in the United States. Jefferson was a deist. He believed in a distant creator God knowable through human reason more than divine revelation. For his private edification, Jefferson even created his own version of the New Testament by cutting and pasting the passages that conformed to his disenchanted worldview into a notebook. Jesus's resurrection did not make the cut. For Jefferson, religion, in its essential "true" form, consisted of opinions about a distant supernatural deity that one reasons over quietly, rationally, and perhaps while taking a penknife to scripture. Earlier in his life, he had thought and hoped that some version of this enlightened religion would become the norm in the United States.[2]

As historian Amanda Porterfield has written, the religious skepticism and worship of "Reason" in the 1790s was under duress amid spirited revivals and enthusiastic new religious movements in the 1800s through the 1830s.[3] The "threatening cloud of fanaticism" that Jefferson forecasted had multiple storm fronts. In his letter to Cooper, Jefferson decried the Presbyterians of Charlottesville, whose "ambition and tyranny would tolerate no rival if they had power." Too much denominational exclusivity. When it came to Richmond, Virginia, he fixated on the women: "They have their night meetings, and praying-parties, where attended by their priests, and sometimes a hen-pecked husband, they pour forth their effusions of their love to Jesus in terms as amatory and carnal as their modesty would permit them to use to a more earthly lover."[4] Too much ritual. Too loud. Too much sex. Elsewhere in the nation, Protestant sectarians damned their theological opponents with heated rhetoric. People, possessed by spirits, shook their bodies and spoke in strange languages and sounds. Narratives of divine exceptionalism and retribution shaped American politics. Revelations abounded. Surely, many thought, the end was near.[5] Like a thunderstorm, American religion was electric.[6]

Whether this electricity constituted a religious energy vital to the national and imperial spirit (what Jefferson called the "empire of liberty") or a storm that threatened human reason and social order was an open question. Americans, including skeptics and Protestants, developed, debated, and deployed the language of fanaticism in the context of this religious environment of innovation, revelation, and newfound freedom enabled by disestablishment and free exercise.[7] The popularization of Protestant revivals, in particular, led to a volley of accusations and refutations of fanatical religion. Revivals, which scholars often identify as the beginning of the evangelical style of Protestantism, took diverse forms.[8] The most infamous involved protracted sessions of crowds praying and singing and passionate preaching with the hope that the work of the Holy Spirit would galvanize conversions to Christianity. Some revivalists, as a demonstration of the efficacy of the conversion experience, would cry, shake, groan, faint, and have visions. Religious skeptics, like Jefferson, and moderate Protestants critiqued revivals as fanatical and called for more disciplined ministerial governance. As Ann Taves has explained, the fear was that such an emphasis on the affections—the feelings and energy of the crowd—could lead to delusions of experiencing the Holy Spirit when it was not truly present. Other critics expressed concern that revivals negatively affected the health and reason of attendees.[9]

This chapter examines two apologists of revivalism who wrote about the nature of fanaticism: American revivalist Charles Finney and British evangelical Anglican writer Isaac Taylor. In the 1820s, Finney was one of the leading defenders of using affective pressures of shame, fear, and joyful certitude to produce conversions. Even if his methods seemed fanatical, the results spoke for themselves, he claimed. Isaac Taylor, who anonymously published *Fanaticism* (1833), the first English-language book dedicated entirely to the concept, aimed to reframe the relationship between revival-style evangelicalism and fanaticism. Though taking on similar concerns as Finney, Taylor's theory of fanaticism had a grander scope: the macro level of white Anglo-American Protestantism and imperialism. The threat of fanaticism was not internal to revivals, Taylor argued, but was ultimately sourced from and embedded in nonwhite and non-Protestant religions, including polytheism, Islam, Judaism, and Catholicism. To be clear from the beginning, Taylor, in truth, knew little about these populations and religions. With reckless abandon, he drew on long-standing stereotypes rather than reputable information.

Despite his lack of empirical research, Taylor's writing helped popularize an early distinction between fanaticism and enthusiasm and contributed to the sense that fanaticism was antithetical to his particular variety of Protestant Christianity. The energies and feelings of evangelical enthusiasm, exemplified in revivals, Taylor argued, were the affective engine and legitimator of Anglo-American Protestant power—"True Religion." Enthusiasm, at least the proper evangelical kind, was based on the affects of love. Fanaticism, however, was based on the affects of hate. He hoped and foresaw in the coming century "the overthrow of old superstitions, and of the universal spread of the Gospel."[10] Americans cited Taylor more than any other theorist of fanaticism, in part because he emphasized the important role that the United States would play in this global mission of love over hate, a form of love that legitimated colonial violence and religio-racial stereotypes.

In the scheme of this book, this chapter provides a general sense of how nineteenth-century Americans were thinking about fanaticism. What was it? Which religious traditions were most susceptible to it? How could it be prevented? When Americans looked to an "expert" to help answer these questions in dictionaries, encyclopedias, and sermons, they often found references to Taylor. Beyond their direct influences, Finney and Taylor, at the very least, provide examples of how evangelical debates and aspirations and ideas of true and false religion shaped the modern American notion of fanaticism and broader ideas of national citizenry in a new republic. Even though the nineteenth century had a formal disestablishment and a legal guarantee of religious free exercise, many Americans still believed religion (that is, true religion, variously defined) had a role to play in the destiny of the nation.

Recent work on secularism has examined the outsized role of Protestant norms in American society. As historian David Sehat has written, Protestants believed themselves to be guardians of a moral establishment that served the US body politic. Scholar of religion John Modern has described how, through the circulation of tracts and itinerants, evangelical presuppositions came to be the judge of one's inclusion into society as a proper social subject in the nineteenth century. "To become truly religious, then," Modern writes, "was to coordinate one's attitudes and behaviors with principles essential to the maintenance of civil society." He calls this "evangelical secularism." Especially in the wake of formal disestablishment, it was up to religious authorities to police morality, religious truth, and, as this chapter shows, agency and religious affects. In doing this work, Protestants heralded myths of Protestant unity and nationalism. Reality was messier. White Protestant polemicists questioned the extent to which Catholics, African Americans, skeptics, and prophetic movements could or should be part of the republican body politic.

Taylor, especially, shows the influence of a specifically white evangelicalism that had an imperial impulse that was violent in and of itself. The evangelical influence stands in contrast to many recent works on fanaticism that emphasize the role of Enlightenment (and Jeffersonian) skepticism. These works have given due attention to European intellectuals like Kant and Hegel, who wrote only snippets on the topic of fanaticism.[11] The religio-racial associations of fanaticism were borne, in part and not reducibly, from this evangelical context. The distinction between fanatical religion and true Christianity was based on religious affects and the specific degree of affectability in question.

Charles Finney and the Evangelical Revival

In 1821, the New York lawyer Charles Finney became electrified. Finney was baptized by the Holy Spirit after a period of emotional turmoil and doubt. Alone in his office, realizing, once broken down, that he needed to pray and volunteer his trust in God, Finney experienced the Holy Spirit. "I could feel the impression," he recollected in his autobiography, "like a wave of electricity, going through and through me."[12] Born again through his conversion experience, he left law and dedicated himself to spreading the gospel as an evangelical Presbyterian preacher. He had a knack for it. Finney sparked large, protracted, and popular revivals through the 1820s and 1830s.

Finney and antebellum revivals in general have long received attention for shaping modern evangelicalism and broader American culture. Scholars have variously examined Finney as someone who democratized religion, incorporated marketplace values into religious practice, contributed to American pragmatism, and helped diminish the influence of Calvinism with his emphasis on individual free will. My analysis focuses on Finney's use and defense of using religious affects (terror, shame, and excitement) to prompt individual conversions in the context of revivals. His techniques drew condemnations of being fanatical, especially by other Protestants. His response influenced Anglo-American Protestantism by securing as acceptable the role of affects and human affectability in terms of religion. Social pressure was on the table. Finney's defense that his revivals were not fanatical had two phases. First, he dismissed the very idea as irrelevant considering the masses of converts revivals gained. Second, later in his life he expressed the importance of preacherly care in governing the affects of a crowd to avoid fanaticism.

Finney innovated revivals and became their foremost defender, but he did not invent them. Revivals had a long history in the Anglo-American world. Influenced by devotional practices of Methodism, colonial Americans such as Jonathan Edwards, Phillis Wheatley, and Sarah Osborn experienced and defended revivalism as an authentic ritual for conversion even as they had some qualms about the more excessive revival practices. Revivals generally included ministers preaching sermons about the dangers of sinfulness and the hope of grace. Sermons could be heated. When the Methodist Englishman George Whitefield visited the British North American colonies to preach in the 1740s, he railed against the sinfulness of humanity and the need to be born again through an emotional transformation that led to a relationship with God. Edwards, for his part, could not help but weep listening to Whitefield in Northampton, Massachusetts.

Even before Finney's innovations, revivals were objects of curiosity and concern, as Taves has examined. Critics assailed the "enthusiastic" and "fanatical" elements of the scene of the revivals. In "Enthusiasm Described and Caution'd Against," moderate Protestant Charles Chauncy decried the revivals for promoting false religion and attacked the affectability of revivalists, or the way that they, thinking themselves being inspired by divine influence, ceded their bodily affections to imaginary powers. The scene of the revival, with its "enthusiastic heat and imagination," "affects their bodies, throws them into convulsions and distortions." Giving in to the "transports of affections," he railed at attendees of revivals, "your reason and judgment . . . will be in great danger of being carried away by your imaginations." The revival wears down people's capacity to willfully reason and judge, opening them up to a rawer form of affectability or influence to the feelings and claims of divine agency. One of the concerns for critics like Chauncy was that revivals could support the theology of Arminianism, or the idea that humans could freely choose to be saved. This was contrasted with Calvinist theology's emphasis on God's providence over salvation and damnation. Worse yet, revivals caused people to act in strange ways—it "gives them such an energy," as Chauncy put it.[13] Using performative bodily gestures and damning rhetoric, the revival minister could have their "intended Effect upon one or two weak women, the Shrieks catch from one to another, till a great part of the Congregation is affected."[14] The presence of women and their open emotional displays were common emphases in critiques of the wild affections of revivals.

For Chauncy, as for defenders of revivals such as Edwards, "enthusiasm" was the dominant term to be debated in the colonial era.[15] Fanaticism was a subtype of enthusiasm. Protestant writers rarely bothered to provide any clear distinction between the two. Importantly, when Chauncy and other colonial writers wrote about enthusiasm or fanaticism, they were usually describing transient events or movements (e.g., revivals). People in the colonial era could act fanatically or enthusiastically, and they could be affected by a fanatical revival, but they were not usually described as irrevocably fanatics. These semantic shifts began to happen in the nineteenth century as revivals, which had died down during the 1780s and 1790s, reawakened during the early 1800s.

As historians have argued, Finney ushered in a more decisive shift away from Calvinism and from Edwards's moderate support of revivalism. In their place, he more fully embraced the naturalistic means by which revivals put social pressure on individuals to convert, freely accepting Christ into their hearts. Finney popularized the use of the anxious bench, wherein sinners in the crowd would come up to the front of the crowd and be broken down through his preaching until they repented. He was not afraid to use intense emotions. For Finney, intense emotions, or what he often called "energy" or "excitability," were the engines of all religions. Humans, stained by sin and prone to ignoring the Gospel, required the *feeling* of Christianity before gaining knowledge about and practices of Christianity. Finney was generally an optimist, but he was pessimistic about the capacity of people to come to Christ only through their will. Humans, and perhaps Protestants in particular, "have so little knowledge, and their principles are so weak, that unless they are excited, they will go back from the path of duty, and do nothing to promote the glory of God."[16] The success or failure of Protestantism was not tied to biblical knowledge alone. The intentional, affective, systematic social cultivation of religious feeling and energy was necessary in a fallen world.

What did this look like? Finney had an experience in mind, but attendees had diverse reactions. Consider this remembrance of a revival from women's rights activist Elizabeth Cady Stanton, who encountered Finney in the 1830s:

> I can see him now, his great eyes rolling around the congregation and his arms flying about in the air like those of a windmill. One evening he described hell and the devil and the long procession of sinners being swept down the rapids, about to make the awful plunge into the burning depths of liquid fire below. . . . He suddenly halted and, pointing his index finger at the supposed procession, he exclaimed: "There, do you not see them!" I was wrought up to such a pitch that I actually jumped up and gazed in the direction to which he pointed. . . . Fear of the judgment seized my soul. Visions of the lost haunted my dreams. Mental anguish prostrated my health. Dethronement of my reason was apprehended by friends.[17]

Stanton, who wrote this passage years after experiencing the revival, clearly remembered Finney's performative power and its effect on the bodies and imaginations of those present. Finney's revivals created an affective environment of intense emotions and fixed attention. For

Stanton, at least, the environment worked as Finney hoped, making Stanton not only ready to see the procession of sinners Finney manufactured, but ready to see herself in a new way. For Stanton, this was a negative experience. In breaking Stanton down to be openly affected by his preaching, Finney harmed her mental health and compromised, temporarily, her reasoning abilities. Her friends were worried.

Others also critiqued revivals as sites of manipulation rather than Christian-nurturing excitement or divine inspiration. The Jewish literary freethinker Samuel B. H. Judah saw little more than calculating ministers' "redoubled energy" stirring up the "animal excitements" of the crowd. The miracle work of the revival was purely the creation of the human, not the divine. In his 1842 satirical poem "The Spirit of Fanaticism: A Poetical Rhapsody," Judah described the scene of a revival, claiming direct experience. The vibe is sensorial overkill: "'Tis noise of the holy devotion we hear, of fanatics frantic with grief and delight. The ranting and canting, and shouting and spouting." He went on,

> Like furies now raving, o'ercharged with blind zeal,
> Excitement soon drives their best senses away;
> When nerves are unstrung, from emotions they feel,
> The priest, like the potter, can manage his clay,
> With coaxing and hoaxing, Beseeching and preaching,
> That all will be lost who may longer delay.[18]

Ministers could shape the imaginations of the revival crowd, made affectably raw through the charge of emotions and the retreat of reason, to find tales of heaven, the Holy Spirit, and their born-again transformation. Worse, for Judah, was the negative moral results of revivals. "What monsters have grown out of fanatic's dreams," he poetically pondered. In a footnote, he situated the revival within Protestant "spiritual warfare," a "vast project of converting the whole human race to what they term orthodoxy, and bringing about the glorious millenium [sic] of ecclesial supremacy, tyranny, and oppression, throughout the world."[19] Judah, like Jefferson, had an anticlerical streak. He blamed the preachers more than laypeople for Christianity's imperial sense of righteousness. This desire to reform the world in one's own image, in addition to the strange sounds and bodily affections, made evangelical revivals fanatical. He distrusted organized religion, especially when it was directed by authority figures who claimed exclusive rights to authentic religion. Judah's life as a Jewish American, living in a community of just four hundred Jews in New York at the time, also likely contributed to his critique of how Christians, especially in the era, viewed Christianity as a universalizing religion destined to supersede all other religions, especially Judaism.[20] The affects of the revival—their overwhelming forcefulness—represented the broader imperial aim of Christianity.

Judah's poetry about the danger of fanatical energies provided a satirical, if a bit exuberant, representation of the scene of the revival. Going beyond the poetics, Judah's poem came armed with footnotes, including a reference to medical doctor Samuel Underhill's 1829 lecture *Mysterious Religious Emotions*. Underhill vaunted the value of reason and the tools of the natural sciences to debunk religion in general and evangelical Protestantism in particular. Judah found Underhill a useful citation for his poem because Underhill so confidently asserted that the excitement of the revival, like all religious rituals, was a natural product of the human body and psychology. The bodily affectations of the revival crowd were the result of the careful coordination of the ministers. By understanding the electric operations of the nervous system, Underhill told the reader, "you will easily perceive how the penitent sinner or the bellowing fanatic witnesses a loss of [willful] muscular power. . . . Prior to all regular motion, excitation from some external object, or from some idea already in the mind, must take place."[21] The imagination, if exercised excessively, can begin to force the body to act "upon opinions correct or incorrect." Affectability to certain objects or ideas was conditioned by social context. The preaching of Islamic doctrine, he says, "throws a Mussulman into raptures" while it "excites disgust in a Christian."[22] Underhill, in his day, alienated most of those around him, including those who were otherwise sympathetic to his socialist utopianism. However, he does represent an early American figure who sought to apply naturalistic scientific study to discern the purely secular anatomic and psychological origins of religious experience. I examine the emergence of psychiatric diagnoses of revivalism in greater detail in chapter 4.

For Finney, the burst of enthusiasm was precisely why modern Protestantism needed revivals to sustain and grow. The obstacles of worldliness, ignorance, and distraction made it so that people "must be so excited . . . before they will obey God."[23] As such, he rejected the idea that revivals were exclusively works of God. "Religion is the work of man," he famously said in his first lecture.[24] However, the fallenness of humanity and the worldliness of modern society required human action and agency. Finney rejected accusations that his revivals were fanatical, but he also admitted many of the claims made by his opponents. His revivals might seem fanatical, and may indeed use fanatical means, but the result of mass conversions was worth it. Further, Finney's ultimately argued that the real power of being spirit-filled, when true, could not be called fanatical. God was not a fanatic. Finney, likely drawing on Isaac Taylor, whom I will examine below, defined fanaticism as a "state of mind in which the malign emotions take the control of the will."[25] His revivals, in contrast, used non-malignant emotions that he believed left the will of individuals intact to freely choose or reject Christ.

Finney confronted the charge that revivals deluded individual imaginations into thinking that they had received the Holy Spirit: "If some people should think they are led by the Spirit of God, when it is nothing but their own imagination, is that any reason why those who know that they are led by the Spirit should not follow?"[26] In other words, Finney expected that his reliance on human feelings would produce some who were deluded into thinking they had a divine experience.

Finney admitted that the use of social pressure and affects was not ideal. Strong religious emotions took a toll. "Our nervous system is so strung that any powerful excitement, if long continued, injures our health and unfits us for duty."[27] However, the "great political, and other worldly excitements" had to be confronted with the same energy. Revival practices, especially for protracted revivals that lasted hours or even days, could have negative effects, beyond theological purity.

This is highlighted in one example from 1833, when a man died in the wake of his participation in a long meeting ministered by Finney. "A Death by Fanaticism" was the title of one sensationalist article originally published in the *Free Enquirer*. The man, the article stated, had "been driven to madness" by Finney. The article placed some blame on Finney, saying that the man did not die but was murdered.[28] Although fanaticism in the 1820s and 1830s largely referred to theological and ritualistic impropriety, Americans were starting to associate it with forms of harm and violence. This would only increase over the nineteenth century.

Finney's argument that his revivals were not producing fanatics relied upon the assumption that (1) God was real and (2) numerous people, including himself, had experienced true spiritual transformations. Regarding whether or not his emphasis on the certitude that God will answer prayers when they are truly, freely offered was a fanatical certitude, he scoffed. In other words, Finney's revivals might be fanatical in form, and might produce fanaticism in certain individuals, but they could not be described as inherently fanatical.

Finney argued that though his revivals did stir religious affections (primarily hope and fear), it was only for the purpose of gaining the attention of his crowds.[29] Finney, though claiming that it was possible that he sometime erred on the side of fanaticism, was largely in control of his crowds, managing their excitements to the appropriate level. Further, he argued that revivals, properly orchestrated by the minister, were a *necessity* to prevent the emergence of "enthusiasm, fanaticism, and spurious excitements" in the nation.[30] Evangelical ministers had "the means in our hand of guiding the public mind, of molding or modifying the excitements that overspread the land."[31] Revivals functioned as a type of emotional outlet that directed Christians' feelings toward Christ. Ministers had to gauge and sway the emotions while also explaining that religious feeling was supposed to be in service of religious intellect. Religious excitement was a necessary tool, not the goal.

What exactly did an overly and improperly energized crowd look like? He provided an anecdote of the type of revival effects he feared. This one occurred at a camp meeting in New York. It was a prime example of the complexities of the proper discernment of the relationship between charismatic authority and a crowd. Finney described a fledgling revival in process. It lacked excitement. Finney then narrated how an attractive young minister—"athletic frame and stentorian voice"—walked into a crowd of women. The man began to clap his hands. "Power! Power! Power!," he shouted. The women, with the man among them, began to shriek and fall from the seats. This was, they all believed, the power of God operating through them. For Finney this was anything but Christian.[32] It was, his writing hints at, sensual, and thus far removed from the Holy Spirit, properly understood. Again: too much sex.

Despite Finney's disapproval, this anecdote laid bare some of the dynamics that powered revivals. These dynamics included the push and pull between bodies, the contagious vocalizations, and the difficulties of discerning what was truly the work of the Holy Spirit and what was the work of more human instincts, such as the attractive young man among the women. Revivals were a human phenomenon. Though the attractive man likely meant "Power!" in the divine sense, he was articulating, and creating in the process, the circulation of power between his authority and the crowd. Starting first with the small group of women, the entire crowd eventually followed his lead. Finney's disgust at this "unintelligent excitement" aside, many revivals had similar dynamics. The men and women at this camp meeting themselves were satisfied that it was the true working of divine power among them. They left the revival "much gratified at the result."[33] The affective work of the revival was the point, at least for the men and women at the camp meeting in New York. Yet the role of affects raised concerns.

Finney's writings on fanaticism reveal his attempts to explain away a problem that scholar of religion Finbarr Curtis has highlighted. Finney subscribed to an Arminian theological framework in which individuals had free will and whose religious convictions were supposed to be freely chosen. But, as Curtis asks, "If sinners were free to make their own choices, what was social pressure doing exactly?"[34] Finney's theories about freedom did not hold that sinners would make the right choices if they were simply left alone. For Curtis the answer lay in how Finney was an exemplary figure in the creation of a "democratic economy of religious freedom," or the production of an environment in which individuals learned to become democratic subjects capable of voluntarily choosing their religion (or in this case, to accept Christ into their life). Like a fanatic under the spell of irrational devotion, sinners had to be first freed from themselves. Finney's writings on fanaticism show how he himself was cognizant of this dynamic, and how he sought to make his theological theories (an emphasis on human free will) and practices (the power of the revivals as directing individuals' energies and choices) compatible.

The management of revival affects was had a certain artfulness. Religious feelings were difficult for ministers to manage. Managing a crowd required producing excitement but avoiding excessive excitement.

Many individuals attended revivals to feel the presence of the Holy Spirit. While Finney felt confident in discerning when the Spirit was operating and when the feeling of the spirit was fabricated by natural and social means, many revivalists did not see or care about this difference. It is in the moments of these determinations of what is fanatical and what is true religion (read: Protestantism) that we can see how the language of fanaticism was a rhetorical ploy, but one that captured concerns about real social practices. Finney wielded fanaticism talk to distinguish himself from the very social phenomena he was helping create. He had less control over the social masses than he claimed.

Finney, like many evangelicals of his day, was progressive on social issues like health care, care for the poor, and slavery. Finney was an abolitionist, and he railed against slavery as a moral abomination to God. On one level, Finney was an egalitarian. He believed that all individual humans had the capacity to reason and, importantly for him, accept Christ. However, Finney also embraced and enforced race-based segregation, including in his own churches and at Oberlin College, where he was president from 1851 to 1865. Commitment to spiritual equality did not necessarily entail social equality.

The centrality of religious affections in Finney's concept of religion was relevant to his idea about racial difference and missionization. On the one hand, Finney believed that revivals, with their capacity to energize through religious affections, were the necessary tool for missionizing peoples he called "heathens." He lectured that it was "improbable that religion will ever make progress among *heathen* nations except through the influence of revivals."[35] Efforts to convert non-Christians through education and a slow introduction to the Bible were not enough. To "wake up the dormant moral powers, and roll back the tide of degradation and sin," you needed to create an affective environment where one's shame could be relieved only through opening up to Christ.[36] Revivals among Christians were also necessary to spur missionary fervor. The job of ministers was to make the "affections rise" and "hearts expand" so that "they have more and more feeling for the heathen, and for all the world. As they increase in piety, they feel more and more a desire that the world should be converted to God."[37] Missionization required not just an appeal to reason and truth, but the cultivation of a Protestant affective atmosphere.

Isaac Taylor's Religio-Racial Theory of Fanaticism

Like Finney, the Englishman Isaac Taylor believed that the heart of religion was feeling. Taylor styled himself a theologian and a historian. Taylor was an "evangelical Anglican," meaning he was a member of the Church of England who shared beliefs, practices, and texts with evangelicals. He lived a quiet life in the English village of Stanford Rivers. He did not work in missionary fields, did not write law, did not command soldiers. He wrote essays and books about abstract concepts. He tried, unsuccessfully, to become a professor, which is one of the more sympathetic events in his life. But in the world of ideas, Americans, and to a lesser extent Britons, viewed Taylor as the expert on fanaticism. Finney almost certainly had read Taylor's book *Fanaticism*, as he claimed that there existed a single authoritative book on fanaticism in history.[38] Numerous other American intellectuals, encyclopedias, and newspaper articles referenced Taylor as *the* prime theorizer of what fanaticism was, where it came from, and why it was a problem that modern Protestant societies needed to combat.[39] Taylor was part of a transatlantic Protestantism that, despite the denominational splits prompted by the American Revolution, found new ways of circulating and articulating a shared Anglo-American Protestant mission in a global context.[40]

Fanaticism was part of a series of books Taylor published on the uses and misuses of what he called the "religious affections." It began with the 1829 publication of *Natural History of Enthusiasm*. Like many other Protestants in this era, he defined fanaticism according to feeling, imagination, and the vacation of the will. Taylor's shorthand definition was a "*fictitious fervour* in religion, rendered turbulent, morose, or rancorous, by junction with some one or more of the unsocial emotions. Or if a definition as brief as possible were demanded, we should say, that fanaticism was enthusiasm inflamed by hatred."[41] It shared some key terms with a definition Finney gave in 1846: "By fanaticism, I mean a state of mind in which the malign emotions take the control of the will, and hurry the individual away into an outrageous and vindictive effort to sustain what he calls right and truth. He contends for what he regards as truth or right with a malign spirit."[42] Finney's definition, in some ways, actually better captures Taylor's argument within *Fanaticism*. For example, by "fictitious fervour," Taylor meant not merely that fanatics were merely performing but that the sources of their fervor were not divine nor based in true Christianity. Finney's use of the vacation of the will, too, captures a key part of Taylor's argument. Fanaticism was an affect, rooted in the emotions.

The ability to govern (to prevent, reform, or eliminate) fanaticism was, for Taylor, a measure of religious and racial superiority. This section argues that what made him distinct is how he redefined the concept in service of a global Christian modernity buttressed by his Anglo-Saxon supremacism. Evangelical Protestantism framed and gave purpose to *Fanaticism*. One of the possible reasons that white Americans (especially of British heritage), more than Britons, favorably cited Taylor's works is the special place he believed the United States had in spreading the Anglo-Saxon version of Protestantism. The fact that evangelicalism had survived and even thrived against the threat of what Taylor called "republicanism," by which he meant a Jeffersonian style of skepticism toward religious feeling is proof of an "indestructible vigour." If the "English race" continued to settle the North American continent, Taylor wrote, then "Christian worship will bless every landscape of the present wilderness that shall then 'blossom as the rose.'"[43] Finney focused on the energies of a particular, local revival; Taylor took a global view of evangelical Protestant revival.

Affectability deals with individual emotions: love, joy, excitement, hope, shame, fear, and so on. In stressing the term "affect" here, I follow many scholars of affect who are interested in how feelings act upon people. Anthropologist William Mazzarella describes "thinking affect" as "a way of apprehending social life that does not start with the bounded, intentional subject while at the same time foregrounding embodiment and sensuous life."[44] Affects, in a way, hit us, mentally and corporeally through our nervous system. Sara Ahmed, in her study of the relationship between love and hate among Aryan white nationalists, described "affective economies" wherein "emotions *do* things, and they align individuals with communities—or bodily space with social space—through the very intensity of their attachments."[45] Emotions are not just individual; they reside and flow between human bodies, symbols, media, spaces, and narratives. This is especially true in relation to religious elements. A cross, a sacred mountain, a mosque, and a flag can be vectors of affective power that can inspire us, surprise us, hurt us in ways not reducible to our conscious beliefs. I, along with affect theorists today, argue that affectability is a key feature of humanity. It is not a sign of a weakness of will or a lack of capacity to reason. It is a condition of life.

However, Taylor, in ways we should question, viewed the fanatic to be *especially*, and perhaps even entirely, affectable. They are driven to fury when hyperenergized with the use of religious elements like rituals, symbols, media, and authority figures. In this process of fanaticization, any sense of will, reality, politics, or strategy disappears. As following chapters will demonstrate, this is a dangerous assumption to make. It misapprehends the complicated personal, political, and intentional reasons why people are drawn to ideas and mass violence that question established religions and social order. Fanatics have their own biographies, and they should not be reduced to their "fanatical-ness." However, Taylor's point here became a key element in the modern figure of the fanatic. When believers crossed the threshold from fanatical to the fanatic, they lost themselves in some substantial way. They became affected subjects.

For Taylor, there was only one God. His God was the benevolent God of the New Testament. Other religious traditions, he wrote in wild speculation, believed in gods who were malignant. This aspect of malignancy is what made fanaticism different from enthusiasm. The relationship between the fanatic and their God had three features. First, the fanatic showed a "deference to malignant invisible power." Second, this deference led to a hatred of the mass of humankind. Third, the fanatic imagined their God to show "corrupt favouritism" to their particular community or population.[46] As the next section examines, Taylor proceeded in a clumsy attempt to argue that most religions, except for evangelical Protestantism, had an understanding of a god or spiritual force that was malignant. Taylor strove to explain that other conceptions of God, though false in the sense that they were not really real, had an effect on fanatics. Fanatics, in other words, were moved by their own religious beliefs and the religious affects that these beliefs produced.

To explain this counterintuitive claim about how people lose themselves, Taylor turned to nascent forms of psychology and especially the concept of the human faculty of imagination. For Taylor, "fanaticism, as we assume, combines always malign and imaginative sentiments."[47] Many nineteenth-century thinkers emphasized the malleability of the human imagination. Fanatics were fanatical because they had a fanatical imagination. Taylor was tapping into a popular understanding of abnormal religious psychology in using this language. Scholar of English literature Emily Ogden has written about nineteenth-century ideas about the faculty of the imagination and its relationship to invisible powers and beings: "Belief's physical effects via the imagination could in fact explain all the enchantments and enthusiasms of the past and present."[48] Because of the power of imagination over human perception, supernatural powers were made real to the believer.

Taylor used this idea to explain how the beliefs of fanatics, spread and impressed through affective channels, came to have a power over their bodies. Further, the beliefs themselves had a type of agency in *causing* violence. Examine, for example, his language in this passage that explains the power of objects (material, textual, or creedal): the imagination "is liable to high excitement from a pressing sense of the reality and the impending nearness of the objects that engage it."[49] Religious imaginations allowed people to be moved by religion, stirred into passionate responses by their beliefs in prophecies, supernatural objects, and deities, even if these things were not empirically real. In their reality these elements of religion not only were imagined to be real but created a pressing sense of their reality. Though intellect was a key faculty, humans, for Taylor, were feeling subjects governed by their own imaginations and the "contagion of sentiments."[50] Religious affects, connected as they were to a sense of divine legitimation, were especially efficacious in shaping the conduct, moral or immoral, of individuals.

Left unchecked, the malignant emotions can fester, leading to a greater sense of righteousness and difference from one's enemies. In this charged atmosphere, fanatics, if the opportunity presents itself, will "rush on ungovernably" to revenge.[51] The result is a fanatic who has forfeited their humanity. "When the wretch," Taylor writes, "shutting out the pleasures of life, its pride and its hopes, clasps his shapeless bags as a sovereign good—we lose hold of him—the last link of human sympathy is snapt, and he seems to go adrift from his species."[52] Earlier accusations of fanaticism during the First Great Awakening often described it as a transient psychological state. For Taylor, the fanatic figure was more someone who had fully succumbed to fanaticism. Fanatics were those who had crossed a line of no return.

Importantly, Taylor's theory of fanaticism was not just about individuals who happened to be fanatical. He situated his theory within a global project to define and differentiate religious and racial groups by their affectability to fanaticism. For him, religion and race were intertwined identities. Taylor took on faith that his religion (Protestant Christianity, especially its evangelical forms) and his race (Anglo-Saxon, according to the taxonomy of his day) were superior. Further, Anglo-Saxon Protestantism represented the ideal of a new modern civilization built on progress, social reform, and global society. As a number of scholars have explored, most nineteenth-century thinkers thought about racial difference through religious difference. The presence and support of fanaticism in other religions and races signaled, for Taylor, a deficient affective and rational disposition to the world. Taylor's knowledge of polytheistic religions, Islam, Judaism, and Catholicism was superficial at best. He relied on tired stereotypes, not evidence or experience. Yet his logic (or lack thereof) is a useful example of how fanaticism was a marker for religious and racial hierarchies in this period.

This gets back to a basic question: What was religion to Taylor? It was not just individual belief. In his 1860 *Ultimate Civilization*, Taylor wrote, "Religious differences, well defined, firmly maintained, and freely developed, and in such a condition that they are not merely *elements*, but are *energies* within the social mass, when duly attempted, stand, if not foremost, yet quite *prominent*, among the forces that are carrying us forward toward a higher civilization."[53] Religion was a form of energy that, through the circulation of beliefs, texts, and affects, shaped individual imaginations and motivated them to act in the world. It was "Christian zeal," Taylor wrote, that carried the "British settler, the traveller, the missionary, or the soldier."[54] Religion had a degree of agency over social masses.

Race, too, was a form of energy that shaped the imaginations and wills of social masses. Race, for Taylor, was flexible and could change over time. He rejected, for example, the increasingly popular racial science phrenology, or the measuring of skull shapes and sizes to determine inherent psychological capabilities.[55] He was also an abolitionist and viewed slavery as an affront to Christianity. Race was more malleable than that for Taylor. Using the popular white-supremacist terminology of the mid-nineteenth century, Taylor wrote that the "Anglo-Saxon race shall maintain its original energy, and shall conserve the vital force of its blood," even while doing the work of colonialism in other lands and among other populations.[56] Religion was the assemblage of energizing forces that bound racial populations together and governed their interactions and mutual influences. Taylor's writings emphasized how it was religion that did much of the work of racial progress, stagnation, or decline. Populations that did not show progress, that were still mired in "inveterate superstitions," did not deserve political rights.

He made this argument on the macro level of civilization as well. As scholar of religion Sylvester Johnson has written, ideas about superior civilizations have long been handmaidens to colonialism. "Colonial conquest," Johnson writes, "was rationalized by claiming that the imperium would disseminate civilization to conquered subjects and thus serve for their benefit."[57] For Taylor, the spread of Christianity could happen through the channels created by imperialism. The spread of the English language and Anglo-Saxon commerce, through both Great Britain and the United States, was, Taylor put it, "pouring itself over all the waste places of the earth." These imperial networks would be the "principal medium of Christian truth and feeling."[58] Superstitions, "a vortex of delusion," draw people to them "as if with a power of fascination." In contrast "true Religion" works as "an expansive force, which, has rendered to a point of radiation, or an emanative centre, whence light and blessings have flowed to the remotest circumference."[59] He was optimistic that this flow would indeed come to pass. The very presence of fanaticism, though negative in and of itself, signaled the presence of religious feelings among different populations. This "susceptibility of the religious emotions" signaled the "capacity to admit the motives of Christian faith."[60] The spirit of Protestantism—in terms of both the Holy Spirit and Protestantism's religious affects—would flow outward from Anglo-Saxon civilization and into the social masses of the rest of the world.

Who needed to be purified, according to Taylor? Like many Enlightenment-inspired Western intellectuals, Taylor had a narrow group of people in mind when he was imagining who *did not* have the seed of fanaticism within their culture and religion. Taylor believed a wide range of religious traditions and communities—Judaism, Islam, Paganism, and Roman Catholicism—were rooted in error and cultivators of violent fanatics. All, he wrote, were "utterly condemned" in the face of the gospel.[61] Taylor's endeavor was not to catalog the number of religious traditions, much less the communities that had engaged in fanatical violence. *Fanaticism* was an attempt to provide a general theory. Nonetheless, a brief exploration of the stereotypes he was drawing on to classify non-Protestant traditions as prone to superstition and violence will help us understand his motivations and the generalizations that his argument rested on.

The bulk of his vitriol was directed at the Roman Catholic Church. The Church hierarchy, he argued, was infected with forms of asceticism, or what he believed to be forms of self-violence. The "superstitions" of the Catholic Church, including the doctrine of purgatory, self-flagellation, residency in cloisters, and other standard anti-Catholic tropes, were the result of the violence and hatred of the fanatic turned inward.[62] In his historical narrative, Roman Catholicism had nearly snuffed out the "love of liberty" he believed to be inherent in European peoples.[63] Taylor's historical narrative made religious difference to be at least partially determinative of political self-determination and, more broadly, the capacity to be free. Taylor's theory of racial difference overlapped with his theory of religious difference.

Similar to other critics of religion, Taylor compared Islam and Catholicism in order to condemn both of them.[64] He relied upon the presumed exoticism of Islam to make Catholicism seem foreign and relied upon centuries of Protestant anti-Catholic rhetoric to make the dangers of Islam clear to readers who in all likelihood had a shallow knowledge of actual Islamic belief and practice. Muslims were, in his writings, a passionately militant religio-racial community who had no shame in cruelty and murderous violence to their enemies. Further, Taylor emphasized that Islam was an exceptionally masculinist religion. Islam, and what Taylor refers to more broadly as "oriental faith," "burst upon the world . . . among an energetic and enterprising race. It was the religion of MEN, and the faith of warriors."[65] He blamed Catholics for their violent wars of persecution more than he blamed Muslims for their violent wars of persecution. At least, he claimed, violent warfare was a natural part of Asiatic racial formation, whereas Catholicism among Europeans was akin to racial betrayal—a turning back from natural racial superiority.[66] Fanaticism's spread among European Christians was a "long invasion of a soil which nature had said should bear nothing that was not generous."[67] Fanaticism, for Taylor, had a distinct theology and a geography in the broad sweep of history.

Taylor's understanding of the Prophet Muhammad interestingly, and perhaps unconsciously, mimicked Taylor's own views of the day. The founder of Islam, he wrote, believed himself surrounded by infidels and "might with reason have regarded the human family as then hastening down a slippery descent towards the bottomless abyss of ignorance and utter atheism."[68] Muhammad was a reformer and a warrior, and his target was primarily superstition and the feminization of cultures in and around the Arabian Peninsula. Islam was a religion of men, Taylor claimed, and its primary emotion toward others was hatred. Muslims were prideful and fully vulnerable to the violent passions. Their "affections are not softened; there is a feverish heat among the passions, but no moisture."[69] Taylor saw in the warfare of seventh-century Islam a model that he was drawn to, one that was contrasted with the twelfth-century Catholic European Crusades, which were the product of "imaginative superstition" and the corrupting power of priests. Taylor critiqued Islam as, at heart, a murderous religion. But it was one that he could not help but identify with, projecting his own motivations and inspirations into his account of the Prophet Muhammad.

Taylor did not spend much time describing cultural and religious specificities of the people he called "heathens." The term generally meant people who did not subscribe to an Abrahamic religion and had the connotation of people who were uncivilized.[70] However, the language he used to describe the source of fanaticism made clear that he understood it in terms of an unnatural disease that had spread from racialized populations, especially from Africans. As Taylor, like Durkheim, invoked the social structure of the primitive clan to elaborate his theory of the sociality of fanaticism, he also viewed "primitive peoples" as its source, not just historically but in his day as well. Fanaticism, in other words, might be present among fellow European Christians, but it was foreign-born. European Christians could not themselves be ultimate sources of fanatical behavior. Taylor identified the source of fanaticism chronologically and geographically, in a passage written with a poetic flair not found elsewhere in his writings: "It is in the heart of forests that are the ancient domain of enormous reptiles, or of savage beasts—it is where horror and death lurk in the way, that the darker passions reach their fullest growth, and are to be seen in their proper force. All the principal or most characteristic forms of fanaticism have had their birth beneath sultry skies, and have thence spread into temperate climates by transportation, or infection."[71] Elsewhere he wrote of the "Natural Religion" of humans that was constituted by "gloomy superstition" that "springs up involuntarily in the human mind."[72] Superstition, which was a precondition for fanaticism to emerge, was a force in and of itself among those credulous enough to believe in a world in which supernatural beings and objects have immediate and innate agency. Taylor's account functioned to make fanaticism a type of social contagion that was *in* but not ultimately *of* Anglo-Protestant Christendom. Instead, the rise of fanaticism, for Taylor, was a result of racial contamination. Despite the evidence of passionate violence justified by Christianity in his own British nation and empire, Taylor sought to make the source of fanaticism always non-Christian and nonwhite. White Protestant evangelicalism was protected and pure from fanatical energies.

What should be done about the persistence and even spread of fanaticism across the globe? How could people, as he wrote, "free themselves from the tyranny of superstition, if the first lesson we are to teach them is that errors has no noxious quality, and truth no prerogative"?[73] As a product and influencer of social relations, fanaticism was firmly within the purview of the state's prerogative to secure social order. Taylor went so far as to say that a government, of whatever form, might "calculate its security by the rule of the amount of religion among the laboring population [lower class] of the country."[74] The churches, too, must play a role in policing the religion of the masses. Moral religion would need to trump natural religion and corrupted forms of ceremonial religion. Moral religion, he argued in *New Model of Christian Missions*, was found in the message of the New Testament in the form of a new divine beneficence, available to the world.[75]

Like Finney, Taylor did not believe feeling was a problem in and of itself. In his interpretation, Christianity tamed Paul's fiery mind and feelings. The "Gospel had made Paul a man of *much* feeling and of *many* feelings." His commentary on the churches of early Christianity emphasized a "paternal tenderness."[76] These populations must be content, he wrote, "to be governed, as they may, for their good."[77] Anglo-Saxon civilization, aided by a strong unified and evangelically infused missionary program, was best suited to do this governance.

Taylor heralded love as the principle of Christian affections, but he embraced the idea that the flow of British civilizational energy was violent. Taylor believed in renewed Christian mission, in which the spread of true Christianity could dispel the powers of fanaticism and a decline of fanaticism could unleash the "impulsive and expansive energies of the Gospel."[78] As philosopher Alberto Toscano has noted, and as much of the material in this book stresses, charges of fanaticism against a population are usually produced to serve as violent calls to action. In the 1841 *Four Lectures on Spiritual Christianity*, Taylor made, by his own definition, his own violent mission clear.[79] He called for and naturalized a "process of colonial purification" wherein the "wastes of the earth must gradually be christanized." This process required evangelical zeal in missionary work, and it would be helped along by "the paternalistic discretion and christianlike feeling of the government."[80] This was, for Taylor, the law of diffusion. Law, here, took on multiple meanings. Law in that Taylor understood the Christianization of the world as a natural teleology. Christianity would inevitably reign supreme, no matter the concerning developments of modern criticism or the persistence of superstition globally. Law in that Taylor took it as a guiding principle for his faith and the faith he preached and wrote about. And, finally, law in that it was the job of secular governments, who were to be "christianlike," to bring this ideal about. Subjects who defied this law, whether they be Muslims, Jews, heathens, or atheists, were doomed to extinction, eventually. The choice of colonized populations was between death or Christianization. And rightly so, Taylor argued. Behind the veneer of his middling intellectual interest in religions and gentlemanly tone in his writing was an acceptance and embrace of a regime of death. The fanaticism he described of the world around him described *him* as well as or better than the religions he wrote about from afar. Isaac Taylor's *Fanaticism* served as a pretext for his own forms of violence justified by his Protestant ideology.

Conclusion

The revivalist Charles Finney defended revivals from accusations of fanaticism and, through his very success as an evangelizer, helped make his methods more mainstream. Isaac Taylor's theory of fanaticism is troubling for its demonizing (and inaccurate) representations of a range of religions, its avowed white supremacy, and its openness to using violence and mechanisms of colonialism to spread Christianity. This is also why Taylor's theory is important and influential. Far more than neutral descriptor, fanaticism so clearly in *Fanaticism* is part of a broader project of religio-racial governance borne from his white evangelicalism.

One of the strange omissions of *Fanaticism* is that Taylor, thinking on such a macro, civilizational level, is never specific about the individual figure of the fanatic. He rarely named people he thought were fanatical, with the notable exception of the Prophet Muhammad. The following chapter examines the emergence of the figure of the fanatic in the early 1830s United States. In governmental archives and in newspapers, the threat of fanaticism is sometimes an abstracted, social contagion. This is related to, but distinct from, the individual fanatic figure subverting or directly, violently, challenging a given social order. The following chapter also examines fanaticism more directly within the dynamic between a specific conflict of governance (in this case the slave regime) and resistance (an antislavery revolt).

2

The Figure of the Fanatic

Nat Turner and Black Religion

The previous chapter ended with an examination of the 1833 book *Fanaticism*. In it, the evangelical Anglican Isaac Taylor aimed to provide a theory of fanaticism across cultures and eras to chart the global destiny of Anglo-American Protestantism. Taylor showed little interest in actual individuals in his sweeping account of the religions and races of the world. That said, his and other general theories of fanaticism as a phenomenon spread alongside concern over individual figures portrayed as fanatics. Taylor's book made its way to US publishers in 1834 amid a wave of prophetic Christians declaring new revelations and cultivating communities that challenged social norms. Joseph Smith began receiving revelations in 1828 and went on to found what is now the Church of Jesus Christ of Latter-day Saints. Robert Matthews, who went by Prophet Matthias, created the utopian Kingdom in upstate New York by claiming he was God incarnate after receiving revelations in the 1820s. Both Smith and Matthews received the charge of being fanatics and have received some scholarly attention in relation to this charge.[1] This chapter focuses on Nat Turner, an enslaved Black man who helped orchestrate a violent and sacralized rebellion against white slave-owning families in Southampton, Virginia, in August 1831. Though scholars have given Turner plenty of academic study, there has been less attention to his role in the popularization of fanaticism in American culture.

Turner's prophetic religion wove together biblical exegesis, Africana spiritual practices, apocalypticism, evangelical fervor, and Black radicalism.[2] White lawyer Thomas Gray interviewed the captured Turner and wrote about his religion and rebellion in *The Confessions of Nat Turner*, published in November 1831, shortly after Turner's execution.[3] In it, Turner described the rebellion as part of a divine plan bestowed upon him by the Holy Spirit. In response, white defenders of the slave regime mobilized the stereotype of the fanatic in attacks on Turner's religious credibility and psychological well-being. Importantly for this book, responses to the Southampton Rebellion included an increased surveillance and policing of Black religion by white Christians.

What did it mean to call Turner a fanatic? The term, from the moment of its popularization, overflowed with meanings and judgments. To simplify, Americans in this period generally understood religious fanaticism to be the product of a "heated" imagination open to being affected by delusions of divine revelations and dangerous feelings, especially hate, terror, hope, certitude, and enthusiasm. Fanaticism was not only an individualized psychological phenomenon but a product of social affects. This conceptualization of fanaticism is why antebellum society found it both powerful and dangerous: fanaticism could spread like a social contagion, leading to subversion and outright violence. Yet accusations of fanaticism produced their own religious feelings of hate, terror, enthusiasm, and hope among the overwhelmingly white media and governmental agents reporting on Turner. Accusations of fanaticism included representations of Turner as a delusional prophet. At the same time, white writers' singular focus on Turner as delusional served to instill hope that the Southampton Rebellion was an aberration and not a result of a broader push for Black liberation. This chapter argues that Nat Turner and his detractors sparred over the meaning and morality of the Southampton Rebellion through diverse appeals to powerful feelings, divine forces, and religious truth. The language of fanaticism was at the center of this sparring.

To make sense of the affective power of fanaticism, this chapter draws on two distinct insights from scholarship on affect. The first comes from theorist Sara Ahmed's concept of "affective economies."[4] Affects, here, refer to the circulation of powerful feelings between bodies, minds, and objects. Ahmed's account of white-nationalist propaganda, with its attention to the ability of texts to produce feelings and social hierarchies in a given context, is a useful model for analyzing the affective work of fanaticism in the antebellum period. Turner described himself as affected by divine messages and powerful feelings that were expressed through natural phenomena including an eclipse that prompted the rebellion. Critics of Turner, in diverse ways, emphasized that these messages and feelings overwhelmed his individual and rational will, leading to forms of madness or delusion.

Attention to affects is relevant for understanding theories of fanaticism, the power of accusing someone of being a fanatic, and the religious narratives and performances of those labeled fanatics like Turner. Taken together, these perspectives and their relevant texts formed an affective economy that this chapter analyzes.

To get at the contested affects and affectability of Turner, this chapter begins with a close reading of *The Confessions of Nat Turner*. It then moves on to examine governmental reports and newspaper coverage of Turner to understand the rhetorical power of framing Turner as a fanatic whose self and whose rebellion was defined *by* his religious affects and affectability, rather than political rationales such as abolitionism. Examining these perspectives highlights how concepts of agency, feeling, and religious truth have, in contested and conflicting ways, been integral to hierarchies of religio-racial difference. Representations of Turner as a fanatic are part of a longer history of pathologizing Black resistance to white supremacy, including its historical entanglement with forms of white Christianity. That said, this chapter suggests a consideration of fanaticism and its associated elements that also provides an opportunity to reconsider Turner. Was Turner a fanatic? Or was he a freedom fighter? To some extent—and with caveats about the dangers of repathologizing Turner—this chapter shows how he presented himself as both.

Scholars have long written about the Southampton insurrection and Turner's role in organizing it. Many have contested or softened the charge that he was a fanatic. At the same time, historians have found Turner's religious claims difficult to interpret, not least because they have access to Turner's voice primarily through the filter of Thomas Gray, as explained below. As historian Douglas Egerton has written, "Many scholars, even those sympathetic to Turner's cause, are uncomfortable with the sort of visions and voices that Turner described."[5] In his work, Egerton aims to normalize Turner's religious views. He notes that Turner's self-description as a divinely inspired figure, though it might seem irrational or abnormal to modern audiences, was not unusual in antislavery uprisings. Similarly, historian Vincent Harding, among others, has argued that Turner's spiritual expectations of a new era were not far from the mainstream of white and Black cultures in the United States.[6]

These arguments are worth noting to show how Turner was drawing on existing religious cultures. However, emphasizing the reasonableness of Turner's religious presuppositions does not necessarily shed light on the particular role of Turner's supernatural claims within the context of his radicalism.

Karl Lampley's *Theological Account of Nat Turner* and Christopher Tomlins's *In the Matter of Nat Turner* both center Turner's religiosity. They argue that some accounts, based as they are on secularist norms, have sidelined Turner's religion in order to emphasize his political radicalism. Gayraud Wilmore, more generally, argues in *Black Religion and Black Radicalism* that religious radicalism and political radicalism are not necessarily incompatible.[7] Lampley examines Turner as a figure in a long tradition of Black Christian radicalism. He uses Turner to think through the scriptural relationship between violence, righteousness, and Jesus Christ's message of peace.[8] Tomlins's account is what he calls a "speculative history" because he aims to get at aspects of Turner's religious consciousness. This consciousness, he writes, is "overwhelmingly one of faith—religious faith, a subject that always tends to make scholars uneasy."[9] This faith is evident in Turner's scriptural exegesis, his figuration of himself as a prophet, and his apocalyptic temporality. These, for Tomlins, are conceptually and causally prior to the politics, or actions, of Turner that led to the rebellion. Tomlins's third chapter, in particular, gives agential priority to Turner's faith as the force that led to political action in the form of the insurrection. Both Lampley and Tomlins influence the portrayal of Turner below.

A quick note on sources is necessary. The historical record for Turner's life is sparse and open to interpretation. Much depends on the trustworthiness of the extant written record composed in the wake of the revolt. White men, for the most part, wrote these sources. Anonymous authors claimed first- or secondhand information in the weeks and months that followed the insurrection. The primary account of Turner's life was *The Confessions of Nat Turner* (1831). Gray was a novice lawyer who defended a number of the people charged with conspiracy and rebellion, though he did not serve as Turner's official lawyer. Gray's prefatory and concluding comments in *Confessions* showed a clear bias against Turner. Especially since the mid-twentieth century, scholars have debated the extent to which *Confessions* offers an accurate portrayal of Turner. Patrick Breen argues that *Confessions* is a historical source that can, when carefully examined, provide information about Nat Turner himself. Breen evaluates *Confessions* on the basis of its corroboration with other descriptions of the insurrection.[10] This chapter shares Breen's approach.

This scholarship has highlighted features of Turner's religion and how he drew on existing religious cultures, especially in the mold of Black prophecy and the spreading of evangelical Protestantism. With attention to the politics of religio-racial affectability, this chapter adds to these analyses a focus on Turner's strategic use of religious affects and his emphasis on his own affectability—his role as a relay for divine messages and forces.

The Affective Power of *The Confessions of Nat Turner*

This section provides a close reading of *The Confessions* as a narrative performance. Turner's narrative mobilized various affects—especially hope and fear—in order to challenge the moral status of the white-supremacist slave regime. Turner's narrative to Gray may or may not have matched Turner's own sincere beliefs about his prophetic status and divine messages. Gray himself wondered this. Turner, he wrote, "is a complete fanatic, or plays his part most admirably."[11] Regardless, Turner made strategic choices in what he told to Gray and how he told it.[12] He did so in the context of his capture and the end of the rebellion. The level of detail and care evident in Turner's story suggests that he may have had some sense that this story might circulate beyond Gray. Turner's confessions were given for an audience. Taking this approach, we can see how Turner, who did not call himself a "fanatic," nonetheless performed the role of the fanatic. The main difference was that Turner's religious beliefs and experiences were, according to him, real, true, and legitimate. In sacralizing the meaning and purpose of the rebellion through the religious narrative in *The Confessions*, Turner produced both hope (among some radical abolitionists) and terror (among defenders of the slave regime), even in the midst of the rebellion's ostensible failure. He impacted the affective economy of the antebellum South.

For the majority of *The Confessions*, Turner told the story of his religious journey in a matter-of-fact manner. He did so with a calm demeanor and with what Gray described as a "natural intelligence and quickness of apprehension."¹³ Turner's narrative relayed to Gray his increasing prophetic certitude as he received divine revelation after revelation. He purposefully described himself as an affectable prophet open to influence from exterior, divine forces. His ability to receive these divine revelations and his miraculous abilities came from what Turner called the "fertility of my own imagination."¹⁴ He did not use the language of imagination to suggest that these messages and abilities were false. Rather, his uses of the language of imagination were an attempt to convince Gray that his powers came not from within him but through divine powers that operated *through* him.

His receptivity to prophetic powers began early in life. He was chosen, or as his parents had told him, he was "intended for some great purpose."¹⁵ As a child, Turner told Gray, he began to talk about events that happened before he was born. Turner said that his childhood miracles left an "indelible impression on my mind, and laid the ground work of that enthusiasm, which has terminated so fatally to many, both white and black, and for which I am about to atone at the gallow."¹⁶ This origin of his prophetic status served to emphasize his ability to know events outside of his timeframe. At first, it was events that happened in the past. Later in his life they were events that were going to happen in the future.

These later revelations informed Turner that the nation was on the cusp of a new age. This new age would be ushered in by a great war, and perhaps even a race war. It would culminate in a day of judgment in which slaveholders would be held responsible for their sins. Enslaved people would end up in power, though it is not clear if Turner meant that this would occur in heaven or in a new world on earth. This prophecy came to him slowly, over time. Its signs were in nature, but it was up to him to properly perceive their meaning. These signs were calamitous or awe-inspiring natural phenomenon. Turner had a vision of "white spirits and black spirits engaged in battle, and the sun was darkened—the thunder rolled in the Heavens, and blood flowed in streams."¹⁷ A voice spoke to him and said, "Such is your luck, such you are called to see, and let it come rough or smooth, you must surely bare [sic] it."¹⁸ The vision of "black and white spirits" could be a forecast for a racial war between white and Black people, though this is speculative considering the common symbolism of Blackness for the demonic and whiteness for the divine. At the very least, Turner's symbolism did seem to equate slavery as an institution with the demonic.

At this point, which was in 1825 according to his narrative in *Confessions*, Turner still did not fully comprehend what was being asked of him or what he was supposed to do. As such, he described removing himself from the company of other enslaved people to ruminate on the meaning of these signs. Further, he took this time to develop, with the aid of the Holy Spirit, "knowledge of the elements, the revolution of the planets, the operation of the tides, and changes of the seasons."[19] Other sources suggested that he began to gain powers. These included "command over the clouds" and the ability to "by the imposition of his hands cure disease."[20] These magical powers over nature, Turner narrated, were the starting point of a process of his sanctification. However, Turner was not clear on the meaning and purpose of the visions and powers.

Clarity eventually came when Turner discovered drops of blood in the cornfields where he labored. He described finding "hieroglyphic characters, and members, with the forms of men in different attitudes, portrayed in blood."[21] This was, he discerned, the blood of Christ and suggested his imminent return. These signs confirmed in him that he was to play a part in preparing Christ's return to earth. The literal shift of the signs in the sky to the signs being on the earth had the metaphysical connotation of Christ's descent from the heavens to the earth. He would be among the crops. That Christ, in Turner's telling, signaled his return within the crops where Turner and other enslaved people labored in hinted at the antislavery politics undergirding Turner's religion.

In 1828 a "loud noise in the heavens" gave way to the Spirit appearing before Turner. Drawing on language from the Book of Revelation, the Spirit told Turner that the Serpent was "loosened, and Christ had laid down the yoke he had borne for the sins of men, and that I should take it on and fight against the Serpent, for the time was fast approaching when the first should be last and the last should be first."[22] This final part of the Spirit's message paraphrased Matthew 20:16. This vision foreshadowed the rebellion and a larger war between the enslaved, who had God on their side, and the slavers, who were identified with the Serpent and inevitable defeat. Turner, who was originally unwilling to challenge his masters and suggested that his own role in divine destiny was a type of "burden," came to accept that it was he who "must commence the great work."[23] Having witnessed an eclipse in the sky on February 12, 1831, he knew it was time to start planning the rebellion. On February 21, he met with his fellow enslaved Black men Henry, Hark, Nelson, and Sam to do just this. Delayed for a variety of reasons, they commenced the rebellion that August.

By downplaying his own willful agency, Turner's narrative sought to make the rebellion a product of divine destiny, not human choice or mere politics in the sense of being produced solely from material conditions. The Southampton Rebellion, in this view, ceased to be an isolated, secular incident. It became, instead, one event on the path to a future of broader conflict and, ultimately, the "Kingdom of God."[24] Turner told this narrative in the midst of the ostensible failure of the rebellion. He was imprisoned. The rest of the rebels had been executed or captured. For Gray, the rebellion was a secular event that had failed. When Gray asked Turner, "Do you find yourself mistaken now?" Turner famously replied, "Was not Christ crucified?"[25] His retort served to reinforce his own confidence in the divine role of the rebellion. It also suggested that its failure and his capture—akin to Jesus's execution on the cross—was not the end of the apocalyptic battle against the Serpent, but the beginning of a new age. In the wake of what at that point seemed like a failed rebellion, Turner's sacralization of it served as a method to argue for its righteousness and abolitionism's ultimate triumph as decreed not by Turner, per se, but by divine messages.

Though the majority of abolitionists rejected the violent means of the Southampton Rebellion, many were affected by the prophetic certitude of Turner's religion. Scholar of abolitionism Manisha Sinha emphasizes the influence of Turner on Black and white abolitionists.[26] Scholar of religion and Black radicalism Vincent Harding poetically noted that despite the fact that few Black people followed Turner's violent means, "it was yet possible to sense the profound disequilibrium building in the society, to feel the underlying, restless, eruptive movement of the river, gaining ground."[27] Though we should not center Turner as *the* cause of increased interest and hope in the righteousness of abolitionism, the circulation of *The Confessions of Nat Turner* certainly played a prominent role across the United States.[28]

Turner was an active participant in the antebellum affective economy. Considering Turner's role in producing affects helps us rebuff white-supremacist claims of his inherent affectability. And, ironically, it was precisely Turner's claims of divine affectability—his role as a vehicle of divine messages and justice—that produced such strong affects in antebellum society. For white defenders of the slave regime, *The Confessions* produced fear, terror, and agitation. Thomas Roderick Dew, who was the president of the College of William and Mary and an ardent proslavery Christian activist, noted the destabilizing affective power of Turner. Although he emphasized the ability of white Christian supremacy to ensure the stability and sustainability of the slave regime, he also admitted white concerns and doubts. In his *Essay on Slavery*, Dew wrote that the rebellion destroyed

> for a time, all feeling of security and confidence, and even when subsequent development had proved, that the conspiracy had been originated by a fanatical negro preacher,—(whose confessions prove beyond a doubt mental aberration)—and that this conspiracy embraced but few slaves . . . still the excitement remained—still the repose of the commonwealth was disturbed—for the ghastly horrors of the Southampton tragedy could not immediately be banished from the mind.[29]

Other accounts affirmed Dew's observation. "There is much *fear* and *feeling* in several of the lower counties of the state," one anonymous letter to the *Niles Register* wrote, "and the white inhabitants seem to be in a constant excitement."[30] The reality of the rebellion and the violence was of course a source of this white agitation. But the details of Turner's account shaped the affective economy of religion, race, and slavery in the antebellum period. Turner's affective legacy lasted far beyond his execution on November 11, 1831.

Representations of Nat Turner as a Fanatic

Americans quickly took to framing Turner as a fanatic. Thomas Gray, in providing his own commentary on the narrative he relayed from Turner, described Turner as a "gloomy fanatic."[31] The chairman of Turner's trial, Jeremiah Cobb, spoke to Turner, telling him that "borne down by this load of guilt, your only justification is, that you were led away by fanaticism."[32] To call Turner a fanatic served to denigrate him and his religion as false and delusional. At the same time, the American interest in the figure of the fanatic helped circulate Turner's religious narrative, including his emphasis on supernatural agency and his mobilization of passionate feelings of hope and terror. Governmental reports and newspaper coverage of Turner helped sow doubt about the morality and destiny of slavery, even as the majority of the white media intended to shore up the authority and sustainability of the institution of slavery. Studied in this way, the discourse of fanaticism, rather than being *only* a tool of demonization, reveals the competition over agency, feeling, and religious truth between Turner and his detractors.

The competition occurred within *The Confessions of Nat Turner* itself. The document reveals the conflicting perspectives of Turner and Gray. This calmness and "gloominess" of Turner that Gray remarked upon exploded into an external spectacle at the end of *The Confessions*, as Gray narrated his visit with Turner in the prison cell. At the conclusion of the interview, Gray described "the expression of his fiend-like face when excited by enthusiasm, still bearing the stains of the blood of helpless innocence about him; clothed with rags and covered with chains; yet daring to raise his manacled hands to heaven, with a spirit soaring above the attributes of man."[33] As with other parts of *Confessions*, Gray was bordering on a romanticist adoration of the willpower of Turner. In another context, with another person, such a picture might be a testament to faith. But here, Turner's "spirit soaring above the attributes of man" was a testament not to his divinity but to the forfeiture of his humanity. Gray immediately dispelled any romanticist reading. "I looked on him," he wrote, "and my blood curdled in my veins."[34] As Harding has written, Turner, especially in this moment, provoked "terror and awe" and "deep levels of rage" among white observers.[35] Whereas the voice of Turner, as presented in the *Confessions*, suggested a religiously inspired prophet operating with a deliberate plan and full knowledge of the rationales and consequences of the insurrection, Turner's face and body, Gray suggested, revealed the irrational, uncontrollable, and wholly otherworldly fanatic underneath. Turner may or may not have actually raised his chained hands as a prophetic act while being interviewed by Gray in Jerusalem, Virginia. Either way,

Gray uses this moment to establish the dominance of his understanding of confession—the confession of Turner's crimes and his inherent fanatical nature. Turner's body, Gray stressed to the readers, betrayed his words.

The attribution of gloominess deserves attention. More so than in *Confessions*, Gray, or at least someone familiar with the substance of Gray's interview with Turner, summarized Turner's religion most succinctly in a chapter published in the *Alexandria Gazette* on November 8, 1831, just a few days after interviewing Turner in prison: "A more gloomy fanatic you have never heard of. He gave, apparently with great candor, a history of the operations of his mind for many years past, of the signs he saw, the spirit he conversed with; of his prayers, fastings, and watchings, and of his supernatural powers and gifts, in curing diseases, controlling the weather, &c."[36] The language of gloomy also appeared in *Confessions*, which was made available to the Virginia legal officials overseeing the trial of Turner in early November and was published for the public later that month. "A gloomy fanatic," Gray narrated, "was revolving in the recesses of his own dark, bewildered, and overwrought mind, schemes of indiscriminate massacre to the whites."[37] The insurrection as a whole was "the offspring of gloomy fanaticism."[38]

The meaning of gloomy, in this case, is not entirely clear. Noah Webster's 1828 dictionary listed a number of meanings for the term: "Obscure; imperfectly illuminated; or dark; dismal; as the gloomy cells of a convent; the gloomy shades of night" and "wearing the aspect of sorrow; melancholy; clouded."[39] The darkness conveyed by gloomy had a few possible meanings here. First, it explained to readers why there was little reason to believe that Turner was a fanatic before the revolt because his fanaticalness was primarily located in his mind, where it simmered and developed over time without much external expression that would have been evident to white surveillance. Many commentators noted that Turner had somehow kept his fanaticalness hidden. He "had acquired a great influence ... without being noticed by the whites," one writer wrote to the *Constitutional Whig*.[40] Second, the language of gloominess signaled his own countenance and isolation. Turner himself said that "having soon discovered to be great, I must appear so, and therefore studiously avoided mixing in society, and wrapped myself in mystery, devoting my time to fasting and prayer."[41] He was not always social with the Black community. He also had a reputation for being severe—rarely smiling and rarely letting his intentions or desires be known.

Turner's gloomy, hidden fanaticism produced fear in white audiences. The idea that fanaticism, which was usually associated with extravagant verbal claims and bodily expressions, could be hidden from white surveillance prompted slaveowners to reflect on the possibility of other Turner-like rebels in their midst. One Virginian delegate, James McDowell Jr., wrote a defense of how white people were hunting down suspected Black people. McDowell wrote that "it was the suspicion eternally attached to the slave himself—the suspicion that a Nat Turner might be in every family—that the same bloody deed could be acted over at any time and in any place."[42] McDowell, and others, even advocated for or threatened the genocide of Black people, especially if there was another revolt.[43]

Ironically, the language of fanaticism did as much work calming white fears as it did in exciting them in an affective economy based on protecting the slave regime. Calling Turner a fanatic helped white critics emphasize that the insurrection was a minor aberration within an otherwise secure and sustainable system of plantation slavery. Early reports emphasized that the rebellion was not the product of a widespread conspiracy. This was a response to rumors about the possibility of a larger, coordinated attack. One anonymous writer in the *Norfolk Herald* assured readers that the conspiracy was contained and that Turner had not influenced many "beyond the circle of the few ignorant wretches whom he had seduced by his artifices to join him."[44] Others explicitly mentioned that the Southampton Rebellion was not the beginning of a revolution on the scale of the Haitian Revolution, an uprising that led to a sovereign Black nation. Since 1804, the example of Haiti had been a source of concern among southern slaveowners. The language of fanaticism was one way that anxious white Virginians sought to contain the insurrection as a local event, not a large-scale attack, even as it made the point that an antislavery rebellion could potentially happen anywhere.

The containment of the insurrection was, rhetorically, a way of depoliticizing the insurrection in that it downplayed that one of the reasons for the rebellion was a wider critique of the system of racial slavery. "He was artful, impudent, and vindictive," one writer wrote, "without any cause or provocation, that could be assigned."[45] Critics saw a delusional fanatic initiating a revolt for no sensible reason. Unsympathetic white writers often framed the violence to be uniquely and, at times, exclusively the cause of misguided religion (or what they at times called "superstition") latent among the Black population and explicit in Nat Turner's own words. Critics intentionally did not mention the material realities of living as a slave within a system of racial slavery as a possible cause. As such, many pointed to the religious aspects of Turner to suggest that the insurrection was caused solely by a corrupted form of religion, and not a larger discontentment or abolitionist sentiment among people who were enslaved. This fit within the larger portrait of slave life that white slaveowners had increasingly articulated in the 1830s—that of the happy slave who would prefer the basic "protections" that the slaveowner, cognizant of their mutual duties, provided.[46]

Other unsympathetic commentators took up the idea of Turner's essential fanaticism, using the religious signs and narratives testified to in the *Confessions* to flip the script on Turner—to make him seem out of control. Turner was an affectable subject, open to misreading natural events as having supernatural meaning and becoming beholden to that meaning. As Thomas Roderick Dew wrote in one newspaper chapter, "Nat, a demented fanatic, was under the impression that heaven had enjoined him to liberate the blacks, and had made its manifestations by loud noises in the air, an eclipse, and by the greenness of the sun—It was these signs which determined *him*, and ignorance and superstition, together with implicit confidence in Nat, determined a few others, and thus the bloody work began."[47] Even in the grammar of these sentences, Nat was not an acting subject: "It was these signs which determined *him*." He was acted upon, affectable. This affectability was based on the way in which Turner granted agency to the external world, primarily to natural events like the eclipse. Dew noted how Turner was careful to put the ultimate authority on the sovereignty of God, not his own politics. But rather than seeing this as a way for Turner to bolster his own authority—by, at the same time, denying it—Dew took this as an opportunity to emphasize how Turner lacked the innate capacity to *interpret* signs. He was simply, as the language of fanaticism and the related language of superstition imply, beholden to them.

One of the cumulative effects of the condemnatory white emphasis on Turner's fanaticism was to deny him any agency in the revolt. Instead of being a person with religion, Turner's agency was vacated to the religious signs themselves. This presentation of Turner brings to mind political theorist Wendy Brown's distinction between "who has religion" and "who is religion."[48] This is ironic because one of the fundamental assumptions of critiques of Turner is that his religion was *wrong*, both in the sense of not being truly Christian and in the sense of misinterpreting natural phenomenon. And yet white critics gave this errant religion a type of possessiveness over Turner. He passively accepted the meaning of the natural signs according to his delusional cosmology that had, at its core, a divine message of Black liberation.

Functionally, this account served to reject Turner as a political subject who had any substantive critique or understanding of slavery as a social system. Any religion based on Black liberation, in this view, was fraudulent and a sign of a weak mental constitution. Worse yet, from the perspective of defenders of the slave regime, Turner seemed to have a knack for mobilizing a similar "superstitious" mentality of the Black community. This was a rhetoric intended to comfort white slaveowners in that it made it seem that enslaved people could not possibly choose on their own volition to rebel. Black liberation, in this racist interpretive framework, was an impossibility as an intentional politics. Black liberation could only be a sign of religious delusion.

Other unsympathetic white people made it a point to question Turner's theological authority and knowledge of Christianity. One writer, sending a letter to the editors of the *Lynchburg Virginian*, took exception to claims the newspaper had published describing Turner as a Baptist preacher. From what this person could tell, Turner "never was a member of the Baptist, or any other church; he assumed the character of his own accord, and has been for several years one of these fanatical scoundrels, that pretended to be divinely inspired." He was "never countenanced," by which the writer implied that he was never taken seriously as a prophet, "except by a very few of his deluded Black associates."[49] Turner, this suggested, was not the Christian authority figure he claimed to be. In the *Confessions*, however, Turner emphasized this very point. His authority came not from credentials or training, but from divine decree.

All this talk about fanaticism was not just an issue of racist rhetoric. It was an issue of policing, which in this case was about discerning and managing the religious authority, affects, and politics of Black figures like Turner. Underlying unsympathetic white people's denigrating portrayal of the superstitious, fake Christian fanatic was an earnest effort to explain the revolt. They were earnest within the racist assumptions of a white slaveholding society whose aim was to preserve white supremacy, to secure the institution of slavery, and to prevent further Black rebellions. The problem of Turner's heated imagination, according to skeptics and anxious white citizens, was also the problem of how this imagination made Turner an effective leader and organizer of the insurrection. Even though writers argued for the falsity of Turner's claims, they made note of the social significance of these claims within their racist understanding of Black affectable psychology. For them, Turner's signs—such as the divine meaning behind the blueish sun rays on August 13, the apocalyptic visions, and the prophetic figure of Turner himself—were all false, but they were real in how they affected him and others. How did unsympathetic writers think Turner's authority worked? How did critics think that superstition explained and even caused the fanatical violence of Southampton?

Many accounts of the insurrection centered the person of Nat Turner. Writers were also interested in the relationship between Turner and the other rebels—at times mentioning specifically the small group of co-conspirators and at times mentioning more broadly all of the enslaved people who ended up joining in the revolt. Rhetorically, the focus on Turner was one way to contain blameworthiness and motivation for rebellion, making it seem the product of a single, demented mind that had somehow influenced others. Strategically, white southerners were invested in finding out the mechanisms and channels of influence in order to prevent a future slave revolt.

Mirroring much of the commentary on Turner as an individual, many wrote that the insurrectionists had no ulterior motive. Drawn in by the power of Turner, the other rebels were "stimulated exclusively by fanatical revenge, and perhaps misled by some hallucination of his imagined spirit of prophecy."[50] The writer does not mention revenge for what, interestingly, and goes on to imply that fellow conspirators followed Turner because of a delusional investment in Turner's divine status. This was a common rhetorical strategy in descriptions of the insurrection. They rarely mentioned slavery as an institution itself. Most white writers buried the fact that liberation was central to the reason slaves were willing to rise up and attack slaveholding families.

The Southampton County Court had similar reasoning. Chairman Jeremiah Cobb presided over Turner's trial. Cobb's use of the language of fanaticism was less about convicting Turner—his fate was already sealed—than about assigning blameworthiness for the insurrection. Though all the participants were legally found guilty (and many more executed extralegally by white militia forces), Cobb singled out Turner as the source of the insurrection. Not only had he massacred the white citizens in their sleep, but he had led his fellow insurrectionaries to an untimely end. Turner was the "author of their misfortune," forcing them "unprepared, from Time to Eternity." "Borne down by this load of guilt," Cobb said, "your only justification is, that you were led away by fanaticism."[51] The effect of this claim was to deny Turner's own agency in the rebellion. The judge was basically saying that Turner did not know what he had done. In some ways this matched Turner's own narrative, which emphasized how he vacated his own agency to serve as a prophetic figure as part of a divine timeline. The affective wrangling over fanaticism—with its attributes of powerful feelings, divine forces, and religious "truth"—reveals the very openness of these questions in the antebellum period.

If Turner was the "author of their misfortunes," with what tools did he write the story of the rebels of the Southampton Insurrection? Or in other words, through what affective appeals and rhetoric did Turner convince other enslaved people to rebel? Most obvious was their oppression within the bounds of slavery and their broader critique of slavery as a regime. But the court and media coverage of the insurrection were not usually interested in the political and social reality of Black rationales for insurrection. Antislavery politics was not legitimate, and the Virginia press studiously avoided making it a prime rationale for the insurrection. Any admission of the possibility of antislavery politics could destabilize southern white arguments about slavery as, ultimately, a beneficial force, including for the Black people who were enslaved.

Even with those possibilities taken into account, Turner was a charismatic, albeit quiet and mysterious, figure and did seem to have some level of authority within his community. One way that unsympathetic white writers sought to explain Southampton as a mass insurrection was by emphasizing Turner's management of the feelings of the Black community. As historian Curtis Evans has argued, white interpreters often viewed Black religion as fundamentally based more on feeling rather than on reason.[52] Primarily, these feelings were hope and fear, made possible by the superstitious credulity that white writers projected onto racial and religious Blackness.

Though described as "gloomy," Turner had an investment in hope. The anonymous September 26 letter to the *Constitutional Whig* mentioned that it was an "imagination like Nat's" that allowed a "mind satisfied of the possibility, of freeing himself and his race from bondage; and this by supernatural means."[53] Religion, here, was both the precondition and the vehicle of hope in the cause of antislavery. The anonymous writer suggested that belief in a divine plan that would lead to freedom was a necessary presupposition for any enslaved person to believe that Black freedom was a possibility. Religion—in this case the belief in the favor of the supernatural and the righteousness of one's cause—was also the means of trying to make that possibility realized. This writer, however, was not an abolitionist. Their frustration here was not with the fact that Turner was willing to fight and die against the slave regime, but with the fact that Turner had the conviction that radical abolitionism *could* prevail in the first place. This divinely inspired conviction was the basis of both the hope and the terror of Turner's confessions.

Policing Slave Religion

The unease among the slaveholding and political white class in the wake of Turner's rebellion led to a lot of questions about what sorts of legal and policing mechanisms might prevent future insurrections. Governor John Floyd of Virginia was one such figure who saw the wider significance of the insurrection. He feared future revolts. Though the language of fanaticism served to rhetorically contain the scale of the rebellion to Turner and the other rebels, southerners were shaken by the insurrection. New measures were needed.

One such measure was that white legislators and slaveowners targeted Black religious authority. Virginians crafted manuals and laws to assert a proslavery Christianity. Whereas many of the sensational accounts of the Southampton Insurrection focused on the unique personality and prophetic claims of Nat Turner, the laws and essays by government officials that followed belied an underlying concern that Turner was a product of abolitionist forms of Christianity as crafted through Black religious authority.

One of the immediate reactions to the Southampton Insurrection among white Virginians was the extralegal murder of anywhere from 25 to 120 Black people.[54] Militias and everyday people with the slightest suspicion of insubordination shot and lynched Black people, both free and enslaved. Turner, somehow, had escaped this fate when he was captured by a local white farmer. Some writers concerned about the violence being directed at Black people nearly charged white militias themselves with fanaticism. Consider the language used by the *Niles Register* on the "indiscriminate slaughter" taking place. "There is much *fear* and *feeling* in several of the lower counties of the state," the anonymous letter wrote, "and the white inhabitants seem to be in a constant excitement."[55] Black preachers, especially, were subject to violence, surveillance, and interrogation.[56]

Members of the Virginian government, to some extent, were concerned about white anti-Black violence. This was more about protecting "property," as slaves were legally defined, than it was about protecting human life.[57] White violence was largely excused as a justified response to the insurrection. On August 28, fifteen days after the initiation of Southampton Insurrection, General Richard Eppes, who headed the Jerusalem, Virginia, militia, sent out an order for civilians and militiamen to "abstain in the future from any acts of violence to any personal property," by which he meant enslaved people.[58] The murders of Black people up to that point would be excused, but General Eppes made it known that any future acts of white anti-Black violence would be prosecuted. The state and the power of law, Eppes pleaded to militants, had secured the situation and would dole out public executions in accordance with the legal process. The state gave white violence directed at Black people legal exemption, at least for a period of time.

In a letter written November 19, 1831, Governor Floyd wrote that Virginia had been "resting in apathetic security" prior to the Southampton Insurrection. To resecuritize Virginia for slaveowners and whites, he turned to lawmaking and the policing of Black religion. Floyd placed ultimate blame on white northern abolitionists, especially William Lloyd Garrison, who had inspired a "spirit of insubordination" through converting Black people to a form of Christianity that stated that "the black man was as good as the white."[59] There is little evidence that white northern abolitionists had inspired Turner. That said, the broad goals of evangelical ministers were a potential threat to giving enslaved people interpretive tools and resources for insubordination. Floyd singled out evangelical women, especially, for teaching Black individuals reading and writing. Governor Floyd, who often referred to Nat Turner as "the Preacher," likely had Turner's biblical literacy in mind when making these comments. In his public speech to the Virginia Senate and House of Delegates on December 6, 1831, Floyd again brought up the problem of Black preachers. "The public good," he wrote, "requires the negro preachers to be silenced, who, full of ignorance, are incapable of inculcating any thing but notions of the wildest superstition, thus preparing fit instruments, in the hands of agitators, to destroy the public tranquility."[60] Black preachers, the idea was, spread a spirit of unruliness. They did not necessarily do so directly. That is, they did not necessarily have to spread a doctrine of antislavery to be a threat. The politics of Black preachers were almost beside the point. By their mere "ignorant" preaching they increased the affectability of the Black community, making it so that any superstitious idea might become believable and real. This made Black people into "fit instruments" whose willpower was suggestible by others. This rehearsed arguments about how Turner had convinced other enslaved people to join the revolt. Without white supervision, Black communities might mobilize themselves through heavenly omens, magical prophets, and apocalyptic timelines. This was not different, of course, from the religious and cultural realities of white communities. The difference was that officials such as Floyd considered it a peculiar problem and potential source of unruliness and violence when it came to the Black population.

Floyd's argument that Black religion was a source of the rebellion seems to have had traction in the Virginia legislature, which in December 1831 passed a number of laws to restrict and surveil Black religious authority figures. The legislature made it illegal for Black people, free or enslaved, to host any type of religious meeting. The punishment for the first offense was a lashing; the punishment for the second offense was a felony, with the potential of offending free Black people to be sold into slavery and transported beyond the boundaries of the United States. The legislature also made it illegal for free and enslaved Black people to attend any meeting "held, or pretended to be held, for religious purposes" at nighttime.[61]

Policing happened not only on the level of the commonwealth, but at the local level as well. This included the level of the plantation. Whitemarsh B. Seabrook, lieutenant governor of South Carolina, published *An Essay on the Management of Slaves, and Especially, on Their Religious Instruction* in 1834. Seabrook evinced the idea that Black people, and especially enslaved Black people, were inherently vulnerable to fanaticism. "Ignorant and fanatical," he wrote, "none are more easily excited."[62] Seabrook's *Essay* is a testament to the widespread idea among proslavery advocates that Christianization was a tool for the soul of people who were enslaved and a tool that disrupted the inclination toward fanaticism among Black people. As scholar of religion Al Raboteau has argued, nineteenth-century US Americans defended slavery as a positive good through Christian claims.[63] The protection of the slave regime required the elimination of African-derived religious beliefs and their replacement with a white proslavery Christianity. Seabrook's *Essay* helps us see the prerogative of slaveowners to discern and destroy any form of religion connected to fanaticism on their plantations.

Seabrook recommended that slaveowners shore up their own religious authority to prevent any "incendiaries," such as Nat Turner, from influencing Black religion. "[The slave] should be practically treated as a slave," he wrote, "and thoroughly taught the true cardinal principles on which our peculiar institutions are founded, viz: that to his owner he is bound by the laws of God and man, and that no human authority can sever the link which unites them."[64] The operation here was to sacralize the order of slavery. Turner mobilized the insurrection through the demonization of slavery. Slavers fought back by doubling down on its sanctification.

Seabrook had ideas on the type of Christianity that should be taught to enslaved peoples. It should be relegated, he suggested, to simple principles that will emphasize their otherworldly salvation. Without this simplicity, the "mind of the negro" would get confused in theological disputations and contradictions, Seabrook thought. "His ambition and curiosity," Seabrook wrote, would become "unduly excited; in anxious and unprofitable meditations his soul becomes absorbed, and, in time we behold him a wild and restless fanatic—an enemy to himself, and useless, if not dangerous to his master."[65] Seabrook, like most Americans in political power, was well aware of Nat Turner's rebellion and cited Turner as an example of someone who outwardly seemed Christian but inwardly was taken by a "maddening zeal," brought on by the fact that he himself was a Black evangelist and had come into contact with other Black ministers and catechists.

Thomas Roderick Dew wrote an influential essay on the question of slavery in the wake of Turner's rebellion. Dew was the writer who emphasized how Turner had been determined *by* the sign of the sun to start the rebellion.[66] He was also an important figure in the debates over slavery that the Virginia assemblies considered in the wake of the insurrection. Gradual abolition was on the table. In response, Dew published *An Essay on Slavery* (1832), which mixed history and political economics to defend the role of slavery in Virginia.

Dew heralded the Christianization of the enslaved population as a moral good. He turned to Christian scripture to cite justifications of slavery. He called on Christian ministers who had abolitionist interests to mind their place. The minister should "beware, lest in their zeal for the black, they suffer too much of the passion and prejudice of the human heart to meddle with those pure principles by which they should be governed."[67] Beyond religious legitimation, he suggested that slavery was simply too profitable, and too beneficial for the increase of white Anglo-American civilization, to be abolished. Insurrections would not be a problem in the future. More slaves, he wrote, allowed for more profit and thus more police to control the slaves.[68] *An Essay on Slavery* was an attempt to exorcise the specter of Turner. Dew wrote that the Southampton Insurrection destroyed

> for a time, all feeling of security and confidence, and even when subsequent development had proved, that the conspiracy had been originated by a fanatical negro preacher,—(whose confessions prove beyond a doubt mental aberration)—and that this conspiracy embraced but few slaves . . .

still the excitement remained—still the repose of the commonwealth was disturbed—for the ghastly horrors of the Southampton tragedy could not immediately be banished from the mind.[69]

Dew's exorcism here reveals the ironic nature of fanaticism talk as white Americans applied it to Nat Turner after his death. On the one hand, fanaticism talk signaled the limited nature of the Southampton Insurrection. The rebel force constituted a minority of the enslaved population of Southampton. They revolted because of the madness of a single individual. Most slaves, this framing implied, were content with their enslavement. On the other hand, despite the rhetoric of superstitions and false religion and delusions, Turner's rebellion in fact happened. Christianity could be a force against slavery, as was becoming increasingly the case with the rise of abolitionists who based their moral critiques against slavery on Christian morals, as chapter 3 explores in greater detail. Turner was a necessary figure to conjure, to constantly bring up as a potential threat against the white population, in order to argue for the increased securitization of the slave regime. Dew brought Turner up, after all, to emphasize the *necessity* of slavery, even as the figure of Turner always brought to mind the instability—the Black religious creativity, the sense of prophecy, and the strategic militancy—lurking underneath and in the heavens above.

Conclusion

Nat Turner's narrative of powerful feelings, divine forces, and religious truth took place in an antebellum period full of prophecies and revelations. In part due to disestablishment and religious free exercise, it was an era of unruly religion and diversification. In lieu of a formal religious establishment, powerful governmental agents, religious authority figures, and writers in the media developed the language of fanaticism to police antebellum religion, especially among marginalized religious and racial communities. The category of fanaticism, then, was a product of power intended to delegitimate those labeled as fanatics. But it was also a response to the reality of figures like Nat Turner, whose narrative drew from and contributed to antebellum supernaturalism for the purpose of Black liberation.

Rather than researching fanaticism as mere discourse, this chapter has approached the term—and the relevant people—within an affective economy. Comparing and contrasting Turner's self-description with the various media and governmental accounts helps clarify the high stakes of the rhetorical and affective push and pull in the wake of the insurrection. The rebellious violence was the point of the rebellion. But the interpretation of the rebellion's causes—political and religious—was also important to Turner, and to a white society made anxious by Black rebellion. The violent actions of Turner and his associates reverberated throughout the nation. Claims and charges of fanaticism circulated among the waves of this reverberation, helping popularize the term in the wider American imagination.

At least according to secular measures, the insurrection failed. Its participants were captured and executed. Turner's conviction in an apocalyptic future and a reversal of fortunes for the enslaved did not come to pass, at least not immediately. Nonetheless, Turner's insurrection and his self-description of a religiously inspired rebel made him a specter of hope and terror in an increasingly polarized nation. White southerners enacted new laws to prevent future Nat Turners and referenced his name in debates over emancipation. The more radical abolitionists embraced Turner's use of violence and his narratives of divine emancipation and retribution. Black and white people debated slavery through recourse to scripture, morality, economics, and politics. Turner's *Confessions* and the diverse responses to it show that people also fought for and against slavery in an affective economy based on competition over agency, feelings, and religious truth.

3

The Feminine Fanatic

Love and Betrayal in Anti-Abolitionist Literature

In the "Concluding Remarks" of the 1852 abolitionist novel *Uncle Tom's Cabin*, Harriet Beecher Stowe raised a question that many readers may have been asking themselves about the unjust nature and violence of the slave regime. "But, what can any individual do?" She answered, "They can see to it that *they feel right.*" She went on, "An atmosphere of sympathetic influence encircles every human being.... See then to your sympathies in this matter! Are they in harmony with the sympathies of Christ?"[1] Scholars of religion, literature, feminism, and affect have long used this quotation, and the novel as a whole, to examine the sentimental culture of nineteenth-century women writers and of abolitionism.[2] For Stowe, sentimentality—the social flow of emotions enabled by the human capacity for sympathy—could guide people to moral truth and serve as conduits for progress. Her novel depicts the cruelties of the slave regime, emphasizing, for example, how it tore Black families apart and denied them (Protestant) Christianity. The influence of *Uncle Tom's Cabin* in galvanizing white northerners against slavery is well known today. So, too, are debates about the limits of sympathetic literature in its confidence in the translatability of experience across racial, gendered, and class identities.[3]

Less well known, except among literary scholars, are the writings of white Americans who critiqued Stowe in editorials and novels referred to as "anti-Tom" literature. Authors of anti-Tom literature attacked Stowe's Christian sentimentality as a form of religious fanaticism. The use of "fanaticism" as an accusation is especially present in anti-Tom novels written by women, who emphasized the danger of ungoverned sentiments, or the trust Stowe put in feeling right as a moral foundation. By one scholar's accounting, thirty-one anti-Tom novels have been published, the bulk in the 1850s. Ten of these novels were written by women, who had a newfound public voice through the genre of the novel. Of that ten, half were northerners, half southerners.[4] The primary works this chapter examines include Rebecca Harrington Smith's *Emma Bartlett; or, Prejudice and Fanaticism* (1856), V. G. Cowdin's *Ellen; or, The Fanatic's Daughter* (1860), Caroline Lee Hentz's *The Planter's Northern Bride* (1854), and Martha Haines Butt's *Antifanaticism: A Tale of the South* (1853). These novels shared many of the same narrative arcs, character archetypes, and moral lessons. All worked to instill in their readers the wrongness of Stowe's "feeling right" through the concept of fanaticism.

These writers, through their dramatic narratives and editorial screeds, worked to convince readers that the excessive fanatical affects of abolitionism constituted a betrayal of the white Christian family. Most nineteenth-century writings on fanaticism focused on men as the archetypical fanatic figures responsible for cultivating fanatical beliefs and practices in a given context. Fanatics, the story often went, were defined by their hatred and intolerance that was often signified as overly masculine. However, many anti-Tom novelists and newspaper editorials reconfigured the concept as they applied it to and blamed northern white women and men for abolitionism. This included Stowe herself. Excessive feeling—and a feminized loving sentimentality for enslaved Black people in particular—was a core feature of fanaticism alongside intolerant hatred. Though critiquing Stowe's sentimentality, these novels articulated and aimed to produce their own sentimental regimes. White women, in particular, had a duty to govern their own sentiments of love, hate, and sympathy toward the white Christian family, which, in the logic of these novels, relied upon Black subjugation for its safety, privileges, and rightful social position.

This chapter has four sections. I begin by situating anti-abolitionist writings within nineteenth-century sentimental literature, in which novelists sought to influence social movements through fictional narratives that *moved* people. I then examine how these writers portrayed the North and the South as having distinct atmospheres of sentiment that either encouraged or moderated fanatical religion. Zooming in from regions to characters, I then describe the archetype of the abolitionist and the imagined operations of how fanaticization, or the radicalization of someone into the abolitionist archetype, occurred. I conclude with the cultural work that I believe these writers were working to do in instilling a sentimental attachment to the white Christian family as dependent on enslavement.

As a warning that should be clear by now, these novels and the quotations I examine below are disturbing in their moral arguments and in particular scenes that are explicitly and bluntly white supremacist, portraying Black people as lacking intelligence, as prone to excessive feeling, and as unable to govern themselves. One of the blunt political strategies of these novels was to elide the agency, strategy, and moral arguments (including Christian moral arguments) of enslaved and freed Black women and men in challenging slavery.[5] White abolitionist literature, at times, has been guilty of this as well. In analyzing anti-Tom novels I am criticizing the logics of a particular white, well-to-do proslavery imagination that is embedded in fictional narratives, characters, and scenes. The upshot of this approach, I assert, is that it helps us understand the contested role of sentiment in an era of calls for social change and stout resistance to such calls.

The Antebellum Contest over Christian Sentiment

From the 1830s to the Civil War in the 1860s, white northerners and southerners debated the question of slavery in increasingly sectionalized and rhetorically violent ways. Mark Noll, among others, has emphasized that the split was also religious, referring to it as a "theological crisis."[6] In this crisis, white Protestants struggled to find unity and clarity on the issue of slavery in the Bible and in their ability to discern God's righteous hand in the nation's destiny. Proslavery literature interpreted the story of the "curse of Ham" in Genesis to legitimate the enslavement of Black people as biblically and divinely ordained. Abolitionist media may have presented its principles as commonsense Christian morality universally available to all, but it contained within it a strong attack on its opponents, many of whom also identified as and drew on Christian ideas. In fact, like so many episodes of nineteenth-century American religion, this media was highly polemical and sectarian, as Claudia Stokes has argued.[7] Further, Tracy Fessenden has examined Stowe's portrayal of the South, tied as it was to the slave regime, as a not-quite-Christian society. Stowe implicitly analogized southern culture to both "heathenism" and Catholicism, two of the dominant others of white Protestants in the era.[8] The white Protestant informal establishment, as David Sehat has put it, was being torn apart.[9] Protestants were also divided in terms of the proper role and use of sentiment in Christianity, a debate that became more pressing with the success of revivals and Methodist styles of preaching. By attending to the language of fanaticism—both what it signified and what forms of Christian sentiment were being cultivated in contrast to it—dueling sentimental regimes emerged.

The idea of sentiment in the nineteenth century did not simply entail feelings, as Stowe's famous quote about feeling right might suggest. Sentimentalism presumed and worked upon the ability of individuals to properly manage what I call their affectability—the relational management of one's willful agency, feelings, and external influence—for the sake of cultivating a moral disposition. Unlike theories that presume emotions to reside within individuals, nineteenth-century Americans understood sentiment to operate at the nexus of the individual and society, with its circulating media, networks of families and citizens, and educational programs. As Glenn Hendler has argued, Americans writing and reading novels in the mid-nineteenth century believed them to be tools of sentiment, especially the sentiment of sympathy.[10]

These theories did not treat sentiment as exclusive to women, but they often did argue that women held a special power over and burden of protecting sentiment for themselves and their families. Lauren Berlant has examined the emergence of this intimate women's culture that "flourishes by circulating as an already felt need, a sense of emotional continuity among women who identify with the expectation that, as women, they will manage their personal life and lubricate emotional worlds."[11] Sentimental literature presumes and works to create a felt moral unity among women, especially well-to-do white women. For Hendler and Berlant, and for most scholarship on sentimental literature, Stowe's *Uncle Tom's Cabin* is exemplary of the genre, in all of its power and limits.

Theories of fanaticism, beyond the genre of anti-Tom literature, also emphasized the role of sentiment. Fanaticism, in this framework, is not a *choice* that an individual makes, nor is it a mental disorder, as later psychologists would try to categorize it. Intellectuals in the nineteenth century dedicated increasing attention to theorize fanaticism. As chapter 1 examined, the most influential theorist in the English-speaking world was the evangelical Anglican Isaac Taylor, who, with the book *Fanaticism* in 1833, wrote the first English-language book dedicated to the topic. The book was published in New York the following year. With this and other writings, Taylor became an oft-cited figure in American encyclopedias, newspapers, and scholarship when it came to violent or excessive forms of religion. Taylor argued that fanaticism was a bodily and psychological disposition wherein the fanatic has vacated control of their will to the passions, has succumbed to supernatural delusions, and is driven by a sense of hatred. Importantly, Taylor believed fanaticism was a product of a particular social atmosphere. Religious fanaticism, as an affective phenomenon, circulates like a contagion across networks of people and media. Fanaticization is a phenomenon that happens to people. If left unchecked (by true Christian moderation, Taylor argued), the fanatics will "rush on ungovernably" for their particular religious cause.[12]

Critical responses to *Uncle Tom's Cabin* in the 1850s at times paralleled and at times explicitly drew on Taylor's concept of fanaticism as an affective phenomenon. One relevant response was "Confessions of an Abolitionist," written in the *Vermont Patriot & State Gazette* by the pseudonymous Omikron. He begins, "I have been in no slight degree affected by the spirit." This was the spirit of concern and outrage at the status of the enslaved. He proceeds to describe how *Uncle Tom's Cabin* made him shed tears for the plight of slaves. His narrative then took a turn. Reflecting on his own affected state, another book sprang to his mind: Taylor's book *Fanaticism*. What Omikron had experienced was, he discovered, "a mere fruitless excitement and love of agitation"—in short, religious fanaticism. The reviewer had fallen for the sentimental trap but, remembering Taylor's warnings about the dangers of fanaticism, proceeded to repossess himself from affective capture. "For no man," he wrote, "to say nothing of a Christian, has a right to yield himself blindly to the guidance of his feelings or emotions." The emotional fervor of abolitionism was a human fabrication. "I suspect," Omikron wrote, "that the spirit which excited these violent feelings was not of heavenly origin."[13] The review sought to model to the reader the seduction of abolitionist sentiment and the necessary wherewithal to resist its trappings. The very concept of fanaticism, here, was a tool that Christians needed to use to discern right and wrong feelings.

Critiques of Stowe and abolitionism more broadly did not uniformly condemn the use of sentiment. As was the case in Omikron's critique, the atmosphere of sympathetic influence necessitated, in this view, Christians to buffer themselves, to carefully regulate the power of affects over them. Fanaticism, as a word and as a theory, was a warning to self-govern one's affectability, or to pay attention to the sources, effects, and underlying "facts" of one's feelings. Of course, these theories and applications of sentiment were not just intellectual exercises. They were part of the polemics over racial slavery.

* * *

There are obvious reasons to conceptualize the Civil War and the rising tensions that precipitated it as a conflict between the North and the South. Certainly, the two regions had distinctive, though mutually imbricated, economies, political systems, and cultures. Anti-Tom novels emphasized another distinction that is a bit less obvious: the North and the South had distinct sentimental atmospheres. Naomi Greyser has theorized this dynamic through the concept of "affective geographies." "As sentimentalism mapped affective geographies by describing interior emotions in externalizing, spatial terms," she writes, "it correspondingly described geophysical space in intimate, emotional terms."[14] As Greyser emphasizes, such association of entire regions with distinct regimes of sentiment must be studied with a degree of caution considering how one's experience of a region was shaped by one's social position. Enslaved and freed Black people, for example, certainly had their own affective associations with American regions. These novelists, however, were concerned with cultivating a specifically white sentimentality.

Anti-Tom novels imagined distinct northern and southern affective atmospheres. Of relevance for this chapter, they represented the North as more prone to cultivating fanaticism and the South as more prone to religious moderation. For these novels, social atmospheres that more or less allow for the circulation of fanaticism are the cumulative result of distinctive regional religious histories, climates, resources, manners, and social relationships between racial groups. This included the very circulation of these texts. Consider the title of Butt's novel, *Antifanaticism: A Tale of the South*. The title refers to both the book and the region of the South as anti-fanatical. "The South," Butt writes in the preface, "is not what it has been represented by fanatical writers" like Stowe.[15] This implies not just that the South is defined by the absence of fanaticism, but that its atmosphere is conducive to a moderate form of religion, generally understood in these novels as a Protestant Christianity governed by white authorities. These regions, as much as individuals, are key characters in these stories.

One of the most striking regional differences was the role of climate, or "clime" according to the parlance of the time. Reading these novels feels, at times, like reading a weather report. The frequency and detailed attention that anti-Tom writers give to climate suggest that such weather reports are not mere filler. The landscapes, weather patterns, and agriculture are key to their sentimental moral argument. In this they paralleled one of Taylor's argument that "all the principal or most characteristic forms of fanaticism have had their birth beneath sultry skies, and have thence spread into temperate climates by transportation, or infection."[16] Nature, here, was a determinative source of religious and racial characteristics.

In one scene in *Ellen; or, The Fanatic's Daughter*, the character Horace Layton, a southerner, is moving his family to the North due to his antislavery commitments, forcing his wife Mary to leave "her luxurious Southern home to find neglect and hardship in the cold, ungenial North."[17] Coldness here referred to both the climate and the lack of warm relationships with fellow white people as the family finds themself isolated and laboring to survive. The language of the "moderate" and the "sunny South" contrasts with the intemperate and cold climate of the North. In *The Planter's Northern Bride*, the southern planter Moreland is courting the young northerner Eulalia. Moreland works to replace her impressions of the South as "dark and forbidding" with the South as having a "sunny clime" of "magnolia bowers and flowery plains." Eulalia, feeling the romance of the courtship and the pleasure of this alternative impression, gives away her changing sentiment as a "dawning colour mingled with the glow of sunset on her cheek."[18] Later, as abolitionists are building out the underground railroad, the narrator remarks on the threat of "darkness for brightness, and angry billows for smoothness, and the storm-gale of the North sweep cold and blighting over her Southern bower."[19] Elsewhere descriptions of the southern climate aimed to naturalize slavery within the harmony of the flora and fauna. For example, *Ellen* begins with a northerner traveling through Louisiana, with verdant fields, chirping birds, and the "chanting of the laborers," which "all appeared in beautiful harmony with Nature's noble panorama." For the northerner, alienated from such harmony and having left the frigid North, "the scene appeared like enchantment" and was full of "pleasurable emotions."[20] Butt, in her preface, wrote of the "warm sympathy" of southern culture that "assures him that the bosom warmed by such feelings cannot be the resting-place of cruelty and oppression."[21] The authors strategically play with scenes of darkness and light, coldness and warmth as literal descriptions of regional climates and symbols of the sentimental atmosphere.

Throughout these novels and nineteenth-century theories, fanaticism is metaphorically tied to storms and bad weather. Near the conclusion of *The Planter's Northern Bride*, the narrator asks the reader to imagine "the full triumph of fanaticism." Though the abolitionists, through encouraging slave rebellions, may have their "lightnings sheathed" at the moment, "they were ready, at any moment, to rend the cloud and dart their fiery bolts around." The end of slavery, here, would destroy the harmonious imagined southern nature of the novels. The "African, *unguided by the white man's influence*, would suffer the fairest portions of God's earth to become uncultivated wilderness."[22] The storm of fanaticism threatened the very climate and nature of the South. Further, the atmospheres of sentiment could, like weather systems, collide and transform each other.

Anti-Tom novels also argued that the fanaticism of abolition was evident in its mixing of religion and politics. Consider the debate between the two ministers Bartlett and Dare in *Emma Bartlett; or, Prejudice and Fanaticism*. Bartlett upbraids Dare for mixing religion and politics, saying they should neither "drag politics *up* to the pulpit, nor religion *down* to the politics."[23] Such a mixture would violate the spirit of not only the First Amendment but also Protestant Christianity. Bartlett suggests that Dare's desire to disobey the law or, worse, his desire to create a theocracy based on his convictions that slavery is unjust was a form of despotism more appropriate to Catholicism, Mormonism, or Judaism, with their presumed willingness to disobey national law for the sake of a "higher law." This strategy of contrasting "true" Protestantism against religious others as incapable of conforming themselves to liberal democracies was common among American Protestants in this era, including abolitionists who likened slavery to a Catholic style of domination. "Render unto Caesar the things which are Caesar's," Bartlett admonished Dare. Slavery and the Fugitive Slave Act were established law that should be respected according to the Protestant ideal of the separation of religion and politics. Categorizing abolitionism as fanatical was a strategy to excise it from proper Protestantism. This obscured, of course, the political dimensions of proslavery Christianity as mere Christianity.

Southern characters frequently brought up a pattern of fanatical religion in the North, and New England in particular. At times, the novels reference the Puritans as a theocratic and zealous precedent of abolitionists. One southerner, in *Ellen*, highlights the "innocent victims and the horrors of the 'Salem Witchcraft.'" He proceeded to lecture the northern abolitionists: "Seek your own reformation—for once keep still when fanaticism and persecution have raised the cry against those whose virtues so far exceed your own."[24] Abolitionism was another example of northern excesses in religion.

The beginning of *The Planter's Northern Bride* highlights the culture shock that the southern planter Moreland experienced during a business trip through New England, accompanied by Albert, a young man who was enslaved. When entering an inn, the owner invites Moreland and Albert to eat at the communal table. The owner, who clearly has negative views of the South as a land of slavery, needles Moreland, telling him that in the North "we look upon everybody here as free and equal," and quotes Proverbs: "When in Rome, do as the Romans do." Moreland, the heroic protagonist of the novel, takes this as a grave insult. A nearby gentleman at the inn explains to him, "In this village, you are in the very hot-bed of fanaticism; and that a Southern planter, accompanied by his slave, can meet by little sympathy, consideration, or toleration."[25] Moreland decides to allow Albert to dine at the table, but himself retires to his room. He would not be compelled to partake in such an equalizing ritual as dining with his slave.

It should be clear by this point that one of the things that these writers believed made abolition fanatical was a commitment to the political and social equality of Black and white people. If anything, these novels probably give too much credit to white northern abolitionists by framing them as proponents of social racial equality. Some whites were invested in equality, but others viewed Black people through a paternalistic Christian framework that argued for the equality of souls but not quite the equality of intellectual capacity, social rights, or political rights. Despite that reality, anti-Tom novels sought to exaggerate the level of equality white abolitionists were arguing for to increase the horror for readers invested in white supremacy and racial slavery.

The affective bonds of the white family extended to slaves, though always in service of the well-being of the white masters. Consider a scene from *The Planter's Northern Bride*. A married white southern couple, Richard and Ildegerte Laurens, have traveled to Cincinnati to seek a specialist doctor for Richard's illness, which turns out to be terminal. They brought with them Crissy, their slave. Another couple, the Softlys, are white abolitionists. Sharing the same inn as the southerners, the Softlys hatch a plan to free Crissy through the underground railroad, believing her misery to be caused by her enslavement. The narrator makes it clear that Crissy's misery is a result of her missing her southern plantation and her concern over Richard. The Softlys proceed to offer Crissy a bribe to let them free her, despite her cries that she would rather die than abandon her masters, whom she loves. However, the bribe and the emotional pleas from the Softlys prove to be too much. Crissy agrees to let Mr. Softly ferry her to a safe house. As they proceed up the Ohio River on a small boat, the novel makes clear the new condition Crissy has accepted. While Mr. Softly is well clothed for the wet and chilly evening, Crissy is left without proper protection from the elements. Shivering, she sees Ildegerte's black hair in the grass of the river banks and sees the eyes of Richard, who happened to pass away that very evening, staring at her from the heavens above. According to the narration, she begins to realize the "bonds of affection and gratitude" she had just rejected and the cruelty of free life in the North for Black people.

The novel frames this as the problem of Black free agency and the need for Black sentiment to be managed by white surveillance. Crissy, under the sentimental spell of the Softlys, was a "poor bewildered creature again yielded herself to their influence, and promised to be guided passively by their will."[26] While ill from losing her husband and her slave, Ildegerte meets Judy, a free Black woman who had come across Crissy and sees an opportunity: to voluntarily enslave herself and return to the southern plantation. The novel stops the narrative to address the reader: freedom "is a glorious possession, but its glory depends upon the character of the nation or individual that owns it."[27] The fact that this scene took place in Cincinnati is relevant as a hub of abolitionism, the Underground Railroad, and the home city of Harriet Beecher Stowe from 1832 to 1850. In the competing destinies of Crissy and Judy, the author Hentz worked to turn the northern Black trek in search of freedom a tragedy and the southern Black trek into slavery a tale of the natural racial order being restored. In historical reality, the Reverse Underground Railroad was a violent affair of forcibly kidnapping Black people to force them into, or back into, slavery.[28]

It is worth noting that abolitionists also used the language of fanaticism against defenders of the slave regime, though not with the same frequency or importance as anti-abolitionists. The abolitionist politician and minister Owen Lovejoy, for example, argued in a speech in the US House of Representatives that it was proslavery advocates who were fanatical. He discerned a shift in defenses of slavery. The "different sentiment" that was emerging in the 1840s and 1850s "deems slavery not an evil but a blessing."[29] This inversed the geography presented in anti-Tom novels by emphasizing white southerners' attachment to slavery as morally corrupt and forcing unnecessary and costly imperial expansion through the Southwest, especially the recent Mexican-American War. "The most impious phase of this fanaticism," Lovejoy went on, "is that it claims the sanction of the Bible for American slavery."[30] Though Lovejoy made a contrasting argument to anti-Tom novels, the territories of the conflict were the same: proper sentiment, biblical sanction, and the role of Christian morality in American civil society.

The Abolitionist and Fanaticization

Although these novels described abolitionism as a growing threat that had a social dimension and drew crowds, actual abolitionists in these narratives are presented as isolated antagonists. Their character arcs signify the irrationality and dangers of abolitionism. There are two generic types of abolitionists in the novels—frauds, who have ulterior motives of fame, wealth, or, when it's a male abolitionist, sexual access to fellow abolitionist women, and fools, who failed to properly govern their wills and sentiments and become ensnared in the seduction of abolitionism. They may be earnest, unlike the first type, but their earnestness in the antislavery cause proves to hurt them and their families.

The most sinister abolitionist character in these novels is Parson Blake in *Ellen; or, The Fanatic's Daughter*. Blake's moral sentiments are insincere, and his motivation for fighting against slavery is to open up the fertile fields of the South for his own purchase. His words when preaching are stirring and aptly use the powerful language of freedom, humanity, and the spread of the gospel. However, his body cannot help but reveal his true intentions from time to time. While preaching, his "excited imagination" prompts him to continually put his hands deep into his pockets, imagining the profit he is working toward. In other scenes, he lusts after the protagonist Ellen. His body and face, again, was "red, full and sensual in expression," giving away his true intentions.[31] The language of Christianity and talk of Black equality are just tools for his own advancement. The parson "used religion as a mere cloak beneath which, for a time, his vices were effectually hid."[32] He had little care for what would happen to the freed Blacks once the abolitionist party triumphed in its real estate scam.

The other abolitionist figure in *Ellen* is Horace Layton, whose moral sentiments are presented as foolish. From the beginning, Layton is described as easily affectable, "nervously sensitive, and religiously inclined—though his religion consisted more of superstitious fears."[33] Such a disposition made him open to manipulation, which Parson Blake, his brother-in-law, had taken advantage of since childhood. The influence of Blake is so great that Layton, from the South, has "forgotten, or suppressed" the facts of the warm, luxurious life he once had in a slave society. In consequence, "his sympathies were all perverted."[34] As we will see, Layton's compromised sentiments, under the control of Blake, made him "worse than a heathen—a traitor to his own fireside."[35] Though Layton is a fool, the novel still takes him to task for failing to properly guard and filter his sentiments.

Some of the most heated scenes in anti-Tom novels are when the protagonists face off against abolitionists. These scenes involve debates over the Constitution and the Bible and, of course, a battle over sentiment. In *The Planter's Northern Bride*, the southerner Moreland's courtship with the northerner Eulalia Hastings is compromised by her father, who resents him for his southern roots and for owning slaves. In a tense meeting between the two men, Moreland feels himself succumbing to Hastings's fiery sentiment. "Moreland," the scene describes, "was losing his usual self-possession. A hot flush crimsoned his cheek; his voice became husky and tremulous."[36] However, the protagonist Moreland is able to recover, to avoid losing command of his argument through "passion or excitement." In contrast, Hastings's voice "shivered and broke, when pitched on too high a key, or became thick and incoherent in the vengeance of argument."[37] The "factual" nature of Moreland's defense of slavery is proved not through facts themselves but through his sentimental control contrasted with Hastings's irrational fanatical drive.

Abolitionists in these novels are always white. Black figures who critique or rebel against slavery are categorized as criminals or as mere pawns of white abolitionists. Indeed, part of the strategy of these novels is to convince readers that slaves themselves generally supported slavery. Any Black resistance occurred only because of northern white interference. Scholar of religion Curtis Evans has examined the discourse of the naturally religious slave prevalent among northern abolitionists like Stowe and defenders of slavery. He argues for a critical approach to both, emphasizing how the very idea of the naturally religious slave, though it could be used for abolitionist arguments, was part of a racializing project that assessed the humanity and capacity of Black people *through* their religiosity.[38] Especially in anti-Tom novels, the naturally religious slave is held up as a liability. Black religion, because of its presumed overreliance on the passions, was susceptible to fanaticization, especially without paternal white southern surveillance. This fanaticism is not inherent to the enslaved, who, as the novels hammer over and over, privilege and appreciate their enslavement, but is open to external manipulation from white abolitionists.

Near the conclusion of *The Planter's Northern Bride*, a northern Methodist minister named Brainard arrives on the plantation to preach to the enslaved. Moreland is at first cautious "for the agents of fanaticism are scattered over the length and breadth of the land, and in the name of the living God endeavoring to destroy our liberties and rights."[39] Brainard assures Moreland that he has no such intention. However, once he begins his sermon at a church attended by nearby slaves, he kindles a "deeper fervour" with "stormy eloquence." The Black attendees begin "to shout and clap their hands in an ecstasy of ungovernable emotion."[40] Moreland, convinced that the minister was truly spreading "the inspiration of religion," allows him to continue to preach on his plantation. Once Brainard has his parishioners enthusiastic and running high on emotions, he shifts gears once the white slaveowners stop attending. He announces that though he "loved his white brethren; but far better he loved the dark and lowly African,—loved him, because, like his Saviour, he was despised and rejected of men."[41] He proceeds to preach of Zion, of the glory of African civilization they were stolen from, and of the possibility of freedom, especially in the North. Brainard's true motives become clear. His preaching is intended to inspire an insurrection along the lines of Nat Turner's Southampton Rebellion. As the previous chapter argued, Turner was an early fanatic figure in American consciousness. The specter of a new Turner engaging in violent resistance against white slave-owning families haunted southern culture.

The Romance of the White Protestant Family

Like *Uncle Tom's Cabin*, these novels tell stories of families being torn apart and coming together. The protagonists are often young white women and men split between northern and southern influences. For example, the titular character of *Ellen* has a delinquent abolitionist father and a nurturing southern mother. The protagonists court each other, but their romance is threatened by the forces of abolitionism and sectional strife. The sympathetic influence that Stowe worked to generate proves powerful, and a protagonist, or an important relative, is seduced by sympathy for the enslaved and outrage over the slave regime. Over time, however, the protagonists come to discover the corrupted, fanatical form of Christianity driving abolitionism and learn the "facts" of northern horrors and southern pleasures through stereotypical scenes of oppressed northern white laborers, singing slaves, and miserable, dangerous freed Black people. The narratives often culminate in a marriage between the white protagonists. Having learned of the wrong feelings of Stowe's "feeling right," the protagonists settle into an idyllic southern domestic life, embracing their role as slaveowners to their happiness and enrichment.

Once in the South, the scenes shift back and forth between domestic romance of the white protagonists and the governance of slaves. These two scenes are connected and together form the central message of anti-Tom novels. Abolitionist sentiment threatened the bonds of the white Protestant family in two ways. First, the fanaticization of white northerners led to a love of enslaved Black people that destroyed their families. Second, the freedom of Black people posed a threat to white families. For both, the South provided a refuge for whiteness, though one under duress by the storm clouds of abolitionism. As Sylvester Johnson, among others, has argued, white freedom and inclusion into the body politic as citizens is discursively and materially intertwined with Black unfreedom.[42] These novels make this case explicitly.

The idea that white abolitionists were investing their sentimental energy into Black people as opposed to their own white family is evident in the relationship of the abolitionist minister Horace Layton to his wife and children in *Ellen*. Layton, in an effort to become an abolitionist influencer and under the sway of the sinister Parson Blake, moves his family from the luxury of the South to the industrial North. In one pivotal scene, Mary Layton, his wife, was fretting over their ten-year-old son Charlie, who had not yet returned from his job at the mill on a dangerously cold day. Horace, however, was too busy writing abolitionist editorials to have any concern. Mary, running out into the weather, eventually finds Charlie, frozen and dead. This narrative may have been a particularly nasty shot at Stowe, whose son Charley died as an infant.

Horace, in trying to process the loss of his son, finds himself conflicted between "nature and fanaticism" and struggles to process where he should be orienting his sympathies.[43] Nature, in this case, is his family. Mary, however, was more discerning of the source and effects of his sentiments. She accuses Parson Black of dragging her family into a northern life of poverty and misery by "enslaving" Horace, "body and soul."[44] Northern fanaticization here is likened to a form of white enslavement. She begs her husband to abandon his antislavery crusade and for the family to move back to the South. He refuses and instead travels by himself to the South to preach and inspire insurrections among the enslaved. However, Horace has a conversion experience in the South, realizing the sinfulness of his zeal after learning the "facts" of the South by a white southern minister who owned slaves and represented the "perfect Christian character."[45] Struggling with his health, he returns to his wife to "crave forgiveness before I die, for the neglect of all of my most sacred duties—the care of my family."[46] With limited time left, he turns to raising their daughter, Ellen. This education and nurturing sets her on a path toward the conclusion of the novel, in which she marries a southern plantation owner.

The novels have a clear moral message for their readers. Martha Haines Butt concludes her picturesque portrayal of the South in the novel *Antifanaticism* with an admonishment: "If the Northern people have any sympathy to spare, let them give it to their poor white servants, for our slaves do not stand in any need of it at all."[47] Moreland's cautionary note to Hastings reflected the unity of whiteness: "Believe not all the tales of the vagrants, who are mostly fugitives from justice, not oppression. In your zeal for one portion of humanity forget not the interests of another, to which you are more closely allied."[48] These novels do not just exalt whiteness but do so in relation to Black degradation. The planter Moreland has to control insurrectionary sentiment among his slaves after they had attended sermons by the abolitionist Brainard. He is successful. In the wake of that moment, his wife Eulalia has a romantic reaction to the scene. "His superiority was manifest," she describes, "in the triumph of mind over matter. He seemed to her an angel of light surrounded by spirits of darkness."[49] This scene, especially, articulates how the protagonists' domestic families are founded upon a white Protestant supremacy.

The romance of the white Protestant family was also a romance of white national unity. In the conclusion to *Emma Bartlett*, the protagonist Emma has survived a dalliance with abolitionists and has just gotten married. She asks her husband to hold her as she contemplates her feelings to plunge into the dark waters of Boston Harbor. Her husband braces her and expresses his concern. She responds, "I was only speaking of my impulses. I would not give way to such feelings for all the world." It is a strange scene that makes sense only in the affective economy of abolitionist and anti-abolitionist literature. Having bracketed her inner feelings, Emma proceeds to recite a poem of her own making about the importance of white union as the legacy of the Constitution. Describing the dangers of abolitionism, she recites,

> For once let the chalice of Union be broke
> And contention will scatter the dew
> That peace and good feeling so long have distilled
> From the blossoms of brotherly love.[50]

Emma's poem provides a redirection of her feelings from individual destruction based on internal impulse to unity through a reenactment of the sacred founding of the nation. She goes on to provide imagery of a bereft George Washington weeping over a wrecked ship that symbolizes a broken body politic. On the one hand, Emma's poem conveys a fairly basic idea of national unity as based on the feeling of togetherness. On the other hand, the fact that this poem comes at the end of a sprawling family drama with an anti-abolitionist message signals a more substantial, and perhaps dangerous, theory of how sentiments can shape, cultivate, and destroy the role of the nation as defined by gendered and racial identities.

Most of the marriages brought together a northerner and southerner, with the northerner often being the wife and the southerner often being the husband. Such unions, the novels suggested, offered a way forward, one that embraced that southern slave system and anti-Black racism as a whole. This hope is also present in the clues at the end of some of the novels that the protagonists are expecting a child. As *The Planter's Northern Bride* put it, the result of these marriages is that "the blood of the North and the South mingles in the veins of their children."[51] This union, or reunion, of whiteness on a national level could occur through reproduction. This urging for white unity across regions foreshadowed what Edward J. Blum described as the postwar reforging of the white republic.[52]

Yet despite the hopeful endings for the protagonists, the novels remind readers of the real danger that abolition presents to the nation. The depth of the conspiracy, anti-Tom novels suggested, was "amalgamation," or marriage and offspring between Blacks and whites. As *Emma Bartlett; or, Prejudice and Fanaticism* put it, "*Amalgamation* will be the next proposed 'reform' as anything else. . . . What's to hinder those who profess such an *ardent attachment* for the blacks, from uniting with them in the holy bonds of wedlock, provided *their consciences approve?*"[53] One anti-abolitionist tract titled "The Conspiracy of Fanaticism" argued that not only was religious fanaticism the driving force for amalgamation, but amalgamation would lead to further fanaticism. The American citizen will become "less manly and intellectual, he will also be more easily governed, without the aid of that dangerous instrument called human reason, which is a sad stumbling-block in the way of fanaticism." This article also used coded language to suggest a Puritanical morality where all Americans will "be immersed in gloom and superstition; our only recreations will be at midnight conventicles, and our only excitements the phrenzy of fanaticism."[54] Fanatical energy, as a type of affective contagion, was exponential.

Conclusion

My aim in this chapter has been primarily historical—the intersection of religion, race, and affect in the social context of primarily white well-to-do writers in the 1850s. I do see this period and the contested role of feelings in social change as part of a broader pattern in US culture. Social movements that challenge powerful institutions and norms often require appeals to sympathy, passion, and outrage to garner success. People who organize against social change, and especially against radical social movements, have numerous rhetorical strategies at their disposal. One is that the social movement for change is based only on *feeling* in contrast to the established social order, based on nature, reason, and, in the case of proslavery arguments, divine decree. Social change requires affective work, of course. But we should also be cautious about rhetoric that implies differential capacity to affect or be affected or that represents a movement as the result of mindless feeling.

Consider recent slogans like "facts over feelings" and "facts don't care about your feelings." These may seem like new phrases, but they represent an old strategy. Consider the anti-abolitionist tract *Fanaticism and Its Results; or, Facts Versus Fancies*, which argued that the spread of abolitionism was due to "appeals addressed to the worst feelings, and most ungovernable passions of mankind. By poisoning their hearts with tales of Negro wrongs and sufferings, by base and vile slanders upon their brethren of the South."[55] At its most basic, this chapter suggests we question such easy binaries of facts versus "fancies" when analyzing movements for and resistance to social change. A more complicated but worthwhile task is to attend the competing sentimental regimes even, or especially, when a social movement presents itself as simply rational, natural, and divinely ordained.

4

The Fanatic Mind

Psychiatry, Law, and the Case of Charles Guiteau

When Charles Guiteau walked up to the gallows to give his final words on June 30, 1882, he chose to sing them. "I saved my party and my land, Glory hallelujah!," he recited. "But they have murdered me for it, And that is the reason I am going to the Lordy. Glory hallelujah! Glory hallelujah! I am going to the Lordy!"[1] Guiteau, at times, seemed unaffected by his execution because he trusted his sense of divine providence. "The worst that men can do is to kill you," he had told the court during his trial, *United States v. Charles J. Guiteau*, in which the jury found him guilty of the murder of President James Garfield. Guiteau had shot Garfield twice in the back on July 2, 1881.[2] Garfield died two months later. Guiteau repeatedly stated that he was serving a higher sovereign than the United States when he assassinated the president. He claimed that "nothing that the Deity directs a man to do can violate any law."[3] Though found guilty and condemned to be executed, he had fulfilled his role in God's plan to protect the destiny of the nation.

Americans were equally fascinated and horrified by the trial, which was one of the most publicized of the nineteenth-century United States. Obviously, Americans followed the case because it involved the murder of a sitting president. Guiteau indisputably shot the president, so a guilty verdict was probable from the beginning. However, the transcript of the trial runs nearly three thousand pages. The length of his trial and public fascination in it had two other factors. First, Guiteau was an eccentric personality who confidently preached a Christian theology that was both familiar and strange to many Americans, especially northern Protestants. Second, *United States v. Charles J. Guiteau* raised the question of insanity and legal culpability. "Without the Deity's pressure," Guiteau had claimed, "I never should have sought to remove the President. This pressure destroyed my free agency. The Deity compelled me to do the act."[4] His attorney argued that such a deific decree amounted to insanity and, importantly, a form of religious insanity. Defying Guiteau's own desires, his legal team deployed an insanity defense. Guiteau himself pleaded that his fellow Americans recognize the divine mission he had acted upon. Like Nat Turner, the antislavery rebel, Guiteau embodied the figure of the fanatic in his time, and the American public pored over the details of his religious biography and debated the religious, political, and medical factors that may have led him to assassinate President Garfield. Indeed, the trial is remarkable for its mixture of debates over legal standards of responsibility, physiological signs of mental disease, and preaching about the nature of sin.

This chapter begins with a survey of the field of psychiatry and diverse understandings of religious fanaticism and insanity. It proceeds to a close reading of the trial transcript and concludes by examining how physicians and psychologists treated mental health as a sign of national, religious, and racial evolutionary development.

The category of religious insanity demonstrates the ongoing significance of fanaticism as concept rooted in Protestant theology but applied across secular fields. Many historians of medicine have traditionally treated the history of psychiatry as one of secularization wherein theological and supernatural ideas fade from relevance.[5] Indeed, scholars have often framed the Guiteau trail as a battle between a traditional Protestant view of individual sinfulness (the view of the prosecution and its expert witnesses) and an emerging argument by neurologists that religious insanity was a physiological and social reality rooted in a hereditary disposition (the view of the defense and its expert witnesses, many of whom were more skeptical about traditional Christianity).[6] However, I see in the Guiteau trial the continuing relevance of religio-racial affectability across the spectrum of legal and psychiatric experts. Psychiatrists aimed to explain behavior and offer remedies to behavior viewed as unhealthy. The courts aimed to assess legal responsibility and dictate appropriate punishments. Both fields in this era aimed to provide secular scientific frames for thinking about religion that were rational, universal, and neutral. Of course, the fields served two different purposes.

For both, the idea of "religious insanity" raised similar anxious questions over the affectability of the fanatic figure. What role did the human will play in one's fanaticization? What caused religious insanity, and where could evidence of its causes be found? Was it located in family history (heredity), social experience, the physical brain, or the cumulative moral choices made by an individual? If fanaticism was not something people willfully chose but something that happened *to* people, how could or should they be judged? Such questions and concerns were implicit in nineteenth-century theories of fanaticism and relevant for the trial.

Born in Illinois in 1841, Guiteau was raised in a devout but abusive Protestant family. He found power in the healthy living promoted by the Young Men's Christian Association. He was for a time a regular attendee at Henry Ward Beecher's abolitionist Plymouth Church in Brooklyn, where he began to regret his past anti-Black racism. He spent time living with the free love utopian Oneida Community. He read, and plagiarized, Oneida founder John Humphrey Noyes's claims that Christ had already returned in 70 CE. He railed against the religious skeptic Robert Ingersoll. His encounters with the revivalist Dwight Moody, whose books he sold, inspired him to become a traveling preacher with a desire to cultivate a revival of true Protestant Christianity. He styled himself a modern-day apostle Paul, though his sermons and publications never garnered a large following. In 1880, he became fixated on the presidential election and believed that President Garfield would grant him a consulship for his loyalty to the Republican Party. This, too, did not come to pass.

Feeling betrayed, he began to view the new administration as a threat and feared, without due reason, that President Garfield was leading the nation into another civil war. In May 1881 he received "inspiration" (his word) that he should "remove" President Garfield. After prayerful reflection, he believed that this was a command from God and not Satan. After a series of aborted assassination attempts, Guiteau shot President Garfield on July 2.[7] Though acknowledging that he felt betrayed by the president during the trial, Guiteau reiterated that his decision to assassinate the president was not his choice and did not result from personal grievance. He believed himself anchored in divine revelation and in the Christian Bible. When his theology came up in the trial he often lashed out at the jury, asking them if they believed in the Bible and the commands God had given to prophets like Noah and Abraham.

Though Guiteau imagined himself a popular hero, few if any Americans found his Christianity particularly compelling. The *Chicago Daily Tribune* claimed that Guiteau "is, according to his own story A FANATIC who has been moved to shoot the President by the command of God, and for the welfare of the Republican party and the American people."[8] The *New York Times*, in covering his execution, condemned the assassin, accusing him of being "conscienceless" and "blasphemous," and emphasized that his "religious professions" were of his own manufacturing and not divine.[9] These were common charges against fanatics. Fanatics were functionally dangerous and epistemologically in error. Such accusations were easy for the press to print, but lawyers and witnesses would find that arguing for or against religious insanity at the nexus of psychology and law would prove more of a challenge. Guiteau's assassination of President Garfield and the criminal trial that followed brought these psychiatric debates over the relation of true religion, insanity, and fanaticism into the public sphere like never before.

Governing Fanaticism and Insanity in Psychiatry

A brief history of Western psychiatry and religion will help contextualize the criminal trial as a showdown over competing theories of religious insanity between psychiatrists associated with asylums and the rising field of neurology. Psychiatrists in the nineteenth century increasingly argued that human behavior and abilities could be understood through the study of biology (nerves, the brain, heredity), psychology (the faculties of the will, feelings, reason), and sociology (family life, social class, and religious experiences). Explanations based on supernatural causes, such as demonic harm, declined. Most believed that insanity was a result of some sort of damage to the brain caused by nerves or blood flow. It is from this context that we received the phrase a "rush of blood to the head" to describe someone losing their senses temporarily and, according to these early psychiatrists, potentially damaging their brain and thus their faculties. Social influence, then, operated through and on the body. Despite this secular immanent frame for studying human psychology, religion continued to play a role in the rise of psychiatry in a way that cannot be assessed as neutral or universal. Three components of religion came under psychiatric debate and scrutiny: moral depravity, egoism, and supernatural experiences.

Psychiatric terms related to religious insanity, including religious excitement, monomania, theomania, and fanaticism, were frequently used to mark abnormal religion and to explain how excessive religion could endanger human health, especially in a society invested in religious free exercise. Though psychiatrists sometimes used the language of fanaticism and insanity interchangeably, they usually referred to fanaticism as a social environment of unruly and unhealthy religion that could lead to individual cases of mental insanity. Most experts who identified with the emerging field of psychiatry believed that religion had a role to play in mental health. As Tanaquil Taubes has written, many "superintendents had definite opinions about the dangers of exposing their patients to 'too much' religion, about the benefits of regular worship, and about the propensity of certain disorders to produce excessive preoccupation with religious themes."[10] However, physicians and psychologists disagreed about which religions and which particular practices constituted moderation or excess.

For many histories of the field, French nosologist Philippe Pinel founded modern psychiatry. Pinel is often heralded for his natural scientific approach to classifying mental disorders and his use of faculty psychology. Faculty psychology was dominant until the rise of Freudian psychology. This philosophy emphasized the semiautonomous features of the mind. Psychiatrists rarely agreed on the number or names for these features. Pinel often emphasized three faculties: understanding (akin to reason), will, and affect (passions). He believed that intense affective states, especially, could disturb the operations of reason.[11]

Fanaticism was one such affective state. Pinel's 1801 *Treatise on Insanity* was translated into English in 1806 and helped influence a shift to viewing insanity as a disease and not a result of demonic activity. Where experts in the past had turned to supernatural phenomena to explain mental health problems, they now became potential evidence of them. In *Treatise on Insanity*, Pinel wrote that "of the numerous illusions to which the imagination is subject, the most difficult to be eradicated are those originating in fanaticism. . . . How extremely difficult to level, with his real situation, the ideas of a man swelled up with morbid pride, solely intent on his high destinies, of thinking himself a privileged being, an emissary of heaven, a prophet from the Almighty, or even a divine personage."[12] His understanding of fanaticism went beyond a self-appointed role of prophetic significance. It included visions of demons, ghosts, and angels. Pinel's support of the French Revolution, and the persecution of the Catholic Church that came with it, is evident in his writings. During his role as a physician at Asylum de Bicêtre, for example, he estimated that 30 percent of patients whom he studied were made mad by the turbulence of the French Revolution and 25 percent by "religious fanaticism." Often, these two demographics were connected. He described the trauma present in priests, monks, and nuns. One "young religious enthusiast" terrified by the thought of eternal torment refused to eat or sleep. There was only one remedy: intimidate the patient with the threat of severe treatment to such an extent that his fear of future eternal torment would be overcome. Pinel wrote that this strategy worked and that the patient's "sleep and strength gradually returned; his reason recovered its empire."[13] Part of the job of early psychiatry was to identify religious beliefs and practices that were harmful and work, through soft and hard treatments, to return the patient to reason.

One of the Americans whom Pinel influenced was Benjamin Rush, who rarely used the language of fanaticism but did speak of religious enthusiasm, which he believed to be a frequent sign of amenomania, or delusions that a patient fixated on but that did not corrupt their reasoning capabilities as a whole. He listed four religious elements he believed signaled amenomania:

> 1. In a belief that they are the peculiar favourites of heaven, and exclusively possessed of just opinions of the divine will, as revealed in the Scriptures. 2. That they see and converse with angels, and the departed spirits of their relations and friends. 3. That they are favoured with visions, and the revelation of future events. And, 4. That they are exalted into beings of the highest order. I have seen two instances of persons, who believed themselves to be the Messiah.[14]

Rush proceeded to write that in previous eras such religious beliefs would be ascribed to impiety. States would fine or imprison such enthusiasts. However, Rush emphasized that in the new era of moral treatment such behaviors are as "devoid of impiety as an epileptic fit."[15]

The treatment was not punishment but medical care within a controlled, ideally caring, environment. The problem was not one of willful disobedience or theological errors as much as a disease. The goal was to reform religious excesses on the individual level.

The psychiatrist Amariah Brigham, influenced by Pinel and his student Jean-Étienne Dominique Esquirol, exceeded Rush in providing, at times, a more aggressive skepticism toward religion as a sign and cause of insanity. Brigham served as superintendent of the State Lunatic Asylum in Utica, New York, created the *American Journal of Insanity* (now the *American Journal of Psychiatry*), and launched what became the American Psychiatric Association. In 1835 Brigham published *Observations on the Influence of Religion upon the Health and Physical Welfare of Mankind*. Variations of the word "fanatic" appeared forty-one times.

Brigham's *Observations* served as a warning sign about the excesses of Protestant evangelicalism, which he implicitly compared with fanatical, more primitive religions. Even in white Protestant societies, citizens, "especially in times of excitement on religious subjects, and in free, democratic countries, they become fanatical, and often licentious, and call for suppression." The solution is clear: religion dictated by "reason, calm and enlightened, should guide us upon these subjects."[16] The fanatical aspects of evangelicalism, in his critique, included revival camp meetings, night prayer meetings, and belief in the Holy Spirit as having supernatural effects.

Such religious excitement and supernaturalism was an important cause of not just insanity but epilepsy, convulsions, and hydrocephalus that were leading to "a generation of men and women, weak and enfeebled in body and mind."[17] As such, Brigham addressed his book to clergy as much as to fellow physicians. Brigham believed religious sentiment to be a universal phenomenon that affected the health of individuals and societies for better or worse. Brigham believed a Protestant style of Christianity to be the supreme model of cultivating rational self-governing. However, Brigham was far more critical of revivals, arguing that ministers like Charles Finney helped "justify the most wild fanaticism the world has ever known."[18] In his reading of the New Testament, "Christ established no ceremonies at all: he exacted virtuous conduct, not the observance of rights."[19] Too much ritual, too much feeling. Summarizing his theological views, Brigham argued that "God has no supernatural dealings with men, that we can observe" and criticized revivals for how they "injure the health—cause insanity, and other diseases." Instead, he recommended that "information on all subjects can be obtained by reading."[20] Brigham seemed to advocate for the subjugation of religious sentiment and supernaturalism as a whole to secular reasoning. This was especially important in the United States. Brigham and others believed that Americans were distinctly susceptible to religious fanaticism, which "prevails most in countries where the people enjoy civil and religious freedom."[21]

Brigham was far from the only early psychiatrist to express concern about American religion. Pliny Earle, a physician known for his service as the superintendent of the Bloomingdale Asylum in New York, described religious excitement as one of the prime causes of insanity in his asylum: "In a country of universal toleration upon religious subjects, and sheltering, under this broad banner, congregations of almost every sect that has ever appeared in Christendom, it is to be supposed that the religious sentiment would act under its greatest possible variety of phases, and in every diversity of gradation between the extremes of apathy and fanaticism." He went on to clarify that while some revivals could cause overexcitement, Christianity, as "true religion," would not "overthrow the powers of the mind to which it was intended to yield the composure of a humble hope and the stability of a confiding faith." Earle kept detailed statistics of his patients. For example, he provided data on alleged physical causes of insanity (which 664 patients had) and alleged moral causes (which 522 patients had). Of the moral causes, "Religious Excitement, &c." accounted for 93, second only to "pecuniary difficulties." Other categories included novel reading (3), dealing in lottery tickets (1), "kick on stomach, from horse" (1), mesmerism (1), and masturbation (37).[22] The behaviors associated with "religious excitement" were quite broad and not uncommon in an age of electric religion.

Some chastised Rush, Brigham, and Earle for being too eager to claim that religious practices, especially Christian practices, could be to blame. Brigham's successor, John Gray, was one such critic. In an 1871 talk, Gray staked his claim that "emotions, sentiments, passions, and affections" could not cause insanity. Only physical impairment, diseases, or injuries could.[23] He castigated his predecessors for a lack of piety. "The sublime faith of Christianity is rather a safeguard against it, and is unquestionably a support under its scourging. We do not believe that insanity is produced by this cause [religion] directly, by a profound impression made through the sentiments and emotions upon the nervous system; or indirectly by gradually undermining the general health."[24] Gray argued that immoral actions, such as murder, were a result of moral depravity, not disease. He was influenced by commonsense realism and rejected many Enlightenment ideas. Gray emerged as a defender of traditional Protestant beliefs in sin and moral culpability in the United States, especially as an expert witness for the prosecution in *United States v. Charles J. Guiteau*.[25]

Charles Spitzka, who had a history of clashing with Gray, served as the expert witness for the defense and carried forward the earlier skepticism of Rush, Brigham, and Earle. Spitzka did not work in an asylum but represented the emerging field of neurology, which was often critical of superintendents and their asylums. Neurologists in this era were generally more liberal in viewing cases of insanity as caused more purely by neurophysiological conditions that were inherited rather than caused by decisions made by the afflicted. Spitzka was born in New York City but studied medicine in Germany. He worked to rehabilitate the theory of monomania, in which religiously insane people could reason properly but whose reasoning went awry when based upon false premises, like that God had a special plan for them. For example, Spitzka wrote a brief diagnosis of the English writer Samuel Johnson. He argued that Johnson had an "impulsive monomania" expressed through gesticulations that appeared like a "superstitious ceremonial." Spitzka noted that if Johnson had attended a revival in modern New York he probably would become overexcited and end up in an asylum, a "living tomb."[26] The affective geography of the United States, and especially northern culture with its history from Puritanism to the revivals of the burned-over district, made it a contributor to mental health issues. And yet, he emphasized, Johnson had a keen intellect and was a productive member of society in the context of eighteenth-century England, which he presumed to be more stable and moderate in its religious culture. Other neurologists also ridiculed the Christianity of figures like Gray. William Hammond, for example, faulted thinkers who "confound the mind and the soul. Science has nothing to do with the latter."[27] This, however, was not universally accepted among psychiatrists, much less the American public.

The trial electrified an already polarized field. Neurologists like Spitzka—through the New York Neurological Society and the *Journal of Nervous and Mental Disease*—had been in conflict with psychiatrists like Gray—through the Association of Superintendents of Asylums for the Insane and their *American Journal of Insanity*—since the mid-1870s. As one historian put it, "No single problem divided American psychiatrists more sharply than the proper definition of criminal responsibility."[28] The issue of criminal responsibility, the role of religion in human mental health, and the assassination of a president all contributed to the sensationalism and public profile of *United States v. Charles J. Guiteau*. The case tested the norms of secularism and reaffirmed the privileged role of Protestant Christianity in assuring the public of Guiteau's distinctive moral depravity and that his religious claims had no commonality with true Christianity.

The Trial and Guiteau's Christianity

The criminal trial, with Judge Walter Smith Cox presiding, took place in the Supreme Court of the District of Columbia from November 1881 to January 1882. George Scoville led the defense. It was a tough job considering that his own client called him a "nuisance" because of his "stinking theory" that Guiteau was insane.[29] Poor Scoville, who was doing his best as an expert in title standards, was there only because he was Guiteau's brother-in-law. In arguing the insanity defense, Scoville was aided by expert testimony from neurologists James Kiernan and Edward Charles Spitzka, who had published his support for the insanity defense before the trial had begun. The prosecution was led by John Porter, with cross-examinations by Walter Davidge. Porter was aided by expert testimony from psychiatrist John Gray. The indictment alleged that Guiteau "feloniously, willfully, and of his malice aforethought, did kill and murder" President Garfield. The fact that Guiteau shot Garfield was indisputable, as was the fact that the murder was premeditated. Few had qualms with calling Guiteau a fanatic. A successful insanity defense, however, would require more argumentative precision.

There were three general theories of Guiteau's insanity. The first was that Guiteau was using religion as cover for his personal, politically motivated vendetta against President Garfield. He was trying to con the jury to save himself. I call this the "insanity dodge theory." This view presupposed Guiteau's will was intact and that his claims about pressure from the deity were insincere. The second interpretation was that the crime was a result of sinful decisions throughout his life that had corrupted his moral capacity, opening up to greater temptations toward immorality and crime. This theory received support from psychiatrist John Gray. I call this the "morally culpable theory." The third interpretation was that his fanaticism was a result of a physiological disorder of the mind and body that made him vulnerable to the religious excesses of the day. Experts like Spitzka referred to this disorder variously as religious insanity, moral insanity, monomania, or fanaticism. I call this the "religious insanity theory." The prosecution primarily argued the morally culpable theory, and at times the insanity dodge theory. The defense relied upon the religious insanity theory.

Expert witnesses representing traditional psychiatry and the more deterministic neurology brought these theories into the courtroom. The court tasked the jury, informed by these medical debates, to assess Guiteau's eccentricity and its relationship to the crime. Was it an inherited disease of the body that affected his will, as the religious insanity theory suggested? Was it caused by his own willful sinfulness, thus diminishing his moral capacities over time, as the morally culpable theory suggested? Or was he willfully conning the court to try to dodge an execution for a crime of personal vengeance? For most of this book, the affectability of the fanatic—that is, their lack of willpower—was a strategy of rhetoric. *United States v. Charles J. Guiteau* put affectability on trial and asked for more precision in order to determine if Guiteau was insane and if such insanity was relevant for his ability to know right from wrong.

Scoville knew that he had a difficult argument to make. Guiteau clearly had reasoning abilities and was actively making arguments in court, including, notably, the argument that he was not insane. Scoville framed the insanity defense as a mark of progress in the justice system, one that befitted an age of beneficence and care for social ills. "It is not always an insanity dodge," he told the courtroom, and "you cannot afford to ignore it in this age of the world."[30] The insanity defense was couched in the language of progress and civilization. Scoville continued, "His reasoning faculties are not all wrong. They may be right after he has once started, but the defect is in the starting point."[31] What caused religious insanity? Scoville argued that much of it was hereditary, though activated by distinct causes, including that "religious emotion may be" a cause, including affects of "love, hate, fear." Such events created an increased flow of blood or bioelectricity, damaging Guiteau's faculties in the process. Because "the operations of the mind proceed from the brain," a damaged brain can lead to damaged perceptions. As such, Guiteau's beliefs that God spoke to him were, at root, a physical disorder. "If his mental operations are not right," Scoville argued, "it is because there is some defect in the brain, in the anatomy, that is beyond the possibility of his influence."[32] Guiteau did not willfully possess his own mind or body.

How could one know if the accused was pretending to be insane? Here, Scoville sought to dispel any confidence in commonsense reactions. Psychiatry experts, with biographical knowledge, family history, and enough time interviewing the accused, alone could know for sure, he emphasized to the jury. Guiteau, in one of his frequent outbursts, clarified his stance on himself: "I never feign; I act myself out, sane or insane."[33] As usual, for Guiteau the question was not one of his individual mind, but one of God's will and national destiny.

Guiteau's biography and family history played an important role in the trial. Early on in his defense, Scoville noted that Guiteau descended from French Huguenots, Calvinists who refused to conform to Catholic rule and fled from France during the sixteenth and seventeenth centuries. The defense noted that this "same intense religious spirit, the same devotion to religious duty . . . has come down through the Guiteau family to the present day." Scoville went on to emphasize that Guiteau's grandparents named their children Abraham, Luther, Martin, Julia, and Mary, which indicated their "religious zeal." One of Julia's daughters, Abby, had been institutionalized after she suffered mental health struggles and began to ask those around her incessantly, "Do you love Jesus?"[34] This was not just insanity that took the form of religion, Scoville argued, but was specifically *religious* insanity that Charles had inherited "in the blood" and that made him affectable to eccentric religious beliefs and strong religious passions from birth.

Scoville's argument that there was evidence of Guiteau's religious insanity throughout his entire life was likely influenced by Spitzka, who two years earlier had written a defense of monomania: "Monomania has all the characters of a constitutional mental affection... there is a permanent undercurrent of perverted mental action peculiar to the individual, running like an unbroken thread through his whole mental life."[35] For Spitzka, religious insanity was an inherent and inherited disease.

Charles Julius Guiteau was born to Jane and Luther Guiteau in New York in 1841. His mother, who suffered from physical health issues, died when Charles was seven years old. Guiteau's father, whom Guiteau himself referred to as a fanatic, had strong Christian convictions and drifted from denomination to denomination trying to discern Christian truth. His father began to believe that "he was part and parcel of the Saviour himself spiritually."[36] He also beat young Charles for his perceived sinfulness. Luther long had respect for and interest in the Oneida Community, a socialist utopian Christian movement founded by John Humphrey Noyes. Noyes, influenced by revivalist Charles Finney's concept of perfectionism, argued for the capacity of humans to fully overcome the stain of sin. As part of this doctrine, Noyes advocated for "complex marriage," or the idea that sexual activity with multiple partners was partaking in a gift from God. The Guiteau family did not reside with the Oneida Community, but Charles grew up learning about them, listening to his father's ideas, and reading the Bible. Like his father, he took it upon himself to discern Christian truth.

After a stint at a prep school in Ann Arbor, he decided to move to the Oneida Community in 1860 after reading the community's journals, the *Circular* and the *Berean*. As he would throughout his life, he framed his choices within a sense of divine providence. He described in a letter from 1861 that he had sent to his brother-in-law George Scoville "an irresistible power which I was *not at liberty to disobey*. I was intellectually convinced, and positively knew from the *feelings* of my *inmost heart*, that this was the beginning of the kingdom of God on earth."[37] Just as he felt called to join the Oneida, he felt called to leave in 1865 after falling out of favor in the community. He explained his decision to the Oneida elders that "just as a musician plays upon the keys of a piano," God worked upon the agency of humans. "God makes no blunders," he told them. "The millions inhabiting the earth are before Him, and he selects the right man every time for the right place; and in this He always successfully check-mates the devil's moves." He was increasingly viewing himself as a messianic figure whose role was not just to discern Christian truth but to publish it. Thus began his efforts to start a Christian magazine, the *Daily Theocrat*. Writing to his father in 1865, Guiteau framed himself as part of the "employ of *Jesus Christ & Co.*, the very ablest and strongest firm in the universe, and what I can do is limited only by their power and purpose."[38] He was responding to his father's critiques that he did not have the physical or mental capacities to succeed in such an endeavor. His belief in God's providence and in the ultimate defeat of evil and his own sense of importance were present a decade and a half before the assassination.

Guiteau bounced around between New York and Chicago after leaving the Oneida Community. Scoville, as part of the insanity defense, emphasized his religious ambitions. The prosecution, however, emphasized Charles's poor work record, debt, and abusive behavior. He tried, unsuccessfully, to extort Noyes and began to rail against the Oneida Community as a type of sex cult. In Chicago, where he had a helping hand from his sister Frances and her husband (Scoville himself!), he was able to pass the bar to become a lawyer and found some success as a bill collector. He married a young librarian, Annie Bunn, whom he verbally and physically abused. In 1874 he reportedly visited a brothel and slept with a prostitute, leading to their divorce. In 1876 he attended a revival by the influential preacher Dwight Moody. Moved by Moody's plain-spoken gospel, Guiteau served as an usher at Moody's revivals and then traveled between towns preaching to anyone who would listen.

The defense and many of the expert witnesses they brought to the stand made the case that Guiteau had inherited a vulnerable psychology easily affected by the religious excitements he encountered and expressed in his life. His biography was the evidence.

Scoville argued that religious fanaticism and insanity were closely linked, with the former signaling social phenomena and the latter individual mental disease. To illustrate this point, Scoville interviewed Thomas Dimon, a physician who served as superintendent of an asylum for insane criminals in Auburn, New York. Dimon had examined Guiteau while he was in prison during the trial. Scoville presented Dimon with hypotheticals meant to reflect Guiteau's mental state, asking Dimon if a patient of his believed that, despite being impoverished and without existing support, was about to "revolutionize religion through the country." Dimon responded by saying that that was not enough information to determine if it was "simply fanaticism or whether it was insanity." Scoville pushed him on this, asking, "Is fanaticism ever near the border-line of insanity?"[39] Dimon was not sure.

Other expert witnesses provided more support for the defense. Spitzka told the court that it was evident that Guiteau had been "in a more or less morbid state throughout his life, and that he was probably insane at the time" of the crime.[40] Guiteau, Spitzka argued, was a "moral monstrosity . . . born with so defective a nervous organization that he is altogether deprived of that moral sense which is an integral and essential constituent of the normal human mind."[41] He cited Guiteau's history of delusive thinking, his family history of religious insanity, and certain physical characteristics that he observed such as his asymmetric cranium. Beyond the trial, Walter Channing, a physician who was a witness for the defense, argued for Guiteau as suffering from insanity throughout his life due to a mixture of genetics and a social environment of religious excess and deviation. He argued that Guiteau attended a revival held by Moody and Sankey, which "worked up" Guiteau "to a high pitch of religious exaltation." Inspired and "unconscious of the absurdity of his" preaching, he was "satisfied that he was working in the vineyard of the Lord, and teaching inspired truth."[42] Scoville framed the impact of the Moody meetings in that Guiteau became "more and more excited" and "his mind seemed entirely absorbed in religious subjects."[43] Though the main argument rested upon inherited insanity as a physical disease, the social environment and evangelical excitement in particular played a role in the defense's narrative.

Countering the defense, the prosecution sought to sketch a life of individual vice, greed, and temptation. Cross-examining Spitzka, Davidge asked him if Guiteau's actions and beliefs were a result of depravity, using a term for the Protestant concept of original sin. Spitzka, either not realizing the theological stakes of the question or rejecting them, corrected him by saying "a diseased depravity," implying a physical, inherited disease, but not a universal human proclivity toward sin. Guiteau, however, discerned the charge here. Interrupting the cross-examination, he told the court that "there is nothing in my record indicating depravity. I have always been a Christian man." Unfortunately for the defense's case, he went on, stating that he "only committed adultery in order to get rid of a woman I did not love and I owe about a hundred dollars in money, and I say that is all there is to it."⁴⁴ Whether strategic or simply his own musings, Guiteau gave voice to a central claim of the prosecution: Guiteau was not insane, he was a sinner.

Like the defense, the prosecution turned to Guiteau's biography to make their case. Davidge, for example, argued that his excitement from attending Moody revivals came not from religious affects but from a realization of a new way to profit. Davidge mimicked Guiteau in court: "What, they make money. One of them has gone to Europe. I can do this."⁴⁵ One of the key portraits of Guiteau that the prosecution highlighted was his effort to start a Christian magazine at a time when he was in debt, roaming the nation, and living in squalor. Scoville worked to make his poor business decisions a sign of insanity, an inability to realize reality. Guiteau, however, saw it differently. It was confirmation of living as an apostle. When Scoville emphasized his poverty, Guiteau shot back that "it is the same kind of business the apostle Paul was engaged in. He got his pay, and I expect to get mine some of these days on that book I wrote."⁴⁶ Gray framed the decision as a sign of Guiteau's moral culpability. His story was not one of sincere religion but a desire for wealth and fame that fueled Guiteau to concoct more and more desperate schemes.

The prosecution also relied upon people who knew Guiteau, often bringing them in as witnesses. The causes of Guiteau's eccentric behavior were long theorized by people who knew him even before the criminal trial. An associate of the Oneida Community, Charles Jocelyn, who had known Guiteau, described his "strong religious bias toward exaltation and even fanaticism." His family, including his father and brother, believed Charles to be possessed by the devil. Luther claimed that his son has "an unsubdued will, the very spirit of disobedience to authority . . . disobedience to God." The brother interpreted Guiteau's life through traditional Christian notions of sin and demonic power. "I believe," he told the court, "that at some time in my brother's life, he must have, through his evil, through his willfulness, through his stubbornness, through his perversity of nature, allowed Satan to gain such a control over him that he was under the power of Satan." Guiteau responded to his brother with a characteristic outburst: "You have that the wrong side up."⁴⁷

Davidge made the sinfulness of Guiteau explicit. In a cross-examination, he attacked Guiteau's phrasing of "divine pressure," blasting him for not being more specific. Was this pressure from God or from the devil? He proceeded, noting that even Charles's brother could see the satanic influence on Guiteau, that what pressure he felt was felt by all humanity. "The pressure was the pressure upon every man when tempted by sin. His struggle was the struggle of every man against what is wrong, what is evil, what is criminal. No more, no less." He then referenced the biblical book of James (1:14–15): "Every man is tempted when he is drawn away of his own lust, and enticed. Then, when lust hath conceived, it bringeth forth sin; and sin, when it is finished, bringeth forth death."[48] References to the scripture and Christian theology were common throughout the trial, especially by the prosecution and Guiteau himself. Importantly for Davidge and many Protestant commentators, the theory of sin was not just a theological concept. It was a theory of human nature necessary for a scientific understanding of the human mind and for holding individuals accountable in the legal system.

The defense noted that there have been times in the Christian tradition when godly pressure has prompted faithful people to do things typically thought of as crimes. The story of Abraham and Isaac became the key example. Guiteau himself was familiar with what he called the "Abraham style of insanity," though he viewed it as a misunderstood phenomenon. He argued that "there are thirty-eight specific cases in the Bible, where the Deity has directed people to kill very good people; not from personal malice, not from ill-will; but where a man has been a ruler of a nation, and has been going wrong; been imperiling the Republic."[49] In response to the defense's argument about Abraham and Isaac, Gray argued that the "ancient record must be taken into account and its authenticity granted. The history is one of supernatural interference and visibly so; and, therefore, furnishes no warrant for any modern parallel."[50] Scoville's references to the Bible to suggest parallels with Guiteau's insanity provoked unease in and beyond the courtroom.

At times the prosecution worked to represent the defense as antagonistic to Christianity as a whole by attacking the character of the expert witnesses. In a cross-examination, prosecutor Walter Davidge asked James Kiernan, after he had vouched for Guiteau's insanity, if he believed "in a future state of rewards and punishments." Kiernan responded, "No, sir." Davidge later brought it up again and asked him to explain. Kiernan did so: "Well, I am simply, like a great many other scientific men, what is called an agonistic." To drive the point home, Davidge interrupted and incredulously asked, "You say you are like other scientific men?"[51] The question of belief in rewards and punishments was not uncommon for expert witnesses in the trial. However, the prosecution, perhaps to some effect with the jury, was able to take Kiernan's personal beliefs and turn them into a sign of a deficient, materialistic theory of the human will. Davidge would again and again bring up the lack of Christian piety among the defense's experts, referring to Spitzka as "this young agnostic expert." This was a legal strategy but also revealed the metaconflict over physiological theories and traditional notions of sin and morality. In other words, by treating religious fanaticism as a scientifically verifiable disease (that is, religious insanity), the defense was removing fanaticism from moral and theological judgment.

* * *

The purview of the medical expert witnesses was to assess sanity or insanity. The purview of the court was to instruct the jury on the standard of the insanity defense to determine responsibility or irresponsibility. Most US jurisdictions relied upon the M'Naghten Test, formulated in Great Britain in 1843 after Daniel M'Naghten shot and killed the secretary to the prime minister. Under this rule, defendants were presumed sane unless, at the time of committing the criminal act, they were in a state of mind in which they did not know what act they were committing or that they did not know the difference between right and wrong. The prosecution and its expert witnesses urged the court to stick with the standard of M'Naghten. Such a test focused on cognition and knowledge of the criminal act's legality. The defense and its experts hoped to push the court to embrace one of the other emerging standards. One was the Irresistible Impulse Test, which made a lack of control over one's actions an extenuating factor. Another wide-ranging test emerged in the New Hampshire courts in the 1870s. With an early form of the Durham Test that later rose to prominence from the 1950s to the 1970s, the New Hampshire courts left it to the jury to decide if a criminal act was caused by a mental disorder. If so, the defendant could potentially be found not guilty by reason of insanity.

These latter two tests could have served Guiteau's defense well. However, Judge Cox was not swayed and for the most part stuck with the M'Naghten Test. The judge's specific instructions to the jury were that insanity could be relevant if the crime was committed "under the influence and as the product of an insane mental delusion that the Deity had commanded him to do the act, which had taken possession of his mind, not as the result of his own reflections, but independently of his will and reason, and with such force as to deprive him of the degree of reason necessary to distinguish between right and wrong, as to this particular act."[52] This charge, again, required a foray into complex philosophical questions that exceeded the mere facts of the case.

By January 25, 1882, the trial and its officials had exhausted themselves. Judge Cox, on this day, provided forty-three instructions to the jury before deliberating. The judge primarily sided with framing insanity and the question of religion with the prosecution, going out of his way to make distinctions between true religion, false religion, and religious insanity. First, he wanted to make clear that the trial could not be viewed as an infringement on Guiteau's right to free exercise of religion. In support of this, he cited *Reynolds v. United States* (1879), in which the US Supreme Court denied that free exercise protections extended to George Reynolds, a Mormon, for practicing polygamy. The case is famous for highlighting the limitations of free exercise in this era. The majority opinion drew from Thomas Jefferson's Letter to the Danbury Baptists (1802) to argue that states could infringe on religious practices (such as polygamy or a God-directed assassination), just not religious beliefs or opinions. Further, that case highlighted the implicit theological and moral norms at the foundation of American religious freedom.

In other charges, the judge sought to clarify the question to the jury and to make a distinction between religious opinions and delusions. The former could be "absurd in the extreme" and included examples such as animal magnetism or spiritualism. Belief in communication with departed spirits was a sign of poor reasoning and ignorance, but still resulted from "some kind of evidence, and liable to be changed by better external evidence or sounder reasoning." An insane delusion, however, was an affection impervious to reasoning or evidence.

Charge 30 to the jury sought to make clear the difference between a general supernaturalism, which could be reasonable or at least sane, and delusions. Judge Cox told the jury that a "great many Christians believe, not only that events generally are providentially ordered, but that they themselves receive special providential guidance . . . and, in an undefined sense, are inspired to pursue a certain course of action." Such a phenomenon was sane in and of itself. The judge wanted to make clear that supernaturalism was not inherently delusional. As demonstrated in the previous sections, the most skeptical psychiatrists were not so sure.

Finally, Judge Cox laid out the choice between "mental and moral obliquity." Channeling the prosecution's argument, the judge told the jury that they all probably knew someone "who have first yielded to temptation with pangs of remorse, but each transgression became easier, until dishonesty became a confirmed habit, and at length all sensitiveness of conscience disappeared."[53] The judge's directions to the jury clearly favored the prosecution and, beyond that, worked to make comforting distinctions between religious fanaticism (e.g., spiritualism or animal magnetism), religion proper, and insanity. There was no such thing, he implied, as religious insanity. The jury agreed, at least in terms of Guiteau. The verdict was unanimous that Guiteau was responsible for the crime, was able to discern right from wrong, and thus was guilty.

Assessing (In)sanity in the Nation, Religion, and Race

The case of Charles Guiteau centered on the religious affections of a single individual. During and after the trial many Americans situated the case and the problem of religious insanity within nationalistic, religious, and racial frameworks. To give just one fairly superficial example, the psychiatrist J. J. Elwell, reflecting on the trial, described Spitzka as from a "class of modern crazy German pagans" working to "break down all the safeguards of our Christian civilization, by destroying if possible all grounds for human responsibility."[54] Elwell leveled that charge in the scientific journal *Alienist and Neurologist*, which suggests how heated moral disagreements were shaping these new sciences of the mind. Craziness is not the same as insanity, but Elwell's hyperbolic claim captured the idea that insanity was viewed as a phenomenon of social psychology as much as individual psychology. Scholar Owen Davies has argued, more specifically, that "the influence of religion and the supernatural became a significant measure of insanity in any given population at any moment in time, and thereby a means of assessing collective and individual mental states."[55] Nineteenth-century experts thought that discerning insanity and working to prevent it required categorizing human difference collectively and in reference to forms of affectability.

The work of psychiatry in producing categories of human difference preceded the Guiteau case. One of the first insanity defense pleas in the United States was in *People v. William Freeman* (1847), in which Freeman, a Black and Indigenous man, was accused and found guilty of murdering a family in Auburn, New York. As the press and public emphasized, the Van Nest family was white and wealthy. His trial gained attention as many whites argued that Freeman, echoing Nat Turner, represented a Black rebellion against white rule and power. William Seward, who would go on to serve as President Lincoln's secretary of state, volunteered to represent Freeman. Drawing on testimony and the ideas of Amariah Brigham, Seward argued that Freeman's abilities to reason and to know right from wrong were compromised, in part because of beatings he had suffered while wrongfully imprisoned. Such beatings were especially brutal, based on the idea that Black people feel less pain that white people. The prosecution and outraged citizens of Auburn, however, used Freeman's Black and Indigenous heritage against him, arguing that his apparent low levels of cognitive function were within a normal range for his race.[56] Seward, in his defense, pleaded with the jury to see past their racial preconceptions of the Indigenous North American "passions with the violent and ferocious character" and the degraded "intellect" of Black people. Instead, Seward asked the jury to hold Freeman to the standard of the "Anglo-Saxon race."[57]

Brigham was eager to help Seward's insanity defense plea for Freeman and in general had progressive ideas about racial difference for his time. That said, Brigham had strong beliefs that fanaticism was a marker of civilizational difference. Brigham opened his book *Observations on the Influence of Religion* with a grand history of what he called "Religious Sentiment," a global force that "continually impels men to the adoration of the invisible and superior powers, and to discover methods of communicating with them." Though he began with the universality of religion, he proceeded to narrate a natural history of religion that framed religion as a developing, ever-progressing force, similar to Isaac Taylor's *Fanaticism* examined in chapter 1. Inferior religions were signs of inferior races, and vice versa. "The negroes and the savages of America profess the worship of the Fetish gods, which erects animals, and inanimate beings the most absurd, into deities." He proceeded to remark that the Jewish God was "jealous, revengeful, and terrible, a God of war." Islam had "served its time, and become stationary and useless." Catholicism, with its emphasis on ritual, had become "useless or injurious." He concluded, "Hence we see that wherever the Christian Religion has been received, the sensual propensities have gradually yielded to the sovereignty of the moral and intellectual powers."[58] The progress of modernity was the progress of Christianity.

Like Thomas Jefferson, he had a narrow view of Christianity, which was primarily white, disenchanted, and Protestant. This was evident in his separate categorization for Black Americans as reduced to "fetishists" in an era of Black Christianity and the perseverance of African-derived religion. This corresponds to scholar of religion Judith Weisenfeld's argument that psychiatrists like Brigham believed that mental disorders in Black Americans and other nonwhite races were often a result of excessive religious emotionalism inherent in their racial constitution.[59]

However, did evangelical revivalism count as Christian for Brigham? When Brigham wrote that "God has no *supernatural* dealings with men" and that such beliefs and related ceremonies were "at the foundation of religious fanaticism," he was arguing that evangelicalism was an unmodern form of religion and was implicitly comparing them to groups he viewed as religiously and racially inferior. Spitzka had similar views about religion and insanity within a framework of social evolution:

> Again, the conduct of a Hindoo fakir, of a religious fanatic, or a revivalist, while it oversteps the boundaries of reason in more than one direction, is not insanity; because, however strange and suggestive of insanity such conduct may be, it is in consonance with the individual's surroundings, and the result of educational influences and mental contagion occurring within physiological limits. . . . Beliefs which in the earlier periods of history were creeds with the majority of mankind would to-day in members of a civilized race rank with the insane delusion.[60]

Though Brigham and Spitzka identified revivalism as a lingering practice from premodernity, they did not treat it as constitutive of a race in the same way as they did, say, Black religious emotionalism or "fetishism." As Weisenfeld notes, experts often treated mental disorders among white American Christians, when instigated by excessive revivalism, as individual affairs and exceptional within the white race and true, Protestant Christianity.[61] For many of these skeptic psychiatrists, white revivalism, then, presented a mental health problem in its excessive affects, but white revivalism was not inherently a sign of an affective racial constitution.

The high stakes of these distinctions and entanglement of religion, race, and mental health help explain the outrage and passions over the Guiteau case. Guiteau's case, too, raised similar questions about heredity in an era of neo-Lamarckism, in which parents passed to their children characteristics from their life. It is worth noting that Guiteau's hereditary features were discussed in terms of his ethnicity and the French Huguenot background of his family, not in terms of whiteness writ large. It is useful to contrast this with Freeman's case. The prosecution framed Freeman's hereditary features as innate and inherited through Blackness and Indigeneity, even though Seward had protested this framing. This distinction is one of race and ethnicity, raising the question of who gets categorized racially and who gets categorized ethnically. Scholar of religion Sylvester Johnson has analyzed how "ethnicity articulated difference among whites through the vocabularies of culture instead of biology."[62] In the specific case of Guiteau as argued through a hereditarian framework, culture and religious practices were products of biology. He, too, was pathologized, but his pathologization was a shield against directing blame to his "whiteness" and, to a lesser extent, blaming the turbulence of the American religious environment.

The discursive protection of whiteness was intertwined with the protection of Protestant Christianity. For John Gray, Spitzka and Scoville had still gone too far and implicated American religion. Their argument collapsed important moral and theological differences between "true religion" and "false religion" into the singular category of religion. In commentary about the trial Gray, wrote about the capaciousness of US religious freedom and how such capaciousness had perhaps gone too far in allowing what he so clearly believed to be counterfeit religion to be treated with the term "religious"—even if it was followed by "insanity." As usual, Gray was implicitly attacking Scoville and Spitzka: "In an age when almost all authority is disregarded as to religious belief and social conduct, it is not extraordinary to find even the most destructive principles as well as the most transparent impostures brought under the cloak of religion, until society is almost forced to inquire how far the 'rights of conscience' are to be respected when the good order and peace of the State begin to be imperiled." Gray went on to rail against the "plague-spot" of Mormonism threatening American civilization and increasingly permissive divorce laws that were putting "constant strain upon the sanctions of family life."[63] Gray saw a threat to the Protestant moral establishment in Guiteau and neurologists' efforts to treat him as a victim of disease.

As scholars have examined, the fields of psychiatry and neurology from the 1880s to the 1910s leaned toward hereditary determinism when it came to mental health and played a role in the prominence of scientific racism.[64] Spitzka and Kiernan were not able to the sway the jury in the trial, but their broader argument about heredity and physicalist explanations for mental disease gained traction. Considering the popular backlash against their arguments during the trial, this was a surprising development. However, it was one bolstered by a number of historical and social trends in the late nineteenth century, including concerns over immigration, freed Black populations, and racial mixing.[65] This was an era of tables and charts wherein experts categorized racial differences and sought to discern and assign intellectual, physical, and mental capacities across them.

Edward Charles Spitzka, too, was invested in measuring psychiatric illnesses across communities as expressions of evolutionary and civilizational development. He paired his emphasis on familial heredity (for example, the argument that religious fanaticism ran in the Guiteau family) with racial heredity. He classified the "higher races" as Anglo-Saxons, Celts, Germans, and Jews. Black people represented the least developed race. He argued that insanity was more prevalent among Anglo-Saxons and Jews, which he attributed to the supposed higher mental functions of these races and their complex civilizations.[66] James Kiernan, who also served as a witness for the defense, took another view, arguing that the increase of paranoia as a disease was caused by immigration of inferior racial groups and thus advocated for immigration restriction.[67] The study of the human mind in this era was not reducible individualistic psychologies. Features and predictions to religious insanity, psychiatrists argued, differed across religio-racial collectivities in an era of concern over immigration and a globalizing US empire.

Conclusion

Fanaticism was not the same thing as insanity in this era. Fanaticism was a general category with theological origins. Insanity was, at least putatively, a term of secular medicine. However, the two categories shared features and raised similar questions. The trial over Guiteau was about the relationship between his will, the affective power of sin (according to the prosecution), and the affective power of mental disease (according to the defense). Further, religious authorities and psychiatrists alike deployed the idea of religious insanity in efforts to maintain the implicit Protestant norms of "true religion." Judging from Gray's commentary about religious freedom and the dangers of Mormonism, the defense of "true religion" was under duress not in spite of the nature of the American society but because of it. The extent of religious free exercise, the cultural emphasis on individualism, new religious movements, and immigration all added to the diverse electrical currents of American religion. Psychological theories of religious insanity were efforts to provide a science of fanaticism by pinpointing its functions in the human body and mind. However, instead of discontinuity from fanaticism to insanity, I see a continuity that defies any easy distinctions between the religious and scientific secular, conceptually or narratively.

The efforts of intellectuals and experts to provide secular scientific theories and studies of fanaticism emerged in other fields beyond psychiatry, neurology, and psychology. The institutionalization of anthropology, framing itself as a natural science, also took on fanaticism, and its close kin term superstition, as objects of study and problems to be solved. As the following chapter examines, US colonial institutions funded and drew on anthropological studies of strange and violent religion for the sake of military strategies, pacification, and governance.

5

Policing Fanaticism Abroad

Militant Prophets in US-Occupied Philippines

In the late nineteenth and early twentieth centuries, the United States' empire continued to expand westward across Indigenous nations and overseas. Many resisted US rule. In the wake of the Spanish-American War in 1898, the United States claimed possession of Spain's colonies, including the Philippines, Cuba, Puerto Rico, and Guam. US Americans once again turned to the language of religious fanaticism to describe unruliness directed against white US power. This was especially the case in the Philippines, where the diversity and mixing of Catholicism, Islam, and Indigenous traditions perplexed American officials.[1] What followed was a wave of government reports and studies on the cultures and religions of the archipelago. These studies, which included anthropological research, were part of a project to assess the religious and racial landscape of the Philippines for the purposes of pacification and colonial governance. Ruperto Rios, whom I opened this book with, was one example of a Filipino whose religious and political movement became of strategic relevance for the United States. He was not alone.

The relevance of religion came to the fore in the early 1900s as religiously inspired militant groups resisted US rule even after the capitulation of the First Philippine Republic. Americans categorized these groups in overlapping and sometimes confused ways. These included *insurrectos* (insurrectionaries), *tulisanes* (outlaws), *bandoleros* (bandits), *babaylanes* (shamans), *ladrones* (thieves), *pulahanes* ("those wearing red"), *juramentados* (Moro jihadists), and Katipunans.[2] Many of these groups were social bandits, revolutionary militants, and religious communities, often all at once. Active membership in these groups constituted a statistically small percentage of the Philippine population. However, they made American forces feel their presence. They conducted raids, fought in skirmishes against the Philippine Constabulary and the US Army, and generally disrupted social order. They were especially active in the central islands of Visayas, the northern reaches of Luzon, and the southern region of Mindanao. Insurrectionaries served as an enduring and embarrassing reminder to the United States that, for some Filipinos at least, US rule was not welcome—and not complete.

Many, but not all, of these insurrectionary groups framed their resistance through appeals to supernatural beings, myths, and forces. White American Luke Wright, who served as secretary of commerce and police for the Philippine Commission in the first few years of the 1900s, sardonically listed the proliferation of divine charismatic figures across the islands: "We have had two or three new popes, several alleged Sons of God, and Virgin Marys, together with here and there a leader who claimed charm-working powers and the ability to make his followers proof against bullets."[3] Some foretold of a new age on the horizon that would lead to Filipino independence and a reversal of the social order. Most important for this chapter, many insurrectionaries across the archipelago utilized sacred objects to protect and enthuse soldiers on the battlefield. Charismatic leaders of insurrectionary bands also used these objects to enhance their spiritual and political authority. US Americans were eager to seize on these religious elements in Filipino culture to denigrate Filipinos as inherently superstitious. Americans were also concerned about religious myths, authorities, and objects as obstacles to Filipino "progress" and US control.

This chapter argues that the policing of fanatics was intimately tied to ideas of Filipino materiality, which was in turn a site of contestation between occupiers and occupied. Americans racialized Filipinos by emphasizing their affectability, which suggested that Filipinos lacked the capacity to exercise autonomous individualized human agency. Colonial reports rendered this affectability by emphasizing how Filipino agency was subsumed by their investment in the divine power of material objects. Though exploring religious stories, authorities, and objects, this chapter focuses on the material culture of the Philippines in part because *things* are easier to police than stories or beliefs. This is one explanation for the US fixation on materiality. Further, the prevalence and importance of spiritually powerful material objects in the Philippines was and has been a sociocultural reality. That is to say that the United States was not entirely off base about Filipino material culture, though it was wrong in many of the details and in its racist interpretations. In the Tagalog language, spiritually powerful charms are often called *anting anting*. These charms could offer various powers such as invulnerability to bullets, invisibility, and sexual prowess. US officials took up the term *anting anting* as a catchall category for spiritually powerful objects that were popular across the archipelago's cultural contexts and traditions. At the end of this chapter I examine the social, religious, and political role of anting anting in the context of a Philippines under colonial duress.

The coterie of powerful white men who controlled the mechanisms of US colonial rule came to theorize resistance as religious fanaticism that was enabled by these material objects. They worked to police fanatics—and their objects—accordingly.[4] The radical religious ideas and practices of insurrectionaries were distinct across different locales. However, Americans tried to argue that these ideas and practices were enabled by an attachment to spiritually powerful material objects that signaled the racial inferiority of inhabitants across the archipelago. Even the well-educated class of Manila was susceptible, Americans claimed.[5] This chapter builds on the work of scholars like Paul Kramer who have argued that the Philippine-American War was a race war.[6] It understands race to be part of the US occupation in two ways. The first was in how US Americans homogenized and essentialized Filipinos as an inherently inferior people. This is racism as generalization—through rhetoric and representation. The second was in how US Americans policed Filipinos as enemy combatants even as it claimed sovereignty over the archipelago. This is racial governance. The occupation was also a religious war, though not in a reductive sense. Americans constructed a racial hierarchy by using religious difference as a marker of racial difference. To be more accurate, Americans claimed a fundamental difference between white US Christianity (claimed as religion proper) and Filipino material culture (claimed as superstition proper). This was part of a long tradition in Christian and Western thought that denigrated cultures that imbued inanimate matter with spiritual agency. Such cultures have been referred to variously as fetishists, idolaters, and animists.[7] However, Americans were encountering forms of resistance and corresponding ideologies that Filipinos developed over decades of resistance to Spanish colonial rule. They were adaptive strategies that brought together religion and politics. Close attention to anting anting can help us see this entanglement.

This chapter begins by introducing the basics of US rule in the Philippines. Second, it explores how Americans, especially the colonial official and ethnologist Dean Worcester, wrote about Filipino religious material culture and the term "superstition," applied as an explanatory category for the existence of anting anting. Third, it shows how Americans presumed Filipino material culture to be the basis of continuing resistance and social disorder. This section focuses on two insurrectionaries: Ruperto Rios and Papa Isio. Finally, this chapter theorizes how anting anting operated within a web of relationships between human and divine authorities who shared radical political and spiritual objectives.

Colonial Knowledge and Governance

In broad strokes, the United States' relationship with the Philippines can be summarized in four historical developments. First, the United States was an ally of the Philippine Revolution in its war against Spain in 1898. Second, after the defeat of Spain, President McKinley decided to claim sovereignty over the islands. This was negotiated in the Treaty of Paris (1898) with Spain. This led to US Americans fighting a war against the First Philippine Republic. Third, the First Philippine Republic was forced to accept US rule. The result was ongoing tensions between an emerging Filipino nationalism and the power of US sovereignty and colonial administration. The United States considered the Philippines unincorporated insular territory.[8] However, resistance against the United States and its Filipino allies continued for decades through guerrilla warfare. Many who had come to accept US rule were *ilustrados*, or middle- and upper-class Filipinos who were landowners and educated by the Spanish. Many of those who continued to resist US rule were rural and from laboring classes. The latter had for decades fought Spanish rule and the socioeconomic power of ilustrados. Violent resistance against the United States largely died down by 1915. However, it lingered on until the fourth broad development in the US-Philippines relationship. In the wake of World War II, the United States and the Philippines signed the Treaty of Manila (1946), granting the Philippines independence.[9]

Throughout the colonization of the Philippines, US American officials utilized religious and racial discourses to legitimize US colonial sovereignty and paternalistic governance over the archipelago. This is evident in Senator Albert Beveridge's 1900 speech to Congress. Beveridge cited commerce with China, the value of the hemp industry, the specter of imperial competition, and Americans' status as God's chosen people as reasons why the United States should maintain sovereignty over the Philippines. He also invoked the figure of the superstitious Filipino:

> It will be hard for Americans who have not studied them to understand the people. They are a barbarous race, modified by three centuries of contact with a decadent race. The Filipino is the South Sea Malay, put through a process of three hundred years of superstition in religion, dishonesty in dealing, disorder in habits of industry, and cruelty, caprice, and corruption in government. It is barely possible that 1,000 men in all the archipelago are capable of self-government in the Anglo-Saxon sense.[10]

Beveridge's speech captures how ideas of a masculinist Anglo-Saxon superiority buttressed by a Protestant-based providential destiny legitimated US warfare and annexation. He and other Protestant Americans believed that Catholic Spanish colonial rule ("three hundred years of superstition in religion") had done little to aid in the progress of Filipinos. The United States' job, Beveridge and many others argued, was to uplift the Filipino, introducing civilizational features such as religious freedom, public education, and capitalism.[11]

Notably lacking from the package of modern civilization that the US Americans promised to provide was self-determination and democracy. Only under the tutelage of the Christian white race living in the United States could Americans' "little brown brothers" develop and progress.[12] This was rhetoric similar to what white Americans had applied to Black communities, Indigenous North Americans, and other racialized groups.[13] The federal government's policing of the Native American Ghost Dance is an apt example, and Tisa Wenger has used the concept of the "settler secular" to describe the colonial prerogatives of the United

States and their relation to shifting categories of religion, primitivity, superstition.[14] White Americans were keen to measure just how Filipinos stacked up in the global racial hierarchy that they projected onto the world. A number of Black Americans who served in the military defected to the Philippine Revolutionary Army after hearing fellow white soldiers refer to Filipinos as racial epithets normally used against Black Americans.[15] They, and many other Black and white Americans, protested the ongoing war.[16] Despite opposition at home, the war continued. Slowly, the United States began to build up a colonial government in the Philippines.

In the early 1900s, US colonial governance was a haphazard affair. By order of President McKinley, two Philippine Commissions were tasked with creating what he called "a civilian agency for the exercise of the powers of a military government."[17] The first commission largely performed survey work, gathering information on material resources, cultural differences, and economic practices, while the US military oversaw governance. The second commission, headed by William H. Taft, did more work building governmental institutions on the islands to pacify and transform Filipino social life according to the norms of white culture. McKinley tasked the commissions, along with the newly created Bureau of Insular Affairs, a division of the War Department, to assess Filipino progress and potential for progress.[18]

Another key figure in the Philippine Commissions and in the forms of colonial governments that followed was Dean Worcester. Worcester's position was at the intersection of scholarship, government, and military strategy. Though he was certainly not alone among powerful US American colonists, Worcester's unique position at these intersections makes him a useful focal point for this chapter. The story of how he got the job is illustrative. Worcester attended the University of Michigan, where he trained primarily as a zoologist. Worcester visited the Philippines before the war on two bird-watching expeditions in the 1880s and 1890s. He did not exactly have the type of experience one might expect for a high-level colonial influencer. However, the McKinley administration had a problem: very few Americans knew anything about the Philippines, much less traveled there. As such, President McKinley felt compelled to ask this ornithologist to take on a privileged leadership position in the colonial administration.[19]

Worcester served a number of administrative positions over the years. This included secretary of the interior for the Insular Government and head of the Bureau of Non-Christian Tribes. His influence went beyond his official roles. His writings about Filipino culture and religion informed the US public and US military forces active in the Philippines. Taft once went so far as to claim that Worcester "knows more about the Philippines than anybody else in the Philippines or anybody out of them."[20] Worcester's articles and massive collection of photographs even helped popularize the nascent *National Geographic Magazine*. His fixation on exoticizing colonized bodies played a role in the magazine finding a template for commercial success. Among other things, this included Worcester's photographs of topless Indigenous women.[21] Worcester's particular white male gaze literally influenced American perceptions about the people who lived in the Philippines.

Amid American public debate about whether or how long the United States should retain sovereignty over the Philippines, Worcester was steadfast in his conviction that Filipinos *needed* the tutelage of US Americans like himself. The purported whiteness, Christianity, and civilizational aspects of the United States represented the only way that Filipinos could develop as a race. Worcester himself had lost his individual belief in certain Christian theological and supernatural precepts. Nonetheless, he held steadfast onto his faith that Christianity (in its white Protestant form) was a necessary component of civilizational development.[22] He was a secular government official who, despite whatever personal religious beliefs he had, saw the management of religion as a tool for secular statecraft. In his public writing and governmental reports, Worcester argued that the unmodern status of Filipino religion was one of *the* chief problems for the United States to deal with to pacify and civilize the archipelago in the image of white men. Though the insurrectionaries constituted a small minority of inhabitants of the archipelago by the 1900s, Worcester made them seem representative of Filipinos as a whole. Worcester turned their willingness to continue to fight the United States into a sign of the religious and racial problem of the Filipinos that the United States would have to solve through force. This belied the fact that the insurrectionaries were fighting *because* of the colonial context, as the theorization section at the end of this chapter explains.

Reporting Superstition

In the early years of the US occupation (1898–1901), Americans were fascinated by the cultures of the Philippines. They gave special attention to cultural beliefs and practices deemed superstitions. For Dean Worcester, a superstitious mentality was a precondition for the emergence of fanatical communities. Other white civil and military officials echoed this idea. There was no single definition of superstition that could capture its various meanings in the context of the US occupation of the Philippines. That said, in state reports and ethnologies, superstition often indicated a haphazard belief in diffuse powers embedded in objects, nature, or persons. For Americans, this signaled a credulousness and an ignorance of natural causality that marked Filipinos as incapable of self-governance. This was, of course, the rationale Americans cited for classifying something as superstitious. However, one person's "superstition" can be another's "religion," and this project pays attention to the function of the term rather any substantive definition. As scholar of religion Jason Josephson-Storm writes, the term "superstition" has been a "marker for beliefs that should not be believed . . . superstition is the inverse of established truths (scientific, political, and religious)."[23] As this chapter shows, US Americans held a haphazard belief in diffuse powers embedded in objects, nature, or persons. But Americans claimed the scholarly and governmental authority to categorize Filipinos as superstitious.

Superstition was a term of racialization, not simply used to describe specific practices and beliefs that seemed odd or even irrational. Colonial officials rendered such practices and beliefs as signs of a more fundamental mentality on the level of the population. This mentality was defined by what it lacked—the capacity to reason. Many, including Taft and, at times, Worcester, emphasized that a superstitious mentality was common across the islands, even among elite and seemingly well-educated Filipinos.[24] As Worcester wrote, to truly "know something of the country and its people" one must "leave cities and towns behind" to "push into the almost unexplored regions where the wild tribes are to be found."[25] Worcester's belief in an underlying superstitious mentality worked alongside ideas about the *appearance* of religious diversity on the archipelago. Indeed, the Philippine Commissions conceptualized and governed the Philippines through distinctions between Catholic, pagan, and Moro territories.[26] Each had its own administration and set of policies. Although this territorialization of religion was key for how the United States imagined the Philippines, Americans were just as likely to emphasize what these religious cultures shared as much as what made them different.[27]

Governmental reports and studies of culture emphasized the presence of anting anting throughout the archipelago. Protestant missionaries described them as demonic. Secular and governmental scholars found them curious and concerning. Anting anting take on many forms and go by many names, including *agimat* and *talisman*. Most often anting anting are small metal objects with an impressed design. In this form, they are worn as a necklace or can be stitched inside one's clothing. They can also take on the form of other manmade objects, including shirts, books, and statuettes. Occasionally, natural objects were referred to as anting anting. These charms do not belong to a single tradition, containing a mix of Indigenous, Catholic, Moro, and even Masonic ideas.[28] They can include symbols, like the eye of providence, crosses, triangles to represent the trinary, and esoteric patterns. Phrases in Latin, Tagalog, and Spanish are common. Moro anting anting often have snippets of Quranic scripture. Others have the initials of the possessor of the anting anting. Some have the initials or signatures of the creator of the anting anting, often a religious, political, and/or military authority figure.

Early on in US rule, Worcester presented Filipino material culture as an exotic curiosity. In the popular 1899 book *The Philippine Islands and Their People*, published just before he received an invitation to serve in the Philippine Commission, Worcester described the practices and objects he encountered and collected during his travels, including anting anting.

He was both attracted to these objects and repulsed by them. One story exemplifies these two reactions in Worcester's early visits to the archipelago. Worcester recounted meeting an unnamed tulisan (bandit leader), who bet Worcester to shoot him while he was wearing a small leather-bound book.[29] The last two people who had tried to shoot the book had died, the tulisan noted. Worcester believed this to be true. Worcester negotiated, offering to shoot the anting anting itself. He offered the tulisan five dollars if the object was undamaged by the bullet. This was a good deal for the tulisan. If the anting anting did take damage, then it signaled that the charm's power had run out. Worcester shot and damaged the book, winning it in the process. The bandits began to believe that Worcester has a more powerful anting anting than those they possessed. The tulisan, after having lost his anting anting book, brought out an even stronger charm—an oval bronze medal. He made another bet that Worcester's bullets would not be able to damage this anting anting. He unfurled the medal from its protective cloth case and placed it on the ground. The tulisanes then proceeded to hide behind nearby trees. Worcester took this as an opportunity to explain the relationship between Filipinos and the sacred objects as one of fear: they feared the objects as if they were gods. Another explanation is just as plausible: the Panay villagers were protecting themselves from Worcester, his gun, and any possible ricochet. Taking cover was reasonable enough. When Worcester shot the bronze medal, it went flying into a nearby river. The powerful anting anting was lost.

Through various similar competitions, Worcester ended up with quite a collection. According to his own words, this collection provided Worcester "a reputation which was worth more to us than two regiments of soldiers would have been."[30] He wrote proudly of how the tulisanes left him and his entourage alone, even as they attacked other visitors and took the local friar hostage, cutting off his arm in the process. Worcester credited his newfound authority and the tulisanes' fear to his own anting anting. Despite his disavowals, Worcester, too, was invested in the power of the divinely infused objects, even if he did not necessarily believe in them. At least in the early publication of *The Philippine Islands and Their People*, he showed some interest in relating stories of incredible coincidences in which the anting anting did seem to have some efficacy, even as he ridiculed Filipinos for their belief in the efficacy of anting anting. Despite these moments of a shared epistemological ground with the local Filipinos he was with, the ethnologist more often emphasized the racial, cultural, and religious gulf between him and Filipinos.

Worcester interpreted these encounters according to white-supremacist theories popular in Western social science of his day. Worcester held an evolutionary understanding of historical progress. He ranked races based on how far they had advanced along the social evolutionary development scale. At the bottom were primitive superstitions. At the top were societies that had evolved to the point of understanding scientific materialism. Protestant Christianity was a stepping stone to this final stage of development. Worcester believed that races were malleable, but only to an extent. Some, like the dark-skinned Negritos who lived on the island of Negros, were doomed for extinction.[31] This was, Worcester believed, the natural way of things.

The historical record provides a good sense of where Worcester got his racist ideas from. As biographer Rodney Sullivan has argued, Worcester interpreted his first-person accounts of Filipinos with the theories of European political philosophers and contemporary ethnologists, many of whom subscribed to social Darwinism. His political theories came, in part, from his admiration for the English philosophers John Locke and David Hume. Worcester was an especially amateurish ethnologist, but he was familiar with the work of Lewis Henry Morgan and John Wesley Powell, who conducted anthropological studies of Indigenous North Americans in a similar vein.[32] As Sullivan notes, Worcester valued the work of British sociologist Benjamin Kidd's book *Social Evolution*, which posited religion's centrality in the work of progress, development, and civilization. Religion, in *Social Evolution*, was a force of energy that either mobilized and energized races or caused their stagnation. Kidd argued that the future was one of racial struggle over rich resources, especially those in the tropics.[33] There is no evidence that Worcester read or was aware of theorist of fanaticism Isaac Taylor (whom chapter 1 analyzes) or Josiah Strong (whom chapter 6 examines). However, they shared certain assumptions and concepts. Kidd conceptualized Christianity as a "force" that through the power of "disciplined enthusiasm" was able to create new orders out of previously disparate nationalities and races.[34] In this Kidd resembled Taylor's emphasis on the affective power of Christianity and the late nineteenth-century white Protestant polemics that viewed enthusiastic fervor as a necessary force for Christian civilization.

Worcester was not alone in operating within this white-supremacist and social Darwinist framework. Other civil and military officials shared this view. Judging by the level of superstition he saw in his province of Tayabas, Colonel Cornelius Gardener remarked that Filipino society was at the same level of progress as Anglo-American society during the witchcraft trials at Salem. "There is no forward movement," he added.[35] When asked why he would not provide a timeline for Filipino independence, William Howard Taft, who served alongside Worcester as a key figure in the colonial administration, argued that it would take *at least* two generations for the Filipinos to learn self-governance. This was because "ninety percent, or more," he wrote, "are densely ignorant, superstitious, and subject to imposition of all sorts."[36] The reports of superstitious beliefs in the islands functioned to highlight the primitive or semicivilized status of Filipinos.

These officials did not view anting anting as authentic religious practices. They represented superstitions that marked Filipinos' deficient sense of human agency. Scholar of religion David Chidester has shown that Victorian anthropological theories of superstition emphasized how superstitious people failed to separate the subjective from the objective.[37] The result was an inadequately agential human. For Filipinos, US ethnologists and colonial officials claimed, spirits and supernatural powers could be arbitrarily created, felt, or sensed anywhere. Any bronze medal, rock, stream, or person had the capacity to become a site of a spiritual agency. For Worcester, especially as a trained zoologist, these practices signaled an improper understanding of natural causality. They inhibited social order, producing subjects who relied on diffuse supernatural powers as opposed to real, secular power—that is, their own labor and scientific inquiry. The superstitiousness of Filipino society, based as it was in material culture, made Filipinos especially subject to being affected. As affectable subjects, they were vulnerable to falling under the sway of charismatic authority figures.

This fits well with a number of studies of coloniality and modernity. To be superstitious meant you were not quite modern. Anthropologist Webb Keane has excavated the role of religion in the narrative of progress Euro-American Protestants told themselves in the context of encounters with diverse populations. "If in the past," Keane writes in summarizing this narrative, "humans were in thrall to illegitimate rulers, rigid traditions, and unreal fetishes, as they become modern they realize the true character of human agency."[38] Emancipation in the political sense was believed to be dependent on emancipation of the agential individual human. Superstitions, signaling the lack of this agency and buffered individuality, were obstacles to this emancipation.

As scholar of African American studies Barnor Hesse argues in his excavation of the whiteness of Western philosophy, race is not merely a social construction nor a misunderstanding based on preexisting biological differences but a product of discourse about modernity that produces and is produced, in large part, by European colonial domination over non-Europeans. Hesse calls attention to the "series of onto-colonial taxonomies of land, climate, history, bodies, customs, language, all of which became sedimented metonymically, metaphorically, and normatively as the assembled attributions of 'race.'"[39] We might add to this series what scholar of religion Robert Orsi calls "unmodern religion"—or the categorization of "superstition" that this chapter has explored.[40]

Religion is an important taxonomy to examine in relation to racist discourses because Westerners had long viewed the cultures of non-Westerners as having inferior religious beliefs and practices. According to these discourses, beliefs and practices were taken not simply as *signs* of racial inferiority but as the very epistemologies that deficient mentalities produced. Worcester argued that these epistemologies—and in particular a willingness to imbue materiality with spiritual power—was a primary factor in one's race. A variety of unmodern religions (which were, in this discourse, "not-quite-religions," as anthropologist J. Brent Crosson suggests) and unmodern races (which were, in this discourse, "not-quite-humans," as African American studies scholar Alex Weheliye suggests) were co-constituted within the US colonial imaginary.[41] This discourse was driven by politics and power. Superstitions marked populations as shackled to the past and resistant to the future, a future accessible only through acceptance of US rule.

Policing Fanaticism

As demonstrated above, American descriptions of Filipinos as inherently prone to superstition formed a rhetorical strategy to depict Filipinos as racially inferior and in need of white, Christian, American paternalism. There was also a practical and urgent problem with Filipino material culture. Americans believed that it helped cultivate fanaticism. This was especially true after 1901, when guerrilla warfare was the main strategic challenge for US efforts to govern the archipelago. In 1899, Worcester found Filipino material culture to be, in part, an exotic curiosity as much as a problem. By 1914, he had changed his tune. The material culture of the Philippines, Worcester suggested, made for a dire problem.

Anting anting was one cause of violent resistance and social disorder. Insurrectionaries were indeed violent, attacking the US military and the Philippine Constabulary. Some insurrectionaries also lived up to their reputation as bandits, attacking livestock and extorting locals. They targeted Catholic priests along with peasants who allied themselves with the occupation.[42] It is fair to say that many of these bandit groups were a problem for many Filipinos. This was, indeed, part of insurrectionaries' anticolonial strategy, though the United States at times overstated their violence. This section focuses on two insurrectionary leaders: Ruperto Rios of the city of Tayabas and Papa Isio of the island of Negros.

The specter of fanaticism became increasingly important for US strategies of pacification and securitization. Racist rhetoric accompanied racial governance. Fanaticism indicated a single-minded zeal to commit divinely sanctioned violence no matter the cost. According to one American newspaper article noting the problematic presence of fanaticism in 1899, the fanatic wanted a "holy war" and was intolerant toward other religions. Despite expressing concern about the future, the article assured its readers that "the new regime will logically bring ... real religious liberty to the Filippinos." This in turn meant the elimination of religious fanaticism.[43] Fanaticism was primarily a religious and criminal formation according to Worcester, not a political one. The insurrectionaries, he wrote, "sought to excuse their lawless acts under the plea of patriotism and opposition to the forces of the United States." But their essence was their identities as "professional bandits" and/or "religious fanatics."[44] The article specifically mentioned the threat of "Moslem fanatics" in Mindanao and Cebu. A number of scholars have expertly explored the figure of the "Moro" in the US imaginary.[45] This chapter focuses on the linkage between fanaticism, anting anting, and insurrectionary groups that had a prophetic authority figure. Most were Catholic, with elements of Indigenous polytheistic religion.

In the colonial archive, references to superstition as imbricated in religious fanaticism became especially common in the early 1900s, when, after the capture of President Emilio Aguinaldo, resistance to US rule splintered into local, largely rural, sects. As Reynaldo Clemeña Ileto has argued, Aguinaldo *and* later revolutionary movements were part of a popular tradition of Filipino revolt that drew on messianic traditions rooted in Catholicism and Indigenous practices related to anting anting.⁴⁶ The presence of religion was not new. Members of the Philippine Constabulary, however, believed a shift was occurring. As Vic Hurley, reminiscing in the 1930s about the history of the constabulary, wrote, "the wave of religious fanaticism" made it so that "no longer were the fighting forces in the Philippines concerned so greatly with political groups; it was pseudo-religion that had succeeded as the force behind the combat."⁴⁷ A once secular resistance was now infused with a religious aura, though one that was not interpreted as properly religious or deserving of the protections of religious freedom. Fanatics came to be what David Scott calls a "target of colonial power."⁴⁸ More specifically, they became military targets. In turn, US strategies of pacification and secularization turned to focus on fanatical leaders and religious ideas and objects believed to cultivate fanaticism.

Who were called fanatics? The decade after 1901 was indeed a time of proliferating insurrectionary authority figures who claimed divine powers or providential favor. This section focuses on Ruperto Rios and Papa Isio, due to the consternation they caused US forces, and the extant descriptions of their material cultures. That said, there were plenty of other insurrectionaries who shared features of Rios's and Isio's militant communities. These religious leaders included Felipe Salvador ("Colorum" or the Santa Iglesia movement), Fransisco (the Solo Dios movement), Andrés Bonifacio (the Katipunan society), Papa Pablo (the pulahan movement), and many others, some of whom no doubt did not make it into the written record. I have not found a recorded instance of a "Virgin Mary," as Luke Wright hinted at, or any woman having much of a record as a religiously inspired insurrectionary. Women, as examined later, did have a role in insurrectionary communities through the production and sanctification of anting anting.

Papa Isio was perhaps the most well-known religiously inspired rebel. He fought occupiers from the 1890s to 1907, when he was caught and imprisoned by US military forces. Americans took a serious interest in him after 1901. The records of Papa Isio are few; most are from the perspective of US colonial officials. He was variously named Dionisio Magbuela, Dionisio Segobela, or Dionisio Seguela. At some point he began to go by Papa Isio to signal that he was the rightful pope of the Philippines. At that point he began to incorporate many of ceremonies and powers attributed to the traditional Roman Catholic pope. That said, he mixed

Catholicism with Indigenous and even Masonic religious symbols, rituals, and associations.

Dionisio was a laborer in his early life. He was forced to move multiple times and frequently came into conflict with wealthier landowners. At some point by the late 1890s, he was emerging as a political, religious, and military authority figure on the island. Papa Isio was operating within the tradition of "babaylanism" on the island. Babaylans were shaman-like religious authority figures, with ritual expertise, prophetic powers, and special authority. Babaylans were traditionally women, with the occasional *asog*, or a male who acted in ways associated with women. In the 1890s, babaylans were increasingly men who embraced more traditional expectations of masculinity. This shift in religious authority was perhaps because Filipinos on Negros were increasingly utilizing the powers of babaylanism for war against occupiers.[49]

Papa Isio and his guerrilla fighters took up residence on the volcanic mountain Kanlaon on Negros. He would order troops to periodically come down to attack American-allied Filipinos and, at times, American forces. Papa Isio was similar to other rebel groups throughout Southeast Asia who found sanction and security in the highlands.[50] Officials estimated his number of followers anywhere from fifty to one thousand. In reality, his number of followers probably ebbed and flowed, and it is difficult to discern in texts when "followers" signaled actively fighting soldiers or more broadly supportive peasants of Negros.

Papa Isio continuously claimed supernatural powers throughout his guerrilla campaigns. Most important were the anting anting he handed out to his soldiers. These charms came in a variety of forms. Many had prayers written on them. One anonymous major in the US Army described Papa Isio handing out belts with "mystic figures" that you would hold over your shoulders.[51] The major also mentioned feathers that soldiers were supposed to keep in their mouths. If they spoke or dropped the feather, it lost its efficaciousness. Another American described Isio's charms as scraps of "paper covered with crude writing and figures, a cross, a few Ave Marias."[52] US government reports emphasized the role of anting anting in keeping Papa Isio's authority afloat and keeping his soldiers in line. John Taylor, who had access to a number of direct sources about Papa Isio, described his powers as such:

Isio was the religious head of his followers; he commanded their implicit faith and obedience, and performed religious rites such as marriage with ceremonies which were intended to resemble those of the Catholic church; but probably most of his influence was due to the belief that he possessed supernatural powers, and owing to this he was able to do a good business in the sale of charms, or anting-anting, to his followers, which, he claimed, would protect them against death by American bullets.[53]

As with Taylor's description, Americans noted Papa Isio's role as a pope with a tinge of anti-Catholicism. Many American Protestants and secularists at this time believed that Catholics were wholly obedient to the pope and too invested in the efficacy of rituals and sacred material objects. Anting anting, indeed, did have similarities to Catholic scapulars. At times Worcester hinted at the Catholic flavor of anting anting. At other times, he emphasized anting anting as pre-Spanish and thus pre-Catholic survivals. In truth, anting anting, in their symbology and supernatural efficacy, drew on multiple lineages, as discussed earlier.

Though there was some debate as to whether Isio himself believed his own claims to be true, most Americans wrote that he was superstitious himself. L. W. V. Kennon, captain of the Sixth Infantry, reporting to Secretary of War Elihu Root, described Papa Isio as "possibly a sincere fanatic, but superstitious and cunning" having "great influence over the ignorant masses, who fear his vengeance and are superstitiously inclined to believe in his sacred character and supernatural powers."[54] Most Americans emphasized that Papa Isio fought primarily because he was deluded in his own religious cosmology. His fanaticism signaled that he was primarily a religious actor, with the assumption that this subsumed all other aspects of his leadership.

Despite this pathologization, the evidence suggests that Papa Isio did avow political principles and rationales for forming his militant community. First, Papa Isio was clearly against any foreign occupation, whether it be Spanish or US. He was well versed in the idea of independence and was allied with the broader Philippine independence movement until the wealthy landowners of Negros capitulated to the United States. He also held political ideals, though it is hard to discern them precisely. Leandro de la Rama Locsin, the civil governor of the province of Negros, struggled to describe Papa Isio's politics. They were, he wrote, a "confused admixture of socialistic principles, anarchistic instincts, and a strange aberration of religious and fanatical notions." Papa Isio posed as a "divine instrument" and helped give the babaylans an aura of being "Christ-sent liberators."[55] By socialistic principles, Locsin likely meant that Papa Isio was critical of the notion of private property, at least in the context of wealthy landowners operating sugar *haciendas* on Negros. Going into the 1900s, Papa Isio was able to attract farm labor against the increasing power of landowner families.[56] He was waging class warfare and anticolonial warfare, which for him were one and the same.

Unfortunately, the historical record offers few words directly from those targeted as fanatics. The colonial archives do contain a few of Papa Isio's letters, which were captured and compiled in the Philippine Insurgent Records, a large collection of reports and sources originally stored with the US Bureau of Insular Affairs. The aforementioned John Taylor was the compiler of these documents. These letters were signed by Papa Isio, but they were likely written by someone else dictating Isio's orders. The letters primarily consist of commands given to Isio's captains, though some were correspondence with other insurrectionaries. They are limited in what they can tell us about the religious aspects of Papa Isio, but they do provide clues.

In his letters, Dionisio reminded his followers of his divine power. He sought to enforce obedience and discipline in his soldiers. Fearful of individuals taking property stolen from the wealthy Americans, Papa Isio made it known that "if the soldiers take any of the property seized, they will speedily be put to death and will surely go to hell."[57] The property was for the community, not individuals. He referred to disorderly soldiers as "evil-minded."[58] The letters show the effort necessary to keep his community and the soldiers in line.

The letters also shed light on Papa Isio's strategic use of violence. Papa Isio did not live up to the caricature of the fanatic in terms of unleashing violence wildly. On the contrary, he was selective in his use of violence, often advocating for discernment when punishing or executing people. Yet he did see the use of spectacular violence as a tool. "It is advisable to punish by decapitation all those who go with the Americans, but it is necessary first to ascertain the existence of the crime, and if it should appear that they are real spies of the enemy, they must be beheaded immediately without any pretext whatsoever against it."[59] He wrote to Rufo Oyos, his loyal captain general, to practice due law when someone was charged with committing a crime. In another letter, Isio cautioned his commanders that he did not want his soldiers becoming overwhelmed by "los resentimeientos y venganzas" (resentment and vengeance). This was "for the good of your soul and body," Papa Isio noted.[60] Though the letters do not shed light on Papa Isio's divine powers, they do show how his roles as a commander and as a religious expert were linked.

At least in interviews with outsiders, Papa Isio's followers seemed to be invested in his supernatural claims as well as his politics and military strategy. As historian Alfred McCoy has described, one anonymous member of Isio's community was interviewed by the Spanish-language newspaper *El Tiempo* in 1907. He said the following:

> Papa Isio is no sort of mortal man, and is nothing other than one of the elect, chosen by God to redeem the Filipino people from slavery. He is immortal, and cannot be hit or wounded by bullets, possessing a supernatural power which you cannot believe if you have not seen it with your own eyes. So that you will be convinced of his infinite power, let me simply say that he can fly through the air if he wishes and can communicate directly with God with whom he holds interesting dialogues in the presence of all his followers. All of us have seen his aerial vapors, seen God, radiant in his glory, and heard his heavenly words on three occasions when Papa Isio called out the complete holy unction.[61]

This loyal follower of Isio still viewed him as a liberator of the Philippines writ large from Spanish, American, and capitalist interests, even as the Philippine-American War had technically ended in 1901, according to US officials. Yet the war had never ended. Though a provincial insurrectionary militant group, the babaylans held messianic nationalistic ideals. This account emphasizes the divine powers of Isio, with a proximity to God. Going further, he served as a medium who could commune with God. The evidence suggests that Papa Isio's supernatural, political, and military claims held at least some sway among those who agreed with him and were willing to fight for him.

Ruperto Rios was not quite as well represented in reports or scholarship as Papa Isio. Like Papa Isio, Rios was one of the first charismatic leaders of the revolutionary sects the United States encountered. In his early life, Rios was a blacksmith. In the late 1890s and early 1900s he had served in the Philippine Revolutionary Army. In the wake of the surrender of the Revolutionary Army in 1901, Rios took residence in the mountains of Quezon province, where he began to build a coalition of resistance fighters. The records do not say when he became an authority figure, though they do capture a common story about how he claimed authority, with which I began this book.

In the early 1900s, a spiritual being radiating a bright light descended upon the city of Tayabas in the Philippines. Amid the crowd that formed to witness the spectacle was Ruperto Rios, a local military chief. The spirit pointed to Rios and bestowed upon him supernatural power and significance. Rios began to talk of building in the Philippines a "New Jerusalem," a reference to Revelation 21. He would help lead the way to this paradise, claiming himself as the rightful pope and the Son of God. Americans interpreted the story of Rios differently. The truth, they reported, was that Rios had dressed one of his officers in black, thrown a mosquito net over him, and poured thousands of fireflies into the net. He then rigged a pully system to make it appear that the officer was floating in midair. Rios, Americans reported, convinced his fellow Filipinos, preying on their superstitious mentality and manufacturing a spiritual experience to gain authority for himself.[62]

The historical accuracy of this story is difficult to assess. Accuracy, in this case, means the question of whether or not some sort of performative spectacle of divine ordination for Rios took place. The story seems to exist only in colonial accounts. Further complicating matters, Baptist missionary Harry Maxfield, who visited the island of Negros, told a similar story. In Maxfield's account it was not Rios of Tayabas who was ordained but Isio of the island of Negros. "The bandits thought he was the Lord," Maxfield reported, "and when he spoke every one groveled on the ground. The manufactured lord then appointed Daniel his mountain pope and called him Papa Ysio."[63] This account is especially untrustworthy. It is possible the story of Rios's ordination was entirely a figment of a colonialist imagination seeking to project religious absurdities onto resistance fighters. Perhaps locals in Quezon province or the island of Negros told similar stories. Maybe the descent of a sacred figure was a common theme. The colonial archive is perilous footing for historical accuracy. That said, all other versions of this tell of Rios as the sanctified figure.

Whatever the case, these stories influenced how colonial officials understood Rios. According to US government reports, Rios "worked upon the superstition of the poor barrio people." He sought to create a semisovereign militarized municipality that he claimed was sanctioned by divine power. This was to be a New Jerusalem on Mount San Cristobal.[64] In the assessments by US officials, Rios was able to do this in two ways: he mobilized Christian messianic myths and circulated anting anting to his followers. As the annual report to the 1903 US secretary of war noted, Rios was in competition with Catholic priests as he "received confessions and granted absolutions considerably below market price, and which he claimed were much more efficacious than those dispensed by an ordinary padre."[65] Insurrectionaries rarely got along with the local official Catholic clergy. In his 1903 report to the US War Department, commander of the constabulary Henry Allen derided Rios as an "inspired prophet," who "found little difficulty in working on the superstitions of the credulous inhabitants of barrios distant from centres of population."[66] Followers seemed to reiterate some of Allen's claims. On September 3, 1903, the constabulary captured a uniformed officer of Rios, who claimed that "Rios was a direct descendant of God and nothing earthly could harm him."[67] Rios's divine status and his ability to dodge capture and harm went hand in hand.

Rios's collection of anting anting was evidence of his proximity to divine power. US officials feared that Rios was participating in and furthering a subversive material culture of spiritual power. Along with the usual small charms (jewelry, shirts, etc.), Rios possessed an especially powerful anting anting. He had a chest with the word *independencia* carved into it. Americans reported that the chest was accompanied by three women who were virgins. Rios told his followers that he would soon open the box. At that moment, one report to the secretary of war stated, "'Independence' would jump out, they could catch her and be ever afterwards happy."[68] This minor deity contained in the box would bring about a new spiritual and political reign in the Philippines. Rios used this to motivate his followers, many of them guerrilla fighters. If they kept fighting, eventually the time would come to open the chest. There would be a new spiritual and political reign in the Philippines. Just around the corner, Rios promised a future with no US military, no taxes, and no jails.

Like Papa Isio, Rios seemed to have a class and political bent in his leadership. This is clear in his anti–US military, anti-tax, and anti-incarceration politics. Chief of the Philippine Constabulary Harry Hill Bandholtz went further in noting that Rios wanted to do away with private property altogether. He described Rios's vision for the future as such: "Each man could help himself to whatever he desired—his neighbor's pony, carabao, or other property."[69] Like with Isio, political independence and a socialistic reimagining of the economy went hand in hand.

Rios and Papa Isio, along with other messianic revolutionary movements, prompted a shift in how Americans wrote about Filipino society. In 1914, Worcester published *The Philippines Past and Present*, which he advertised as an updated version of his 1899 survey *The Philippine Islands and Their People*. By this time, Worcester had become frustrated and bitter about the slow progress and continued resistance Americans like himself faced. In *Philippines Past and Present*, he noted that some anti-imperialist Americans had referred to movements in the Philippines as "independence movements." Indeed, some US writers had sympathy for the lingering insurrectionaries. Worcester disagreed: "As a matter of fact, the bulk of the common people have little idea what the word [independence] really means."[70] Worcester had in mind Rios and his independencia box.

For Worcester, Rios did not have a sincere desire for independence. Independence was supposed to be a political ideal, not a spiritual being who resided in a literal material box. Rios's desire for independence was corrupted by his superstitious beliefs that manifested in irrational resistance. Worcester wrote that "until it ceases to be so readily possible to prey on the superstitions, the credulity and the passions of the common people, efforts on the part of the Filipinos to establish and maintain unaided a stable government are not likely to be crowned with very abundant successes."[71] In 1898 Worcester suggested that it might take ten years to "civilize" Filipinos. By 1914 he wrote that if the United States had civilized and pacified Filipinos by the end of a century, then it should be counted as a success.⁷² Belief in anting anting was targeted for being a precondition for fanatical cults to form, ensnaring the credulous into an irrational and suicidal mission against the United States.

A number of developments can help contextualize Worcester's emboldened claims about the problem of fanaticism in the Philippines. First, Worcester, as biographer Rodney Sullivan writes, was in need of money in the early 1910s and looked forward to profits from publishing *Philippines Past and Present*. Worcester, spurned in part by his extreme unpopularity among Filipinos, was rightly fearful for his job as secretary of the interior. Anticipating his dismissal, he resigned in 1913, turning to a career of extractive corporate ventures in the Philippines. Beyond his own economic well-being, Worcester also had motivations to once again impact public perception. With the election of Woodrow Wilson, the status of the Philippines as a colonial possession was once more up in the air. Democrats, then in power, were publicly talking about the possibility of an independent Philippines. Worcester no doubt found the story of Rios as one that could sway public opinion. He employed other stories to emphasize the degree of Filipino savagery, including the practice of slavery. By the assessment of Sullivan, Worcester indeed swayed public opinion and pressured the federal government to sign the Jones Bill in 1916. Instead of granting the Philippines independence, the Jones Bill made small, though significant, changes to the colonial constitution, including an elected Philippine legislature. On the national level, the Philippines had slightly more autonomy than before.⁷³ Worcester's descriptions of a degraded Filipino culture had as much to do with Rios as with Worcester's careerism and desire for the United States to maintain sovereignty over the archipelago, a lucrative possession to the nation and to Worcester.

Rios's own voice is even more difficult to discern than Papa Isio's. There is at least one letter allegedly written by Rios. It contains three sentences. Rios refers to himself as "jefe politico-militar de Tayabas" (the politico-military chief of Tayabas). He then goes on to elevate a citizen to the rank of "Second Corporal of Volunteers."⁷⁴ At the very least, this letter indicates that similarly to Papa Isio, Rios was working to build a chain of command and was strategic in his efforts. He, too, saw himself as a political and military figure. The strategic nature of Rios and Isio rarely showed up in colonial reports, focused as they were on the supernatural aspects of these two popes.

How did the US police the insurrectionaries? The United States and its Filipino allies did so through the military and law. Attention to the efforts to police fanatics reveals the extent to which to be labeled a fanatic by a powerful occupying state meant being a primary target. To be a fanatic was to already have a death sentence. This was especially true of fanatic leaders.

First, the United States needed to catch the insurrectionaries, which was no easy task. New military strategies were needed to counteract the insurrectionaries. To this end, in 1901 Governor-General Taft created the Philippine Constabulary, a paramilitary force. It was organized and directed by officers of the US Army and enlisted largely Filipino men. Worcester wrote favorably of the constabulary as exactly the type of force that was necessary to combat fanaticism. He counterposed the dutiful and nationalized constabulary against the provincial nature of the rebels: "The head-hunters of the Mountain Province, the Mohammedan Moros of Mindanao, Jolo and Palawan, the bloody *pulájanes* of Samar and Leyte, the wily *tulisanes* of Luzon, all unrestrained by any regard for the rules of civilized warfare, have for twelve years matched their fanatical bravery against the gallantry of the khaki-clad Filipino soldiers."[75] He specifically noted that the constabulary was necessary to handle the emergence of "popes" like Papa Isio.

General Henry Allen, chief of the Philippine Constabulary in the early 1900s, also wrote assessments of fanatics and argued that the presence of fanaticism required that the United States not lessen the presence of US troops. The *New York Times* summarized Allen's call: "The susceptibility of the natives to religious deceptions is another reason why there should be sufficient American troops kept in the islands. Through a fanatical uprising, it would be possible in some sections to bring on a large insurrection, which would give this Government considerable trouble and expense to deal with."[76] In less public reports, Allen's writing displayed an ambivalence about the religious, social, or political factors that could be motivating armed bands, describing them as "quasi religious or political movements, which were, for the most part, ordinary brigandage faintly disguised." Religion and political commitments were excuses for simple criminality. But that said, he could not help but note the power of religion in motivating Filipinos for rebellion: "It is a curious fact, however, that among the various religious sects found in the Archipelago there is an invariable effort and desire on their part to become possessed of arms to reinforce the propaganda of their creeds."[77] Though skeptical and ambivalent about the role of religion as an instigator of political agitation, Allen seems to have found himself compelled by the wave of evidence. No doubt he also found it a politically expedient way to legitimate the power of the Philippine Constabulary.

The creation of the constabulary and continued presence of the US Army to fight the insurrectionaries led to a cycle of violence. Despite the official rhetoric on both sides of sharp differentiation, occupiers and the occupied mirrored each other in many ways, including tactics and the uses of violence. They were, after all, at war. In his chapter "Murder as a Governmental Agency," Worcester emphasized how insurrectionaries like Papa Isio were willing to use terror against both American forces and Filipinos who had not joined the resistance. He claimed Filipinos were at first friendly toward the Americans, only to be turned against them out of fear of fanatics like Papa Isio. He quoted Papa Isio's command about the decapitation of allies of the United States: "To be considered a 'real spy,' it was necessary only to be seen talking to Americans." Papa Isio's meaning was not as clear as Worcester made it seem. As mentioned, Papa Isio also wrote that "it is necessary first to ascertain the existence of the crime."[78] Mirroring Papa Isio's strategy—though with the threat of incarceration or occupation rather than decapitation—Bandholtz threatened Filipino town leaders. He told them that he would "hold them responsible for bands existing within their respective jurisdictions."[79] Proximity to the enemy meant guilt by association for both sides. Though the Philippine Constabulary referred to its members as peace officers, the paramilitary presence made clear that in many ways the Philippine-American War was ongoing. Not all Filipinos had accepted US rule, and many promoted violent resistance.

What did the fight against insurrectionaries look like on the ground for US and US-allied military forces? A few sources shed light on the troops' understandings of fanaticism. The *Manual for the Philippines Constabulary* tasked the members of the PC with doing their best to study fanaticism. "In dealing with outlawry or fanaticism," it continued, "the best information and results can be obtained from the people themselves." The manual also emphasized that leaders, rather than followers, should be the ones made an example of.⁸⁰ This fit the theory of fanaticism as an energizing force produced primarily by a charismatic leader. Eliminate the leader, and you can potentially moderate the fanaticism. The Filipinos might be a superstitious people, according to this theory, but that made them only susceptible to being fanaticized, not inherently fanatic. Resistance, in this view, was caused only by authority figures who dressed themselves up with the aura of religious authority. It had no mass appeal. To be sure, many Filipinos welcomed US rule and actively worked with the colonial administration, some more or less enthusiastically. The political situation of rising national sentiment and the question of colonial rule was complicated. The United States, however, underestimated the extent of resistance that it would receive.

John White provided another perspective from a soldier. White was an officer of the constabulary who fought on the front lines against the insurrectionary leaders. In the early 1900s, he was actively battling Papa Isio's forces and trying to capture Isio himself. He later published a memoir on his experiences in the Philippines. Similar to Worcester and other top-level leaders, White blamed anting anting for Papa Isio's power. "Papa Isio was strong on the dispensation of these charms," White wrote, "giving one to each of his followers."⁸¹ White was fixated on the capture of Isio to stop the circulation of anting anting.

Fanatics were killed in battle, executed immediately, or, more often, sent to the colonial courts. Fanaticism was not a legal concept during the colonial occupation. Though the colonial government and the constabulary made known that they were targeting superstition, no laws name the elimination of superstition or fanaticism as their aim. Rather, the US colonial government targeted superstitions and fanatical characteristics through legal accusations of other crimes, primarily banditry. According to the US census, which included qualitative ethnological writings alongside quantitative data, superstitions not only would "interfere with the daily affairs of life" but could lead to "serious crimes."⁸² Especially after Aguinaldo's capture, revolutionary movements were associated with bandits, outlaws, and cults.⁸³ These sects were often policed under the language of *bandolerismo*, which was used to mark a particular strain of banditry flourishing in the wake of the Aguinaldo's capture. A 1902 act made this type of banditry a crime against public order and punishable by twenty-five to thirty years' imprisonment or execution.⁸⁴ The extreme policing of bandolerismo was part and parcel of the policing of bands of fighters resisting US rule. What is interesting for the purposes of this chapter is how bandolerismo was tied up with superstitious beliefs. Reports referred to both Papa Isio and Ruperto Rios as bandits. Banditry was the technical charge leveled against them.

For those deemed fanatics, however, law was often beside the point. To be labeled as a fanatic was to be outside of the population of citizens who deserved due process. This was, in some ways, true of Filipinos as a whole. But it was especially true for Filipinos labeled as fanatics. As Bandholtz wrote, "The courts have invariably put a beautiful polish upon all cases turned over to them by the constabulary, in this way contributing their full share to the work of pacification."⁸⁵ Bandholtz's phrasing of "beautiful polish" makes clear that the law was simply putting a stamp on cases that were already a foregone conclusion. The legal cases of insurrectionaries, or at least the ringleaders of insurrectionary groups, served simply to keep the illusion of due process. To be a fanatic was to be, from the perspective of the colonial state, righteously executed. In a report, Captain L. W. V. Kennon emphasized this point: "Papa Isio, I believe, is a hopeless case. He should be exterminated."⁸⁶

The US materialization of Filipinos (that is, the emphasis on Filipino culture as tied down by its emphasis on the potency of objects) was a convenient way of dismissing all resistance as outside the acceptable realm of liberal politics, as noted in studies of other imperial regimes.⁸⁷ But it was more than just rhetoric. Soldiers made killing enemy combatants wearing anting anting a point of emphasis. After describing how he removed a glass stopper charm from the neck of a dead insurrectionary, John White exclaimed, "Poor, deluded folk of the mountains! How often have I seen their still bodies with anting-anting pierced by bullets."⁸⁸ On nearly all of the charms, White claimed, was Papa Isio's signature. Other examples abound. Lieutenant A. C. Allen wrote of anting anting shirts, which were worn by Filipino rebels who could afford them. Like many accounts, Allen emphasized the ineffectual nature of these charms. "We have often found bodies with the shirt upon them, perforated with American bullets," he wrote, "and dyed with insurgent blood."⁸⁹ Another account relayed in US newspapers described a battle between the Seventeenth Infantry, led by Lieutenant H. P. Hobbs, and a band of Moros who were attacking a village protected by US forces on the island of Pata. A local prophet came to the front of the Moro troops and defied US forces, claiming invincibility. He was immediately shot dead. Examining the body afterward, US forces described the prophet's "look of unutterable surprise." The author interpreted this look as his surprise at his own mortality. Of the seventy-five killed by US forces, almost each one wore some sort of anting anting.[90]

The gratuitousness of the violence directed at remaining resistance fighters was the point. Ending the lives of the insurrectionary authorities was not enough. Governor-General Taft, writing to the secretary of war, described the fight against insurrectionaries: "We are getting rid of the bad men and we are not offering any terms of any sort. A number have been sentenced to be hanged, and most of the others have received long sentences. It is not quite so spectacular to kill them in battle, but it has I think a better affect."[91] That type of resistance needed to be an example, complete with a threat to future potential fanatics. This was a logic of fanaticism talk: the strategy against uncompromising insurrectionaries was to be uncompromising in the pursual and punishment of them.

Women, too, were targeted as producers and sanctifiers of anting anting. Indeed, women had a traditional role in parts of the Philippines where they were ritual experts. Before Papa Isio on the island of Negros, most babaylans, or shamans, had been women. Unfortunately, I have found only hints of the role of women in the production of anting anting in the colonial archives. Allen notes the capture of "two women who posed as 'saints'" trying to distribute anting anting.[92] The role of women in later revivals of resistance, like the anti-US Sakdalista uprising in the 1930s, suggests that women certainly played a more prominent role in active, violent resistance than suggested in the colonial archive.[93]

American soldiers often collected anting anting, either through raids or by taking them off the bodies of the deceased. Through troops returning home, anting anting, insurrectionary flags, and weapons made their way into the United States. Brought to home by Lieutenant M. Colmenares, a book of prayers from Papa Isio was displayed at the Philippine exposition at the St. Louis World's Fair in 1904. At that time, Isio was still at large.[94]

The constabulary and US military interpreted the collection of anting anting and the success of its spectacles of violence as the ultimate demonstration of the falsity of superstition and of the colonial state's prerogative to ban superstition. At least in regions with known insurrectionists, the constabulary was on the lookout for charms, messianic sects, and charismatic figures who might foment rebellion. Rios's independencia box was captured by Captain Murphy on March 8, 1903.[95] Rios himself was captured and executed shortly thereafter. Papa Isio, who outlasted most insurrectionaries, was captured in 1907. He was incarcerated at Bilibid Prison. Charged with banditry, the pope of the Philippines died behind bars in 1911.

Theorizing Religion, Power, and Rebellion in Filipino Material Culture

As discussed throughout this book, fanaticism was an overflowing signifier that requires care to understand the strategic aims of people using the term and discerning fact from fiction. This chapter has explained how Worcester's use and understanding of anting anting bore similarities to how insurrectionaries themselves described anting anting. In other words, Worcester was not *always* inaccurate in his descriptions of Filipino material culture. This chapter argues this is the case even as it has emphasized skepticism about his interpretations and assessments. What this section provides is a more careful analysis of how anting anting operated within the social and material cultures of the insurrectionary groups. This is necessary to understand how Americans did not quite grasp the social and political functions of these charms as religious objects. The language of anting anting referred to an array of distinct beliefs, objects, and practices that differed from region to region. The work of this language flattened out these distinctions, providing an intelligible account of Filipino religion for those whose main goal was to master it, rather than study and learn from it. That said, the distinct practices that US Americans studied and recorded were often real. Charms are used today in the Philippines and have been worn by recent political leaders.[96] And despite the differences across cultures and regions in the archipelago, the mixture of Catholic, Indigenous, and Masonic religious ideas has historically helped create robust material and religious cultures that Filipinos can draw on in times of crisis.

Anting anting as understood and operating in the Philippines were relational objects. Filipinos did not believe supernatural power to be embedded in the objects themselves, as Worcester and others argued. The power of these charms emerged in a web of relationships between humans and divine beings. Further, the power of anting anting was produced by and helped produce authority in this web of relationships. Filipinos utilized anting anting in efforts to enact their collective political, economic, and religious aspirations as much as individual supernatural powers. For the insurrectionaries, these aspirations included the mobilization of guerrilla fighters against US rule and, ultimately, communal self-determination led by charismatic leaders. Anting anting were important for both fighting the enemy and creating authority within insurrectionary groups. To build this case, this section draws on theories from historian Reynaldo Clemeña Ileto, social theorist Émile Durkheim, and scholar of religion Robert Orsi.

Existing work on religiously inspired rebellions in the early twentieth-century Philippines has done an excellent job examining the economic and, to a lesser extent, the political forces that compelled insurrectionaries to organize as they did. These accounts sideline religion and study it only as a side effect of these materialist forces.[97] Working to recenter religion, this section turns to Reynaldo Clemeña Ileto's insights into anting anting in his work on popular culture and its relationship to revolutionary movements in the Philippines. Drawing on the work of historian Benedict Anderson, Ileto pushes academics—and, pointedly, Western-trained academics—to "suspend temporarily our common-sense notions of what power is all about in order to understand" phenomena like anting anting.[98] He poses questions: How do so-called superstitions function in society? What do they make possible to create, imagine, solidify?

Anting anting were relational objects, operating at the nexus of the individual, charismatic authority, and divine power. Orsi, for one, has advocated for studies of religion to attend to the webs of relationships that constitute religious worlds.[99] Importantly, these webs of relationships should include spiritual beings and presences (saints, spirits, gods, etc.). We might add objects, too, for the way that they help mediate, crystallize, and define these relationships. To understand this web, it is helpful to consider the possible relationships one by one.

The first relationship was between the individual and the object. Ileto has written about how in Filipino culture the self and the supernatural powers of the charm were interconnected. A common element in Southeast Asian culture, evident from the precolonial period but not exclusive to it, was that of *loób*, a Tagalog term that means the state of one's inner being. One's loób was cultivated through asceticism, meditation, sacrifices, and self-discipline. Anting anting, Ileto argues, were representations of the status of one's inner power. This cut both ways. A failure on the part of the anting anting to live up to its powers was often linked to failures of the individual. These failures could be ritualistic or ethical.[100]

The second relationship was between the individual and the charismatic authority figure. This relationship was mediated through anting anting. Papa Isio was believed to craft anting anting, or at least he had a large collection of anting anting to give to people committed to his authority and willing to fight. The power of the anting anting that protected individuals from bullets derived from Papa Isio's divine powers. As one loyal follower commented, Isio "is immortal, and cannot be hit or wounded by bullets."[101] Anting anting offered fighters a piece of this power. They also bound the fighter and leader together. Papa Isio's charms bore his signature. In this, they served as a reminder of their origin and the source of their power. Some anting anting also served the function as edicts or indulgences. John White notes how one babaylan's anting anting, a sheet of folded paper, contained an "absolution in full from Papa Isio for a murder committed by the wearer in the lowlands."[102] Papa Isio, in this case, was operating as a sovereign. He was fulfilling his claim to be the political and religious leader of Negros, complete with the ability to define law and morality. The circulation of charms reiterated this power.

The third relationship was between individuals and divine power. Divine power could be God, but it could also be a more general sense of a divine force that permeates the world. This force was an energy whose flow can be directed, collected, or blocked.[103] For some anting anting, the divine power was separable from the material object. Though it is difficult to access its accuracy, Vic Hurley recounted an interrogation between Captain Murphy and a captured member of Ruperto Rios's guerrilla group. Murphy wanted to know more about the independencia box and asked the insurrectionary where it was. He responded that the spirit had left the box:

"Si, senor; in the box it was [the spirit], but by now it has flown away."

"Flown away?"

"Si, Senor Capitan—to the 'Pope,' to be enclosed again in another box."

The fanatic rolled his glistening eyes as he drank in the thought of the approach of the millennium. "When *independencia* flies from the box, there will be no labor, Senor, and no jails and no taxes."[104]

Evident in this quote is the culmination of these relationships. The anting anting of the independencia chest mediates these relationships. Ruperto Rios had the power to enclose the spirit of independence in a box. The opening of the box to release the spirit for good was dependent on the actions and merit of Rios's fighters. This interrogation also points to another important aspect of insurrectionary material cultures. They were weaponized for the sake of imagining and creating a future. "What really made the movement 'subversive,'" Ileto writes, "is that Rios's followers had an image of the future that shaped their activities."[105] Rather than an expression of an inherent racial incredulousness, the power of anting anting was generative in this world.

This was true generally of insurrectionaries: their religious beliefs and objects housed and mediated their social and political aspirations. These religious aspects of insurrectionary groups were inseparable from these more worldly political aspirations. These relationships were the basis for the formation—or attempted formation—of communities that espoused communal self-determination and sovereignty. At times this was highly localized, as with Ruperto Rios and his New Jerusalem. At times it was more nationalistic, as with Papa Isio. Scholar of Filipino religion and politics Evelyn Tan Cullamar discerned this entanglement when she described babaylanism and Papa Isio as constituting a "religio-political protest movement."[106] Insurrectionaries were fighting not just colonial but also class-based battles. Indeed, Papa Isio and Ruperto Rios fit the template of white British historian Eric Hobsbawm's idea of the social bandit who engaged in criminal practices like theft, ransom, and threats of violence for collective gain and with a sense of righteousness.[107] John White even claimed that Papa Isio was something akin to "the Robin Hood of the Philippines."[108]

Some early twentieth-century antiwar Americans wrote of the function of the language of fanaticism in obscuring the reality of the conflict.

One anonymous writer of "Those Filipino 'Fanatics': Such Is the Latest Title Our 'New Subjects' Get for Daring to Wish to Be Free," originally published in the *Columbus Daily Press* in 1903, specifically mentioned a dispatch about Ruperto Rios as a "fanatical leader." Exploring the contradictions of the language of fanaticism, the writer concluded that "Ruperto Rios is neither a fanatic nor a murder, but a native in arms against American invasion of his country.... Is it not a new and peculiar species of fanaticism to resist invasion and fight for freedom?" George Washington, they noted, did just that.[109]

My point is not to romanticize the insurrectionaries but to emphasize that US reports, when brandishing the category of religious fanatics or the legal charge of bandolerismo, failed to capture, or willfully ignored, the intentions and strategies of insurrectionaries. Which is not to say that plunder, violence, and self-enrichment were not real aspects of insurrectionary groups. They were. Such were the conditions of a war and occupation. Scholars studying fanaticism talk must proceed with caution in working through the overflow of claims, connotations, and judgments.

Anting anting formed a microcosm of the nearly impossible circumstances that insurrectionaries faced when resisting US colonial rule. This was the case on two levels. The difficult circumstances included the overall threat of the US occupation to Filipino independence and the threat of American bullets to individuals. Rios's independencia box speaks to this symbolism. Anting anting were potent symbols. They were more than symbols, too. It was also true in what anting anting made possible through their circulation: the creation of new communities mobilized for counterinsurgency. Anting anting produced feelings and oriented insurrectionaries into collectivities allied against common enemies. As some accounts suggested, Papa Isio's anting anting protected possessors from *US American* bullets in particular. These were religious objects of war crafted for the moment.

There are aspects of French social theorist Émile Durkheim that are useful in interpreting anting anting to help understand that these relationships were constituted through the transfer and crystallization of energy. Durkheim describes the flow of energy between a charismatic leader and a crowd: the speaker "feels filled to overflowing, as though with a phenomenal oversupply of forces that spill over and tend to spread around him ... This extraordinary surplus of forces is quite real and comes to him from the very group he is addressing. The passionate energies that he arouses reecho in turn within him, and they increase his dynamism." This was, Durkheim notes, the type of "general effervescence that is characteristic of revolutionary or creative epochs."[110]

Durkheim writes that at its most intense levels, this social effervescence changes a person. "He is stirred by passions so intense that they can be satisfied only by violent and extreme acts: by acts of superhuman heroism or blood barbarism."[111] In many ways, Durkheim's writing is similar to Worcester's understanding of fanaticism, including his racializing fanaticism talk. But for Durkheim, this was not a sign of a lack of rationality. Such effervescence was the basis of social organization, including in the West. "There is virtually no instant of our lives in which a certain rush of energy fails to come to us from outside ourselves." This rush of energy was even the basis of our feelings of moral duty, creating a "moral power that, while immanent in us, also represents something in us that is other than ourselves."[112] But there are moments when that rush of energy is more intense, when a collective group of people helps generate it at a higher level. Such intense feelings of collectivity and duty are necessary for going to war. They can give soldiers the confidence to go into battle with a sense that they will overcome. Perhaps they can avoid injury or death. And even if they are killed, they will at least have died for a cause bigger than themselves.

Durkheim, in describing the "rush of energy," was largely writing about a situation of a charismatic authority figure addressing a crowd through speech. But material objects, too, can be containers and purveyors of social effervescence, as he outlines elsewhere. Durkheim is useful for his nonreductive theories of the affectability of religion that aimed to take into account the relationality between materiality, mentality, society, and the individual. Objects are sources of power and gain this status not by an inherent energy, but through relationality. Further, the energy transferred, blocked, or accrued in this web of relationships is felt as real. "When I speak of these principles as forces," Durkheim wrote, "I do not use the word in a metaphorical sense; they behave like real forces. In a sense, they are even physical forces that bring about physical effects mechanically."[113] This might not always match the way that subjects describe the effect of an object, but social analyses of community formation attuned to lived religion can discern the power of objects.

Anting anting *did* things. Those in favor of Filipino independence and US rule alike marveled at the capacity of these objects, in tandem with prophetic religious ideals, to mobilize Filipinos. John Taylor remarked on the power of fanatics, and the Katipunan society in particular. Though he had a condescending view of the masses of fanatics, who "speak little and perhaps think little," he admitted that "that which they believe is their faith, is fanaticism in them, and works miracles, moves mountains, creates new worlds and other prodigies."[114] In his condescension lay a hint of truth. The point is to suggest not that anting anting were, after all, rational, but that they had a *rationale*. Supernatural charms objectified the imaginative political and economic aspirations. They were compelling objects toward certain ends. As Rios envisioned, no US military, no taxes, and no jails.

The power of affects and materiality in the Philippines was distinct, but not entirely unique. US Americans, too, relied on the power of objects to mobilize themselves for the occupation of the Philippines. This chapter has already shown how Worcester himself was half invested in the power of anting anting. So, too, was John White, who frequently bragged about the powers of the anting anting he possessed. During one battle he encouraged his Filipino soldiers to be brave. "I told them," he wrote, "that I was like Papa Islo and that rifle balls would not touch me. I enlarged on the virtues of an *anting-anting* that I possessed."[115] One might question whether or not White or Worcester actually *believed* in the power of anting anting. The same can be argued for Filipinos. The efficacy of anting anting is tied less to *belief* than to their collection, their circulation, and the levels of authority they help produce. From their writings, White and Worcester certainly seem to feel emboldened and more secure in possession of powerful anting anting.

Even beyond the halfway investment in anting anting that occupiers had, Americans at home and abroad have long had their own divine object: the American flag. Durkheim himself noted the similarities between the Indigenous totems and the flags of Western nations. The flag is a powerful collective representation:

> The soldier who died for his flag dies for his country, but the idea of the flag is actually in the foreground of his consciousness. Indeed the flag sometimes causes action directly. Although the country will not be lost if

a solitary flag remains in the hand of the enemy of won if it is regained, the soldier is killed in retaking it. He forgets that the flag is only a symbol that has no value in itself but only brings to mind the reality it represents. The flag itself is treated as if it was that reality.[116]

The flag is a symbol and more. US Americans have imbued it with a powerful aura, such that the object of the flag itself becomes an agent in a web of relationships.

The flag is an important object of colonial power as much as national collective representation. As Paul Kramer notes, US Americans' emphasis on the flag as a symbol and agent of US control in the Philippines was a substitute for words that Americans were less comfortable with: colony, possession, territory, and so on.[117] US Americans often referred to questions of sovereignty under the metaphor of the flag. This was captured in the pithy formulation of a complicated legal question popular in debates over the legal status of Filipinos: "Does the Constitution follow the flag?" That is, did Filipinos gain constitutional rights because the Philippines was technically a territory? The answer, "not necessarily." The power of flags was evident in the Flag Law of 1907, which outlawed the display of the Philippine flag, created by Filipino nationalist Emilio Aguinaldo. In its place the colonial government required the display of the US American flag.[118] Coincidentally, in that same year the US Supreme Court heard its first case on flag desecration with *Halter v. Nebraska* (1907). The court ruled that states had the right to ban desecration of the flag as they saw fit.

The flag objectified two things: the right to kill and the will to sacrifice one's self. Consider, for example, this US Army song:

> Damn, damn, damn, the Filipinos!
> Cut-throat khakiac ladrones!
> Underneath the starry flag,
> Civilize 'em with a Krag,
> And return us to our own beloved homes.[119]

The flag served as a symbol of sovereignty, conveying a sense of sanction for the United States to do as it pleased with colonized subjects. A "Krag" was a Krag–Jørgensen, a bolt-action rifle used by many US troops. The line "Civilize 'em with a Krag" discloses the close relationship between the desire to civilize and the desire to enact violence. This relationship was sanctified by its position "underneath the starry flag."

The flag served as a repository for the blood sacrifice of US soldiers. In response to a letter from General H. C. Corbin about the death of his son, Secretary of War Elihu Root wrote that "the flag under which he sacrificed his life in defense of his country's rightful sovereignty will remain the emblem and guarantee of peace and justice throughout the land, and your boy's sacrifice hard as it is, will not have been in vain."[120] Senator Beveridge also heavily relied on the power of the flag in arguing for US empire: "The republic never retreats. Its flag is the only flag that has never known defeat. Where the flag leads, we follow, for we know that the hand that bears it onward, is the unseen hand of God. We follow the flag, and independence is ours."[121] The flag and divine providence together sanctioned the US empire.

Durkheim himself wrote about how his theories applied to Western colonists' engagement with non-Westerners. Colonists, feeling that they were operating beyond the sphere of their own home society, felt enabled and justified in exercising their worst violent desires against the colonized. Moral forces, a product of society, were no longer felt as valid. "The superiority that he arrogates," Durkheim wrote of the colonist, "produces a veritable intoxication of self, a sort of megalomania, which goes to the worst extremes. . . . The violence is a game with him, a spectacle in which he indulges himself, a way of demonstrating that superiority he sees in himself."[122] The Stars and Stripes was a powerful object for Americans to affectively produce a sense of superiority and even invulnerability.

Critics of the war and occupation were keen to highlight how the discourse of the flag obfuscated the work of colonialism. One critic of Worcester questioned his impartiality and scientific qualifications by noting that at a speech in New York in 1900, Worcester gave a toast to the flag, saying, "May it always stay wherever it is raised."[123] Worcester's books, the critic argued after noting Worcester's toast, might not be as trustworthy as they look. The flag inspired, helped produce feelings, and mobilized people for war.[124] It was also a site of contestation.

I want to end this chapter with an anecdote that discloses a scene of Filipino contestation over fanaticism talk. At times, Americans' misinterpretations of the stories and objects they collected in the Philippines were rather blunt. Not everything was alive with effervescent power. At times, the stories Filipinos told were just stories—and the objects in these stories were mere symbols. Stories could be political too. Some stories that Filipinos told were thinly veiled critiques of white colonizers. When Worcester was on the island of Panay, he described a story that the people he was staying with told him about a local parasitic tree species called *balete*. This tree clings onto neighboring plants, draining them of life and has indeed been a source for mythic narratives and supernatural ideas.[125] Locals told him "that there were white men inside of this tree, and that its branches would bleed if cut."[126] Worcester noted this, decried it as an odd and inexplicable superstition, and moved on. Worcester's religio-racial presuppositions limited his own ability to discern the potential meanings in the stories that Filipinos told him. White men like Worcester were akin to parasites that expanded their power at the expense of other plants, killing them in the process. White men were trying to establish roots in the Philippines. White men, however, were not invulnerable and would indeed bleed if cut.

Conclusion

Insurrectionaries, especially those in remote regions of the archipelago, never fully went away. By the 1910s they were, however, largely contained and US colonial officials did not view them as an existential threat to US rule. This was due to the executions, imprisonments, and spectacles of colonial violence that William Howard Taft described. The weaponization of anting anting in anticolonial religio-political guerrilla fighters served as a reminder of the nonconsensual nature of US rule in the Philippines.

This chapter has attended to the materialities of governance, or how states govern populations through acts of classification *and* through the more visceral and direct policing of bodies, texts, and objects taken to be of significance by the subjects in question. It has focused on Filipino material culture, as rendered in the colonial imaginary and as practiced by insurrectionary groups in the late nineteenth-century and early twentieth-century Philippines. For strategic purposes, US Americans concerned about securing their colonial possession could not afford to dismiss superstition and fanaticism as only unreal. Colonial power players like Worcester, Bandholtz, and Taft had to engage. They might not have believed in anting anting or Papa Isio's messianic claims, but they would, in practice, have treated them as powerful—dangerously powerful. Colonial and white-supremacist frameworks notwithstanding, they were not entirely wrong.

6

Enthusiasm Against Fanaticism

The US Empire and Its Critics

Chapter 1 of this book examined the emerging differentiation that Protestants, and especially evangelicals Charles Finney and Isaac Taylor, were making between fanaticism and enthusiasm. This chapter returns to the discursive fates of these two terms in the late nineteenth and early twentieth centuries. Protestants increasingly argued for a more radical distinction between enthusiasm and fanaticism. The former, with its passions, energy, and imagination, was necessary for Christian mission and, at times, US imperial power. The latter was a source of moral degradation and violence. Christians expressed such views in reference works, sermons, and reflections on the role of Protestantism in the US nation. Dissenting voices, including antiwar activists and Black intellectuals, critiqued US power as in and of itself fanatical or, flipping the script, argued that fanatical energy was necessary to fuel radical political movements.

In 1888 Methodist George Milton Hammell wrote "Religion and Fanaticism" in *Methodist Review*. He provided examples of fanatical behavior and theorized causes of fanaticism. Though focused on the theological errors of fanaticism, he noted that in "some of its phases fanaticism is a mental as well as a moral aberration, and may so be treated." Fanaticism was a disease of religion and, at times, natural science. Presuming an audience of Protestant ministers, he went on to recommend ministerial vigilance and affective management so that congregants "avoid the Scylla rock of formalism on the one hand and the Charybdis whirlpool of fanaticism on the other." Protestants needed religious sentimentality for their own moral piety and for their missionary efforts. Hammell, in writing this article, relied heavily on Isaac Taylor's theory of fanaticism: "Taylor's work is still quoted with tacit approval by the compilers of the best theological dictionaries and encyclopedias; and, though old, is not yet obsolete."[1] The world at the turn of the century was far different from the world of the 1830s, when Taylor first published *Fanaticism*. American Protestants, however, continued to draw on Taylor in an age of Christian enthusiasm, an affective style categorized as the middle ground between formalism (associated with Catholicism) and fanaticism (associated with nonwhite and non-Christian groups).

Enthusiasm Against Fanaticism in Reference Works

As Hammell claimed, Americans continued to cite Taylor as the expert on fanaticism in reference works. Admittedly, reference works such as dictionaries and encyclopedias are imperfect sources for tracking semantic change over time. However, a survey of religious reference works suggests the amelioration of enthusiasm and the continued denigration of fanaticism. Some reference works continued to present both enthusiasm and fanaticism as descriptors of false and dangerous religion. This was evident in *A Religious Encyclopædia*, edited by Protestant theologian Philip Schaff, founder of the American Society of Church History. The entry defined enthusiasm as an "intense moral impulse or all-engrossing temper of mind." However, the entry went on to prescribe that there should be a distinction between genuine and morbid enthusiasm. In its morbid sense, "enthusiasm is almost synonymous with fanaticism." That said, enthusiasm, properly practiced and understood, was a positive for the sake of freedom.[2] The dictionary cited and agreed with Isaac Taylor's writings.

Other reference works made clearer distinctions. *A Dictionary of Religious Knowledge, for Popular and Professional Use*, edited by influential progressive evangelical Lyman Abbott, argued that Taylor did not go far enough. The entry commented that "fanaticism has been, though not we think with entire accuracy, defined as 'enthusiasm inflamed by hatred.' It differs from enthusiasm rather in involving the idea that the reason is practically dethroned."[3] Abbott here borrowed Taylor's formula of "enthusiasm inflamed by hatred" but articulated a stronger differentiation based on the use of reason. *The Dictionary of Doctrinal and Historical Theology* (1872), also drawing on Taylor, prescribed to readers that "fanaticism must be clearly distinguished from enthusiasm. The latter may be animated by the pure love of God and man; whereas the former is fired with the worst passions." Fanaticism was "an overwrought fancy, working by passion and not by reason, a master-thought that becomes a monomania, narrow-minded, blind, and cruel." Fanaticism had been at times evident in the Christian tradition, and especially Catholicism, but the entry frames examples of fanaticism in Hinduism, Judaism, Islam, the atheism of the French Revolution, and paganism as more essential expressions. This replicated Taylor's argument that Christian fanaticism could exist, but Christianity was not inherently fanatical. The majority of other traditions across the world, however, had an essential affectability to fanaticism.[4]

Reference works for other fields also contained entries on fanaticism. The *Dictionary of Philosophy and Psychology* described it as such: "As Taylor says, fanaticism is enthusiasm inflamed by hatred . . . so far as it can be treated scientifically, fanaticism belongs to the province of psychology. It is often considered to be a form of abnormal brain action affecting persons predisposed to mental disease. It is very susceptible to the influences of contagion, and may be certainly regarded as belonging to the borderland between sanity and insanity."[5] This definition is useful for seeing the imbricated nature of secular and religious theories of fanaticism. Taylor's theory in 1833 was based on his Anglo-American Protestant mission and apologetics against other traditions. He remained a source of expertise on fanaticism even in a dictionary invested in the science of psychology.

Evangelical Enthusiasm Against Global Fanaticism

Reference works provide evidence of broad semantic shifts, but they are less useful in providing deeper explanations as to why these changes occurred in US society. Protestant publications provide more explicit reasoning. Consider Dwight Moody, one of the most influential evangelists of his time and the preacher who had inspired Charles Guiteau to try his hand at missionizing. "I don't think a little enthusiasm would hurt the church at the present time," Moody wrote. Critics of enthusiasm may "raise the cry, 'Ah, enthusiasm—false excitement—I am afraid of it.' . . . I had a good deal rather have zeal without knowledge than knowledge without zeal, and it won't hurt us to have a little more of this enthusiasm."[6] In flipping the formula from Proverbs 19:2, Moody expressed confidence in the value of enthusiasm. This signaled an uneven, though perceptible, shift in the social power and legitimation of evangelical affections.

Enthusiasm was in the atmosphere of US culture. As Moody put it when responding to critics of religious enthusiasm, "We can have enthusiasm in business, we can have enthusiasm in politics, and no one complains of that."[7] John Mac Kilgore, in his history of enthusiasm as a revolutionary affective ideology, has argued that it is nearly an "impossibility . . . to demarcate the sacred and the secular with respect to enthusiastic politics."[8] Enthusiasm was contagious. Historian Andrew Preston framed the national mood this way: "The end of the nineteenth century witnessed a sharp rise in national assertiveness . . . its underlying message was one of intense pride in the United States and confidence that it would soon become the world's leading power. The new self-assurance was no less active within religion than it was in other aspects of society."[9] This was an era of missionary enthusiasm, social gospel enthusiasm, and imperial enthusiasm that took place within a global framework in which the United States was playing a greater role than before.

The enthusiastic global ambitions of American Protestants rose alongside the (sometimes contested) enthusiastic global ambitions of the US empire. In 1898, the year before Moody died, the United States claimed sovereignty over Puerto Rico, Guam, the Philippines, and Hawaii. The US war against Spain and the occupation of these new colonies provided new optimism and energy for white Protestants. Subsequent US interventions in Latin America (e.g., Honduras, Nicaragua, Haiti, and the Dominican Republic) also opened up new opportunities for missions. Missionaries did not always support imperial ambitions, and imperial ambitions did not always support missions. However, as scholars have argued, they could benefit from each other, and many influential Protestants explicitly articulated Protestant mission and US empire as conjoined projects, especially in regard to the occupation of the Philippines. This opportunity of territorial expansion, made possible through the US victory in the Spanish-American War, helped sway many prominent social gospel progressives such as Lyman Abbott, Washington Gladden, and Walter Rauschenbusch.[10]

Protestant clergyman Josiah Strong certainly agreed. The historian Sydney Ahlstrom, in his magisterial survey of US religion, described

Strong as a clear "spokesman for the 'Protestant Establishment.'"[11] Strong viewed himself as such, and he explicitly traced his lineage through white Protestant men before him. This is evident in his 1913 book *The Next Great Awakening*, in which he provided a short history of Protestant enthusiasm starting in the eighteenth century, in which "religion had lost all spirituality." He cited, funny enough, Isaac Taylor for this claim. Strong proceeded to describe how revivalist Charles Finney was able to work the religious affects of a crowd into "manifestations of overwhelming conviction" and how Dwight Moody spread a simple message of God's love, thus persuading "multitudes who had become indifferent to the staple presentations of the pulpit."[12] The era of US global empire provided a new opportunity for a third great awakening.

In the 1880s and 1890s, however, Strong's imperialism was evangelical, not political, in nature. If anything, he leaned toward isolationism in this early era. Strong's focus in the 1885 *Our Country* was missioning the US West, articulating Anglo-Saxon supremacy, raising concern about Catholic immigration, and promoting civilizing projects through Christianization.[13] In 1893 he described the social mission of the church as such: to save society, the churched needed love. "Such love," he wrote, "is remedial; and such a love widening until its arms embrace mankind becomes *an enthusiasm for humanity*."[14] "The essence of Christianity is love," he went on, "and love always gives. It can never be satisfied so long as there is anyone who has not received it. By its very nature, therefore, Christianity is expansive. It will have no banks, it must flood the world as the waters cover the sea."[15] Strong's concept of enthusiasm for humanity was driven by the affect of love with the goal of uniting humanity in the creation of the kingdom of heaven on earth. Love motivated missionary work, but Strong was ambivalent about the extension of US political power abroad.[16]

In the midst of the Spanish-American War and the opportunity to claim sovereignty over the Philippines, Strong began to change his rhetoric. In March 1898, he published "The Preacher in Relation to the New Expansion." He began to argue that missionizing through appeals to reason and affect were not enough. Force and perhaps even violence were warranted when dealing with inferior races whose affectability made reasoning ineffective. "Superstition and fanaticism," he explained, "are not amenable to reason, and ignorance and prejudice are often invulnerable to it." Force, for the sake of love, was appropriate, as "when a parent punishes a child." The child, here, was the Filipinos, the parent Anglo-Saxon Protestants.[17] This reflected a concept of religio-racial human social evolution.

In making the case for the United States claiming the Philippines, Strong relied on the testimony of anthropologist Dean Worcester, whom Strong referred to "as one of the highest authorities on all questions relating to them." Strong relayed from Worcester that the Filipinos are "utterly unfit for self-government."[18] As chapter 5 examined, Worcester's assessment of Filipino civilization was in part based on the continuing "fanaticalness" of resistance against the United States. The sciences of fanaticism, when in service of colonial power, had relevance on the ground and in the world of citations and publications.

Strong's idea of "enthusiasm for humanity" is useful to capture the sense of Christian mission that was emerging in the late nineteenth century. Christian mission meant both Christian institutions whose mission it was to convert people to Christianity and the broader sense of the United States having a providential role in world history to bring about a new Christian era. For Strong, these aims were connected. Enthusiasm would transform the masses of people who constitute the Church. Once transformed, the Church, through its enthusiasm, could transform the world. Anglo-Saxons, especially those in the United States, had a special mission from God to achieve this transformation.[19]

What was this transformation? It was the process of civilizing, which called for a radical reconfiguration of other nations and races in the realms of religion, political economy, and culture. Africans, the "Orient," Mormons, and Roman Catholicism would all need to be reformed. Strong's "enthusiasm for humanity" signaled the means (enthusiastic mission) and the ends (a self-realization of humanity). He believed that Christianity, founded through the process of God becoming a man, must be the religion to serve in this self-realization of humanity. Strong wanted to turn the people of the world into humanity. Strong's racism and conviction that this task must happen reveal the violence that lay behind his ideas.

Critical ethnic studies scholar Sylvia Wynter helps put Strong's normative conception of humanity in the broader context of secular modernity. Wynter provides a wide-ranging theoretical narrative of what she calls the invention of man in the Western world. The Western conception of man, which is simultaneously racialized and gendered in its being overrepresented as a white man, is in its origins a religious figure. She describes the discursive transformation as such:

> In the wake of the West's reinvention of its True Christian Self in the transumed terms of the Rational Self of Man, however, it was to be the peoples of the militarily expropriated New World territories (i.e., Indians), as well as the enslaved peoples of black Africa (i.e., Negroes), that were made to reoccupy the matrix slot of otherness—to be made into the physical reference of the idea of the irrational/subrational Human Other, to this first degodded (if still hybridly religio-secular) "descriptive statement" of the human in history, as the descriptive statement that would be foundational to modernity.[20]

Along with Wynter, this book has considered the continued relevance of Christian theological ideas in the ongoing and changing markers that constitute religio-racial difference. When Strong posited his "enthusiasm for humanity," the humanity he imagined was singular and of his own image. Christian engagement with humanity was premised on humanity's transformation into Strong's own Protestantism. Similar to Isaac Taylor, Strong believed the Protestant white man to be the end point of history. All other possible humanities would be destroyed or assimilated in the process. Enthusiasm was the affective vehicle for achieving this.

With Strong's writings and Wynter's macro narrative in mind, fanaticism in the late nineteenth and early twentieth centuries came to represent the ultimate resistance to Strong's narrow conception of "humanity." Fanatics were not only "Others" but "Others" who resisted—violently at times—colonizing and racializing projects of governance that sought to conscript them into Strong's Protestant Anglo-Saxon modernity.[21]

Critiques of American Fanaticism

This early era of US global imperialism was also an era of enthusiastic intellectual critique and activism that challenged US global imperialism, among many other social issues, including women's suffrage, temperance, racism, and economic inequality. Critiques and reclamations of the word "fanaticism" were useful for these political projects as well.

The satirist and anti-imperialist Mark Twain's "War Prayer" was one such critique. He wrote the prayer around 1905, as the United States was continuing to fight Filipino insurrectionaries in the Philippine-American War. "It was a time," Twain begins the scene, "of great and exalting excitement." In churches "packed mass meetings listened, panting, to patriot oratory which stirred the deepest deeps of their hearts . . . the tears running down their cheeks the while; in the churches the pastors preached devotion to flag and country." But then a stranger arrives "bearing a message from Almighty God." The stranger interrupts the preacher and proceeds to give a prophetic sermon. He prays to God to guide American soldiers for success against the enemy so that we "tear their soldiers to bloody shreds with our shells; help us to cover their smiling fields with the pale forms of their patriot dead." "We ask it," the stranger concludes, "in the spirit of love, of Him Who is the Source of Love." Twain's stranger served to reveal the flip side of the patriotic prayers. They implied the defeat, death, and maiming of the enemy. The packed church does not comprehend the critique from the stranger. "It was believed afterward that the man was a lunatic, because there was no sense in what he said."[22]

Twain believed that the American public, like the parishioners of the fictional church, were not ready for the truth. The "War Prayer" remained unpublished until after Twain's death. He had also feared public backlash. Twain was responding to evangelical imperial enthusiasm of the sort Strong had preached. The stranger, in their skewering sermon, brought to the surface the effects of a Christian love legitimating colonial warfare. Patriotic prayers had as their implied effect the defeated, dead, and maimed enemy. This was, the stranger put it to the church, "that part which the pastor—and also you in your hearts—fervently prayed silently." Such love, Twain suggested, was intimately connected to hate, or at least a desire for dominance.

Late nineteenth- and early twentieth-century Black intellectuals and activists adopted and adapted the language of the fanatic to critique the persistence of white supremacy and the unfreedom of Black people after the failure of radical Reconstruction.[23] Historian Gayraud S. Wilmore has defined Black radicalism according to three features: independence from white control, revalorization of Africa, and acceptance of protest and agitation as necessary for Black liberation.[24] Additionally, Black radical thought has critically analyzed, among many other things, the interrelated construction of Protestantism, white supremacy, and the US nation-state.[25] If more moderate intellectuals and politicians saw the promise of Black freedom within the structures of the US nation-state (as did the white abolitionist James Brown, who believed that US law, even if misused by slavers, ultimately reflected divine law), more radical thinkers saw the structures of the US nation-state as the very cause of Black unfreedom, both during and after the period of formal racial slavery. The question became how to transform or transcend the nation-state, along with how to transform or transcend the bounds of evangelical Protestantism. In thinking through these questions, Black radicals offered new conceptualizations and applications of fanaticism. At the same time, Black radicals, especially those who were well educated, maintained a complicated relationship with evangelicalism. In some ways, they shared the critique of evangelicalism as potentially fanatic inducing.

Some Black writers engaged the idea of fanaticism before the war. Those who did were usually advocates for immediate emancipation, and they accepted the South's charges that abolitionism sought the end of slavery at all costs. Abolitionist Frederick Douglass was one example. In his speeches and writings, Douglass rarely mentioned fanaticism or enthusiasm, though he did have one speech that, if not titled, was at least advertised as *Abolition Fanaticism in New York* (1847). What was fanaticism, for Douglass? In the speech, he spoke with a prophetic voice in denouncing slavery. Along with slavery, he denounced the United States. "I have no love for America, as such; I have no patriotism," he wrote, "I have no country. What country have I?" If Brown was compelled by the founding documents of the United States and a general spirit of liberty, Douglass had his doubts. Even as a free man, Douglass recognized how he was not a full member of the nation. Slavery had been sanctioned by religious institutions, political institutions, and the US Constitution. Douglass gave his speech and embraced, if not the word itself precisely, then certainly the spirit of fanaticism in his totalizing critique of the nation. Working within a Black radical tradition, Douglass believed that progress would come not from within the structure of US religion and politics but through its destruction. "I desire," he told the crowd to both hisses and cheers, "to see it overthrown as speedily as possible and its Constitution shattered in a thousand fragments, rather than this foul curse should continue to remain as now."[26] Douglass's pessimism, which went alongside and informed his optimism, was shared by many Black radicals in the late nineteenth and early twentieth centuries. Other Black radicals did not self-describe as fanatics, but reconceptualized it.

Black intellectuals provided theories of fanaticism that challenged those of Isaac Taylor and Josiah Strong. Alexander Crummell, an Episcopalian priest, Pan-African thinker, and colonist of Liberia, contested popular notions of Black fanaticism. For him, Black Americans had, at times, contracted fanatical ideas from proximity to white Christians. "We have unlearned," he wrote in regard to Black Americans, "the savagery and the fanaticism of blatant American democracy. Of all classes of the American freemen, we have come to a clearer knowledge and appreciation of Law which guarantees freedom; of freedom, regulated by Law."[27] Crummell reversed white theories that saw white fanaticism as necessarily a type of racial contagion contracted through proximity with "inferior" religio-racial groups. The truth was the opposite, he suggested. Black Americans had had to learn to survive and work to transcend the fanaticisms inherent in US white supremacy.

W. E. B. Du Bois, a student of Crummell's, also had a complicated and shifting relationship with fanaticism. Du Bois is now recognized as a pivotal figure in the study of society, race, and religion. Throughout his intellectual career Du Bois was critical of the affective power of evangelicalism, in both its white and its Black forms. Barbara Dianne Savage has written generally about Du Bois's criticisms of Black religious leadership and the role of emotion in Black worship.[28] His criticism of evangelical styles of revival was evident in his 1903 publication of *The Souls of Black Folk*. Dedicated to a largely secular vision of education, Du Bois emphasized the power of Black higher education to uplift individuals out of the mass of social life, with all of its compromises to individual agency. Du Bois wrote that Black colleges could pull people "out of the worship of the mass" and bring to them a "higher individualism" that had a "loftier respect for the sovereign human soul that seeks to know itself and the world about it; that seeks a freedom for expansion and self-development; that will love and hate and labor in its own way."²⁹ This was a self-sovereign subject who even had power over the emotions of love and hate. What was the contrasting subject to this self-sovereign subject? In some ways the contrasting figure was the Black evangelical.

Though this suggests that Du Bois was simply reifying a harmful binary, he at times complicated this portrait. As scholar Curtis Evans puts it, Du Bois, like other Black leaders, wrestled with tensions in his interpretation and evaluation of Black religiosity.³⁰ This tension and self-reflection of Du Bois is evident in the chapter "Of the Coming of John." Contained in *The Souls of Black Folk*, this chapter presents a fictional story of John, an educated Black man who returns to his home in Altamaha, Georgia. John goes to a Black Baptist meeting, where he is to be the first of three preachers. Going up to the pulpit, John is "cold and preoccupied." He proceeds to lecture the crowd about the limits of Christian salvation and the need for progress, charity, education, and investing in Black businesses. Du Bois, drawing on his own ethnographic descriptions of his visits to Black churches in the South, described the scene that followed John's failed sermon:³¹

> A painful hush seized the crowded mass . . . an old bent man arose, walked over the seats, and climbed straight up into the pulpit. He was wrinkled and black, with scant gray and tufted hair; his voice and hand shook as with palsy; but on his face lay the intense rapt look of the religious fanatic. . . . He quivered, swayed, and bent; then rose aloft in perfect majesty, till the people moaned and wept, wailed and shouted, and a wild shrieking arose from the corners where all the pent-up feeling of the hour gathered itself and rushed into the air. John never knew clearly what the old man said; he only felt himself held up to scorn and scathing denunciation for trampling on the true Religion, and he realized with amazement that all unknowingly he had put rough, rude hands on something this little world held sacred.³²

Though Du Bois (or perhaps John?) referred to the older preacher as a fanatic, this passage emphasized the affective power that the sermon had on John, despite his individualistic ethos and education. The sermon worked.

Scholar of religion William D. Hart has asked the question of whether Du Bois reified some of the more harmful colonialist tropes about Black religion as excessively religious. Hart's focus is on the categories of fetishism, voodoo, and frenzy. Of the three terms, frenzy had the closest meaning to fanaticism. Frenzy, Hart describes, signaled "emotionally unhinged (frenzied) bodily expressions."[33] Noting some ambiguity, Hart argues that these terms do indeed operate within the legacy of racist colonial depictions of Black religion as uncontrolled. For the purposes of this chapter, the side-by-side reading of Du Bois's depiction of the figure of the educated, individualized Black man in contrast to the depiction of the Black congregation does reify the type of ideas that writers such as Isaac Taylor depicted in justifying Western Christian colonialism. However, Du Bois's emphasis on the affective power of the old Black preacher also starts to undo this binary. John's sermon failed. The elder Black preacher's sermon succeeded. Intellectual language failed. Affective exhortations succeeded. John does not understand the preacher's meaning. But the preacher successfully affects John's feelings, making him feel the heat of his own shame. He is, in this moment and perhaps productively, fanatically affected. As with *The Souls of Black Folk* writ large, Du Bois was diligent in thinking through the relationship between his politics, his views on religion, and his own positionality—truly, Du Bois is part of the canon of the academic study of religion, among his influence on other academic fields.

Later in his life, Du Bois conveyed a different sense of fanaticism. Like Douglass, Du Bois saw fanaticism as politically powerful. If fanaticism meant movements that challenged white supremacy in the nation, then it was desirable. Du Bois viewed white and Black churches as, in some ways and at times, obstacles to Black freedom. They were moderating institutions. Du Bois wrote about the Christian church as an inefficacious source of radical reform in bringing together the racial groups across the globe. This radicalism, he believed, was the only force that could address the "problem of the color line." In a 1931 essay, he wrote that the church "will be found consistently on the wrong side and that when, by the blood and tears of radicals and fanatics of the despised and rejected largely outside the church, some settlement of these problems is found, the church will be among the first to claim full and original credit for this result."[34] Du Bois reimagined the language of the fanatic and associated it with political radicalism. Fanaticism, here, was not a pathology but a strategic political affectation, and one that marginalized communities were imagining and enacting on the periphery of "true" or "proper" religion.

Conclusion

This chapter has examined evangelical discourses of enthusiasm against fanaticism in the late nineteenth and early twentieth centuries. Studying the causes and influences of semantic change is a difficult task. The continued references to figures such as Isaac Taylor suggest at least some level of influence on turn-of-the-century evangelicals and the existence of a white evangelical secular, wherein evangelical imaginations existed in relation to ostensibly secular political movements, especially foreign interventions. Fanaticism, in this context, was not just a word but a key node in a constellation of categories, rituals, movements, identities, and projects.

The evangelical secular was increasingly hegemonic, but it was never monolithic nor without challengers. Antiwar activists and Black intellectuals developed counterdiscourses that critiqued imperialism, racism, and Protestant Christian supremacy. Some highlighted the selective nature of whom white Protestants considered fanatical. Others adapted the term to argue that the white American establishment had its own forms of irrationality, affective appeals, and violence. For all, fanaticism was an overflowing signifier to contend with and mobilize in an era of social conflict at home and expansion abroad.

Conclusion

This book has offered a history of fanaticism as a concept. Through the past six chapters we have traced broad semantic shifts in the language of fanaticism and delved into closer analyses of the role the concept has played in social conflicts. In the eighteenth century, most British North Americans treated fanaticism as a subcategory of enthusiasm and used both to critique evangelical revivals. In the 1830s evangelical writers such as Isaac Taylor started to defend revivalism by differentiating enthusiasm from fanaticism. Americans, at times explicitly citing Taylor, began to contrast the two terms. Chapters 2 and 3 examined how Americans in the antebellum era applied the term in racial, regional, and gendered conflicts. Chapter 4 analyzed emerging theories of religious insanity within law and psychiatry. Experts sought to provide scientific analyses of fanaticism as a phenomenon but never fully abandoned the theological import of the term. Chapter 5 focused on the US occupation of the Philippines to situate religious fanaticism as a term of colonial anthropology. By the early twentieth century, as chapter 6 explained, Americans, especially evangelical Protestants, asserted a definitional and moral difference between fanaticism and enthusiasm.

Enthusiasm was the force—political and religious—necessary to combat fanaticism. These two terms were not limited to religious figures or texts. They became key terms for secular modernity and secular governance as well. Enthusiasm was a spiritual, national, and imperial drive based on love for humanity. Fanaticism was a provincial hatred that threated the global power of Protestantism (Anglo-American style) and the United States. Americans in the nineteenth century developed and turned to the language of fanaticism to demonize opponents and make distinctions within the category of religion: between true and false, good and bad, and reasonable and unreasonable.

Going beyond the production of simple binaries, we have employed the term "religio-racial affectability" to capture the role of affects and affectability in the construction of these hierarchies of human difference. Our focus has been religion and race, but the concept of affectability is also useful for understanding issues related to gender, disability, class, and education. The term's key operation has been to suggest that fanatics were fanatics because they could be nothing else. In this Protestant secular imagination, fanatics never chose to be violent, never chose to feel the Holy Spirit when gazing upon an attractive young man, never chose to see a sign from God in an eclipse, and never chose to believe that freedom was a spiritual being that emanated from a wooden box to put an end to taxation, jails, and the military. The fault lay in their religious affects (their credulity to "superstitions" or "delusions"). Or maybe in their presumed inherent racial characteristics. With attention to affectability, we have seen that uses of fanaticism show that notions of religion and race were not wholly distinct from each other in this era. Religious beliefs and practices could signify racial essence. Racial essence could signify religious beliefs and practices. Whatever the forms of difference being articulated, fanaticism talk functioned to remove individuals and entire populations from the realms of history, agency, and, at times, humanity.

Methodologically, I have tried to have it both ways: to capture the politics of fanaticism talk and to provide some sense of the political and religious commitments of those called fanatics. Fanaticism is what I have called an overflowing signifier. Uses of it draw from a thick constellation of presuppositions, definitions, and moral judgments. Because of this overflow, fanaticism talk must be studied in the context of its uses. This book has highlighted the term's problems and instances of blunt demonization. It has also aimed to recuperate something from it by taking fanaticism talk as a starting point to think through the entanglements between religion, politics, affects, and radicalism. It has suggested that an overly secular approach that aims to redeem the targets of fanaticism—people such as Nat Turner, Papa Isio, Ruperto Rios, abolitionist women, and evangelical revivalists—leaves something to be desired in terms of explaining their worldviews and motivations.

If this book had taken what I would call a secularizing methodology, its focus would have been about recovering the politics undergirding religious claims of those targeted as fanatics. Instead, it has dwelled on the reasons and effects of nineteenth-century Americans invested in prophecy, the efficacy of ritual, divine fear or hope, or providentialism. It has critiqued the reductionism inherent in fanaticism talk. Such reductionism implies that religious people do what their religion tells them to do. Or, as character and religious skeptic Fox Mulder once put it in an episode of the *X-Files*, "These people are simply fanatics behaving fanatically."[1] Chapter 2, for example, took up the question of whether Nat Turner was a fanatic or a freedom fighter. Our starting point with Turner was to say he was both. We then worked to unpack and discredit the harmful racist assumptions behind calling Turner a fanatic even as we worked to think through descriptions of Turner's supernatural cosmology as a constitutive part of Turner's worldview and not a mere religious *expression* of more materialist politics. This book, then, has maintained a constant tension between politics and religion, aiming not to reduce one to the other. Cumulatively, this approach has hopefully brought into question this very binary.

This is a fitting methodology to study fanaticism. After all, the language of Protestants in the nineteenth century explained the causes of fanaticism in terms of both theological metaphysics and naturalistic descriptions of human emotions, reason, and imagination. This tension is what John Modern has highlighted in his account of "evangelical secularism."[2] Fanaticism in this period was caught in the median of the process of being secularized from Protestant theological speculation about divine and demonic forces to the forces of natural science and human psychology. The very idea of secularization as a process fails to capture the ongoing work of religion within putatively secular norms. This is similar to Kathryn Gin Lum's analysis of the term "heathen," which emphasizes continuity and discontinuity between the word as a religious category and a racial category.[3] Dean Worcester, the ethnologist and colonial agent for the US occupation of the Philippines examined in chapter 4, subscribed to the theory that fanaticism was both non-Christian (despite the Catholicism of the Philippines) and a result of a deficient understanding of the natural world. We should be skeptical of such modernist dichotomies. Both those who wielded the language of fanaticism in positions of power and those described as fanatics shaped their politics through appeals to supernatural signs, efficacious material objects, the flows of affects, and stories of gods operating in history.

In the twenty-first century, accusations of fanaticism do not necessarily have anything to do with supernatural beings or inherent differential human capacities. They are just as likely to be about excessive sports fandom (which is, perhaps, a certain form of religion). The term lost its teeth in the late twentieth century.[4] More relevant contemporary terms that resemble fanaticism, in definition or function, include terrorism, radicalism, extremism, and cult. Though terrorism has replaced fanaticism as the dominant terminology to describe political and religious violence, the two have shared overlapping conceptual space going back to at least the French Revolution.[5] Anthropologist Darryl Li's gloss on the function of terrorism talk today matches much of what this book has argued regarding fanaticism. Li writes that "to call someone a terrorist is to deny any political dimension to their use of violence—and, paradoxically, only serves to reconfirm that this violence is political."[6] Whereas Li suggests that the language of terrorism can only get in the way of analysis, I have found it useful to think *through* the questions that fanaticism talk raises when studying individuals and communities who were called fanatics. I do not think academics can or should simply ban influential though problematic terms like "fanaticism" from our lexicon.

Careful attention to the strategies, affects, and effects of "fanatical" or "enthusiastic" movements—whatever our moral judgments—reveals and challenges secular modern norms on the progress and separation of religion and politics. In 1932 white Protestant theologian Reinhold Niebuhr published *Moral Man and Immoral Society*. Niebuhr was a proponent of Christian realism who applied Calvinist principles to explain the social struggles of his day. These included the world wars, the conditions in Henry Ford's factories, and white supremacy in Detroit, where he preached at Bethel Evangelical Church.

Though influenced by the optimism of the social gospel, Niebuhr ultimately believed that human sinfulness necessitated a more chastened view of human progress. On the level of the individual, and especially at the level of modern states, egoism and imperial drives prevailed and would continue to prevail. So, too, would countermovements. He concluded his book with a call about the dangers, inevitability, and necessity of what he called the "sublime madness of the soul," or, as I interpret it, the very affective, theological, and political drives that have filled this book. He reflected,

> The most important of these illusions is that the collective life of mankind can achieve perfect justice. It is a very valuable illusion for the moment; for justice cannot be approximated if the hope of its perfect realization does not generate a sublime madness in the soul. Nothing but such madness will do battle with malignant power and "spiritual wickedness in high places." The illusion is dangerous because it encourages terrible fanaticisms. It must therefore be brought under the control of reason. One can only hope that reason will not destroy it before its work is done.[7]

I am not certain that such sublime madness always rises in service of progress and justice. Nor do I think Niebuhr is providing a clear or "useful" definition or theory of fanaticism. That said, I see his commentary as a rare realistic approach to "fanaticism"—acknowledging its overflowing meanings—as a common facet of human struggle and one that is neither inherently laudable *nor* condemnable, but is a particular style to effect change, for better or worse.

Modern narratives of secularization, disenchantment, and rationalization have not meant the end of fanatical or enthusiastic movements. Rather, they are the conceptual frameworks that give rise to such terminology and give such movements power, either in concealing the continued relevance of provincial theological and supernatural worldviews or as narratives to be transgressed. Such tensions, I have argued, are what necessitates a method of sifting through the overflow of religious fanaticism as blunt rhetoric, target of governance, lived practice, and affective economy in any given context. To return to Emily Dickinson's poem "Much Madness is divinest Sense" from the epigraph of this book, we can do better to develop and practice a "discerning Eye." Discernment, here, is not based on certitude in our capacity to quickly unearth the religious/political, irrational/rational, voluntary/coercive essence of a given movement. This is discernment as the embrace of methodological uncertainty and the embrace of the work—self-reflection, research, empathy, and criticism—necessary to gain understanding. It may feel good to call someone a fanatic. I can attest to the fact that it feels good to call someone a fanatic. Perhaps, at times, such an accusation serves a moral or political good. More good and truth, however, can come from embracing a "discerning Eye" and handling such loaded terms with care.

ACKNOWLEDGMENTS

I will admit here that I am an affectable subject. My will, enthusiasm, and sense of self have been affected substantially by my time in academia, my friends, and my family. Catherine O'Donnell converted me to American religion at Arizona State University. She encouraged my shy undergraduate self to express my thoughts beyond my internal dialogue. John Corrigan taught me the field of American religious history and inspired me to ask bigger questions. Robert Orsi pushed me to give due attention to lived realities and lived consequences of the ideas we study. Elizabeth Shakman Hurd, Brannon Ingram, and Pamela Klassen provided needed criticisms and support as I wrote this book. Sylvester Johnson has inspired me with his brilliance, generosity, and insistence that we put our work in the perspective of the lives we live and the people we love. They are model mentors and scholars. I miss the dedicated time I had with them.

I am fortunate to have an incredible support network of peers who have provided community and feedback throughout the years. Thank you to the Florida State University diaspora of Tara Baldrick-Morrone, Cara Burnidge, Talia Burnside, Michael Graziano, Haley Iliff, Charles McCrary, and Adam Park. I cannot imagine my life without the formative experience I had at FSU. Thank you to the Northwestern crew of Jennifer Callaghan, Laura Dingeldein, Ashley King, Marlon Millner, Courtney Rabada, Aram Sarkisian, Matt Smith, and Lily Stewart. More recently, my Young Scholars of American Religion cohort provided intellectual community at a time when I needed it most.

This book would not be possible without the research and fellowship support I received. These include graduate fellowships from the Buffett Institute, the Luce Foundation, and the Franke Fellowship at the Alice Kaplan Center for the Humanities. More recently, Iowa State University's LAS Research and Travel Grant and the American Academy of Religion Research Grant enabled necessary archival research. Undergraduate research assistants Dawson Weathers, Kara Green, Allison Steinkamp, and Noah Cummins provided invaluable research support through the PhilRS Lab at Iowa State University. Many spaces and staff have tolerated me as I have written this book. Thank you to Dog-Eared Books, London Underground, and Waffle Houses across the nation. The New York University Press editorial team helped make this book a reality. Joseph Dahm was a perceptive copy editor. Jennifer Hammer is one of the best in the business, and I appreciate her support and guidance over the years.

My dearest friends—from the lovely lands of Arizona, Florida, Chicago, Iowa—have kept me grounded and laughing. My partner, Meghan, has provided love and patience, especially in the final months editing this book. Meghan, I apologize that you now have academic stress dreams despite not being in academia. My bad. When I was a baby, my parents Janeen and Jack believed I would grow up to become a minister, and I appreciate that they view my academic teaching and research as "close enough." I owe my parents for their empathy, work ethic, and curiosity about the world. This book is for them.

NOTES

EPIGRAPH
The poem "Much Madness is divinest Sense," by Emily Dickinson, is in the public domain.

INTRODUCTION
1. US Philippine Commission, *Report of the Philippine Commission*, 3:101.
2. US War Department, *Annual Report of the Secretary of War*, 926.
3. US Philippine Commission, *Report of the Philippine Commission*, 3:100.
4. Ngozi-Brown, "African-American Soldiers and Filipinos."
5. For a use of "race war" to describe the Philippine-American War, see Kramer, *Blood of Government*.
6. Hurley, *Jungle Patrol*.
7. *Chicago Daily Tribune*, "Rios Sentenced to Hang."
8. Wenger, *Religious Freedom*.
9. For an account that reframes the politics of Filipino guerrilla militants, see Reynaldo Clemeña Ileto, *Pasyon and Revolution*.
10. See Fluhman, *"A Peculiar People,"* chap. 3; Weisenfeld, *Black Religion in the Madhouse*, chap. 1.
11. Asad, *On Suicide Bombing*.
12. Pellegrini and Jakobsen, *Secularisms*, 3.
13. Brooks, "How to Roll Back Fanaticism."
14. Howard and Christopherson, "Pluralism," 139.
15. *Oxford English Dictionary*, "fanaticism," accessed June 16, 2025, www.oed.com.
16. Burnett, "Luther and the Schwärmer."
17. Colas, *Civil Society and Fanaticism*, 6.
18. Casson, *Liberating Judgment*, 137.
19. Kant, "Essay on the Maladies of the Head," 213.
20. McCrary and Wheatley, "Protestant Secular."
21. Fessenden, *Culture and Redemption*, 4.
22. Josephson-Storm, *Invention of Religion in Japan*.
23. See Gin Lum, *Heathen*; Goodwin, *Abusing Religion*; Matory, *Fetish Revisited*.
24. Modern, *Secularism in Antebellum America*, 5.
25. Weisenfeld, *New World A-Coming*, 5.
26. Johnson, *African American Religions*, 88.

27 Kahn and Lloyd, *Race and Secularism in America*, 6.
28 This project braids together Sara Ahmed's concept of affective economies and Denise Ferreira da Silva's argument that racialized figures in the modernity have been defined by their affectability. See Ahmed, "Affective Economies," and Ferreira da Silva, *Toward a Global Idea of Race*.
29 Howard and Christopherson, "Pluralism," 139.
30 Brown, *Regulating Aversion*, 152.
31 McCrary, *Sincerely Held*.
32 As Ferreira da Silva has argued, the very idea of especially affectable subjects has been a central part of race-making in the modern world. She provides the term "affectability" to describe this. With this in mind, what is necessary is not just to catalog the management and governance of affects but to examine how the measure of a population's capacity to affect or to be affected was a marker of inclusion or exclusion into the body politic, normatively defined. See Ferreira da Silva, *Toward a Global Idea of Race*. For an account of how the governance of affectability was tied to constructions of sex and race, see Schuller, *Biopolitics of Feeling*.
33 Orsi, *History and Presence*, 41.
34 Keane, *Christian Moderns*, 6.
35 Logan, "It Was Never About the Snakes."
36 General James Rusling, "Interview with President William McKinley," *Christian Advocate*, January 22, 1903, 17, from Schirmer and Shalom, *Philippines Reader*, 22–23.
37 The quote is from Graham, *Christianity vs Communism*. For scholarship on these conflicts and occupations that attends to the politics of religion, see Ramsey, *Spirits and the Law*, esp. chap. 3; Thomas, *Faking Liberties*, esp. chap. 5; Mamdani, *Good Muslim, Bad Muslim*.
38 See Johnson, *African American Religions*; Evans, *Move*; Wright, *Armageddon in Waco*.
39 For work focused on theories of fanaticism among European enlightenment skeptics, see Katsafanas, "Fanaticism and Sacred Values," and Zuckert, "Kant's Account of Practical Fanaticism."

CHAPTER 1. EVANGELICAL ENTHUSIASM

1 "From Thomas Jefferson to Thomas Cooper, 2 November 1822," *Founders Online*, National Archives, https://founders.archives.gov.
2 For more on Jefferson and his "Bible," see Manseau, *Jefferson Bible*.
3 Porterfield, *Conceived in Doubt*.
4 "From Thomas Jefferson to Thomas Cooper, 2 November 1822."
5 For broad accounts of the supernaturalism and rowdiness of American religion in this era, see Jortner, *Blood from the Sky*.
6 Although scholars of religion have always been quick to examine the influence of Protestantism on the modern general definition of "religion" as centered on

internal, individual belief, I find it telling that in the nineteenth century many Americans talked about religion in terms of electricity as a metaphor (and perhaps something more than a metaphor) for passions, social imitation, and divine revelation. For more on "electric religion," see Klassen, *Story of Radio Mind*; Supp-Montgomerie, *When the Medium Was the Mission*; and Beliso-de Jesús, *Electric Santería*.

7 My focus here is on religious fanaticism, though Americans also wrote about forms of fanaticism that were purely political. In 1800, for example, Alexander Hamilton privately wrote to John Jay about potential legal steps "to prevent an *Atheist* in Religion and a *Fanatic* in politics from getting possession of the helm of the State." Funny enough, Hamilton was describing Jefferson, who had just been elected president and who had received criticism for his support of the French Revolution. Jefferson, accuser and accused, knew the word from both sides. The use of fanaticism to describe a purely political form of fanaticism has a distinct enough history to be beyond the scope of this book. Syrett, *Papers of Alexander Hamilton*, 464–67.

8 Historians have largely attributed this energy to the emergence of what we now call evangelicalism, a cross-denominational and transatlantic movement that emphasized the centrality of Christ, the Bible, missionizing, and personal experiences of conversions. As Linford Fisher has noted, the term "evangelical" has been contested throughout history. In the eighteenth century, Protestants mostly used it as an adjective to describe authentic practices and experiences. It became a noun of self-designation in the early nineteenth century. I am less interested in determining who was and was not an evangelical than I am in how the language of evangelical, fanatical, and enthusiastic all related to the governance of religious energy—its vital role among more charismatic Protestants and the concerns of more moderate Protestants that too much energy suggested a human, rather than divine, inspiration. Fisher, "Evangelicals and Unevangelicals."

9 Taves, *Fits, Trances, and Visions*.
10 Taylor, *Fanaticism*, 5.
11 See, for example, Pocock, "Enthusiasm."
12 Finney, *Memoirs*, 20.
13 Taves, *Fits, Trances, and Visions*.
14 Charles Chauncy, "A Letter from a Gentleman in Boston to Mr. George Wishart ... of Edinburgh ... ," quoted in Taves, *Fits, Trances, and Visions*, 30.
15 See Ngram search for "enthusiasm" and "fanaticism" on Google Books.
16 Finney, *Lectures*, 10.
17 Stanton, *Eighty Years and More*, 41–43.
18 Judah, *Spirit of Fanaticism*, 5.
19 Judah, *Spirit of Fanaticism*, 10.
20 Feffer, "Judas the Maccabeas."
21 Underhill, *Lecture on Mysterious Religious Emotions*, 12.
22 Underhill, *Lecture on Mysterious Religious Emotions*, 13.

23 Finney, *Lectures*, 10.
24 Finney, *Lectures*, 9.
25 Finney, *Revival Fire*, 39.
26 Finney, *Lectures*, 64.
27 Finney, *Lectures*, 11.
28 *Free Enquirer*, "Death by Fanaticism."
29 Finney, *Revival Fire*, 12.
30 Finney, *Revival Fire*, 90.
31 Finney, *Revival Fire*, 91.
32 Finney, *Revival Fire*, 37–38.
33 Finney, *Revival Fire*, 37.
34 Curtis, *Production of American Religious Freedom*, 7.
35 Finney, *Lectures*, 12.
36 Finney, *Lectures*, 12.
37 Finney, *Lectures*, 453.
38 Finney, *Revival Fire*, 42.
39 Finney, *Revival Fire*, 42.
40 See Carté, *Religion and the American Revolution*, esp. chaps. 7, 8.
41 Taylor, *Fanaticism*, 21.
42 Finney, "Letters on Revivals No. 9."
43 Taylor, *Natural History of Enthusiasm*, 235.
44 Mazzarella, "Affect," 291.
45 Ahmed, "Affective Economies," 119.
46 Taylor, *Fanaticism*, 54.
47 Taylor, *Fanaticism*, 233.
48 Ogden, *Credulity*, 18.
49 Taylor, *Fanaticism*, 220.
50 Taylor, *Fanaticism*, 58.
51 Taylor, *Fanaticism*, 223.
52 Taylor, *Fanaticism*, 225.
53 Taylor, *Ultimate Civilization*, 20–21.
54 Taylor, *Ultimate Civilization*, 117.
55 Taylor, *Ultimate Civilization*, 271.
56 Taylor, *Ultimate Civilization*, 117.
57 Johnson, *African American Religions*, 251.
58 Taylor, *Natural History of Enthusiasm*, 253.
59 Taylor, *Fanaticism*, 102.
60 Taylor, *Natural History of Enthusiasm*, 252.
61 Taylor, *Fanaticism*, 58, 313.
62 Taylor, *Fanaticism*, 63–64.
63 Taylor, *Fanaticism*, 120.
64 This was not an uncommon strategy of comparative religion among critical voices. Voltaire, for example, wrote the play *Fanaticism, or Mahomet the Prophet*

in 1736 with the expressed purpose to paint Islam and the Prophet Muhammad as violent and self-serving. Many took the play to be a thinly veiled criticism of the Catholic hierarchy, and Catholic clergy successfully censured the play in 1741. Voltaire, *Fanaticism*.

65 Taylor, *Fanaticism*, 78.
66 Taylor was unsure if this natural tendency toward violence among "Asiatics" was a product of climate or the "physical conformation" of the race. Taylor, *Fanaticism*, 119.
67 Taylor, *Fanaticism*, 120.
68 Taylor, *Fanaticism*, 162.
69 Taylor, *Fanaticism*, 169.
70 For more on usage of the term, see Gin Lum, "Historyless Heathen," 56–58.
71 Taylor, *Fanaticism*, 53.
72 Taylor, *Fanaticism*, 55.
73 Taylor, *Fanaticism*, 219.
74 Taylor, *Fanaticism*, 256.
75 Taylor, *New Model of Christian Missions*. Interestingly, Isaac Taylor's son, named Isaac Taylor (1829–1901), argued against his father. The younger Taylor claimed that it was Islam, more than Christianity, that had been the most successful civilizing force in Africa. See Prasch, "Which God for Africa."
76 Taylor, *Fanaticism*, 356.
77 Taylor, *Ultimate Civilization*, 110.
78 Taylor, *Fanaticism*, 368.
79 Taylor mentions that he has encountered the argument that Christian evangelization efforts among heathens are "fanatical in principle, and are injudiciously managed." He allows that Christian missions might utilize horrid tactics, but, somewhat confusingly, claims that Christian missionaries "feel more sensitively" to the oppression and misery of colonized populations. Taylor, *Four Lectures on Spiritual Christianity*, 174.
80 Taylor, *Four Lectures on Spiritual Christianity*, 182.

CHAPTER 2. THE FIGURE OF THE FANATIC

1 See Parsons and Nickerson, *Mormon Fanaticism Exposed*; Stone, *Matthias and His Impostures*; Vale, *Fanaticism*.
2 Literature on Turner is vast. For work that emphasizes Turner and Africana religion, see Akinyela, "Battling the Serpent"; Chireau, *Black Magic*, 68. For work on Turner's religion in relation to Black radicalism, see Harding, *There Is a River*; Wilmore, *Black Religion and Black Radicalism*. For work that situates Turner in broader antebellum supernaturalism and apocalypticism, see Durrill, "Nat Turner and Signs of the Apocalypse." For work on Turner, Christianity, and exegesis, see Lampley, *Theological Account*; Tomlins, *In the Matter of Nat Turner*, xii–xiii. Historian Patrick Breen provides a general historical account of Turner that is attentive to religion. See Breen, *Land Shall Be Deluged in Blood*.

3 Gray and Turner, *Confessions of Nat Turner*.
4 Ahmed, "Affective Economies." For work on religion and affect in particular, see Corrigan, "Introduction"; Hazard, "Evangelical Encounters"; Hamner, "Theorizing Religion and the Public Sphere."
5 Egerton, "Nat Turner in a Hemispheric Context," 136.
6 Harding, *There Is a River*, 76.
7 Wilmore, *Black Religion and Black Radicalism*.
8 Lampley, *Theological Account*.
9 Tomlins, *In the Matter of Nat Turner*, xii–xiii.
10 Breen, *Land Shall Be Deluged in Blood*.
11 Gray and Turner, *Confessions*, 19.
12 Gray and Turner, *Confessions*, 20.
13 Gray and Turner, *Confessions*, 19.
14 Gray and Turner, *Confessions*, 8.
15 Gray and Turner, *Confessions*, 8.
16 Gray and Turner, *Confessions*, 7.
17 Gray and Turner, *Confessions*, 10.
18 Gray and Turner, *Confessions*, 10.
19 Gray and Turner, *Confessions*, 10.
20 The idea that Turner had the ability to heal is only briefly mentioned in *Confessions*. Turner declares that he got a white man to cease his "wickedness" and that after days of fasting and praying the man was healed. In early newspaper reports and in the record of Turner's trial in the Southampton County Court, Turner was represented as having a more direct role as a healer. Jeremiah Cobb, "Trial of Nat" (November 5, 1831), in Tragle, *Southampton Slave Revolt of 1831*, 90.
21 Gray and Turner, *Confessions*, 10.
22 Gray and Turner, *Confessions*, 11.
23 Gray and Turner, *Confessions*, 11.
24 Gray and Turner, *Confessions*, 11.
25 Gray and Turner, *Confessions*, 11.
26 Sinha, *Slave's Cause*, esp. 210–13.
27 Harding, *There Is a River*, 103.
28 As scholars have noted, the spectacular violence of antislavery uprisings should not distract from the other forms of resistance. For an account that focuses on antislavery resistance among women in Southampton, Virginia, see Holden, *Surviving Southampton*.
29 Dew, *Essay on Slavery*, 4.
30 Miscellaneous, *Niles Register*, September 10, 1831, in Tragle, *Southampton Slave Revolt of 1831*, 76.
31 Gray and Turner, *Confessions*, 4.
32 Gray and Turner, *Confessions*, 22.
33 Gray and Turner, *Confessions*, 19.
34 Gray and Turner, *Confessions*, 19.

35 Harding, *There Is a River*, 99.
36 "Extract of a Letter Received in Richmond Dated Southampton, Nov. 1," *Alexandria Gazette*, November 8, 1831.
37 Gray and Turner, *Confessions*, 4.
38 Gray and Turner, *Confessions*, 5.
39 *American Dictionary of the English Language* (1828), "gloomy."
40 Letter to the editor, *Constitutional Whig*, September 26, 1831, in Tragle, *Southampton Slave Revolt of 1831*, 93.
41 Gray and Turner, *Confessions*, 9.
42 McDowell, *Speech*.
43 Such threats were reported in the *Daily Advertiser*, September 1831, in Tragle, *Southampton Slave Revolt of 1831*, 83; "Slave Insurrection," *Worcester Spy*, September 1831, in Tragle, *Southampton Slave Revolt of 1831*, 84; McDowell, *Speech*.
44 "Nat Turner Certainly Taken," *Enquirer*, November 8, 1831, originally published in the *Norfolk Herald*.
45 "Extract of a Letter from Jerusalem," *Richmond Enquirer*, August 30, 1831, in Tragle, *Southampton Slave Revolt of 1831*.
46 Raboteau, *Slave Religion*, 152–210.
47 Dew, "Abolition of Slavery."
48 Brown, *Regulating Aversion*, 152.
49 Letter to the editor, *Lynchburg Virginian*, September 15, 1831, in Tragle, *Southampton Slave Revolt of 1831*, 80.
50 Letter from senior editor, *Constitutional Whig*, August 27, 1831, in Tragle, *Southampton Slave Revolt of 1831*, 55.
51 Gray and Turner, *Confessions*, 22.
52 Evans, *Burden of Black Religion*, 17–63.
53 Letter to the editor, *Constitutional Whig*, September 26, 1831, in Tragle, *Southampton Slave Revolt of 1831*, 92.
54 See Breen, *Land Shall be Deluged in Blood*, 231n23.
55 Miscellaneous, *Niles Register*, September 10, 1831, in Tragle, *Southampton Slave Revolt of 1831*, 76.
56 "The Disturbers of the Peace," *Alexandria Gazette*, September 5, 1831; "Letter from T. B. Emmons to the Editor," *Boston Christian Herald*, September 28, 1831; "[United States; Secretary; Governor; Monday; Orange]," *Daily National Intelligencer*, September 17, 1831; To the Editors of the Enquirer, *Richmond Enquirer*, October 4, 1831, in Tragle, *Southampton Slave Revolt of 1831*, 117; "The Banditti," *Richmond Enquirer*, September 2, 1831, in Tragle, *Southampton Slave Revolt of 1831*, 58.
57 This logic is also important to keep in mind when considering the careful legal procedures that sought empirical evidence of participation or knowledge of conspiring to revolt when deciding guilt or innocence.
58 "Order of General Eppes," *Lynchburg Virginian*, September 8, 1831, in Tragle, *Southampton Slave Revolt of 1831*, 74.

59 John Floyd to James Hamilton Jr., November 19, 1831, in Tragle, *Southampton Slave Revolt of 1831*, 275.
60 John Floyd, "Governor's Message and Accompanying Documents," December 6, 1831, in Tragle, *Southampton Slave Revolt of 1831*, 433.
61 Virginia Legislature, "Draft of a Bill Concerning 'Slaves, Free Negros, and Mulatoes,'" in Tragle, *Southampton Slave Revolt of 1831*, 455.
62 Seabrook, *Essay on the Management of Slaves*, 7.
63 Raboteau, *Slave Religion*, 152.
64 Seabrook, *Essay on the Management of Slaves*, 7.
65 Seabrook, *Essay on the Management of Slaves*, 15.
66 Dew, "Abolition of Slavery."
67 Dew, *Essay on Slavery*, 98.
68 Dew, *Essay on Slavery*, 102–4.
69 Dew, *Essay on Slavery*, 4.

CHAPTER 3. THE FEMININE FANATIC

1 Stowe, *Uncle Tom's Cabin*, 632.
2 For classic treatments, see Douglas, *Feminization of American Culture*; Tompkins, *Sensational Designs*; Berlant, *Female Complaint*.
3 Baldwin, "Everybody's Protest Novel"; Hartman, *Scenes of Subjection*; Evans, *Burden of Black Religion*, 37–41.
4 Jordan-Lake, *Whitewashing Uncle Tom's Cabin*, xvii, xix.
5 For a survey of recent insights into abolitionism as a wide-ranging, radical, and diverse movement, see Sinha, *Slave's Cause*.
6 Noll, *Civil War as a Theological Crisis*.
7 Stokes, *Altar at Home*.
8 Fessenden, *Culture and Redemption*, chap. 5.
9 Sehat, *Myth of American Religious Freedom*.
10 Hendler, *Public Sentiments*.
11 Berlant, *Female Complaint*, 5.
12 Taylor, *Fanaticism*, 223.
13 Omikron, "Confessions of an Abolitionist," *Vermont Patriot & State Gazette*, December 14, 1855.
14 Greyser, *On Sympathetic Grounds*, 2.
15 Butt, *Antifanaticism*, vi.
16 Taylor, *Fanaticism*, 53.
17 Cowdin, *Ellen*, 52.
18 Hentz, *Planter's Northern Bride*, 54.
19 Hentz, *Planter's Northern Bride*, 244.
20 Cowdin, *Ellen*, 3–4.
21 Butt, *Antifanaticism*, 1.
22 Hentz, *Planter's Northern Bride*, 511–12.
23 Smith, *Emma Bartlett*, 213.

24 Cowdin, *Ellen*, 125–26.
25 Hentz, *Planter's Northern Bride*, 22–23.
26 Hentz, *Planter's Northern Bride*, 280.
27 Hentz, *Planter's Northern Bride*, 294.
28 Wilson, *Freedom at Risk*, chap. 1.
29 Lovejoy, "Fanaticism of the Democratic Party," 1.
30 Lovejoy, "Fanaticism of the Democratic Party," 3.
31 Cowdin, *Ellen*, 40.
32 Cowdin, *Ellen*, 5–6.
33 Cowdin, *Ellen*, 4–5.
34 Cowdin, *Ellen*, 53.
35 Cowdin, *Ellen*, 7.
36 Hentz, *Planter's Northern Bride*, 106–7.
37 Hentz, *Planter's Northern Bride*, 87.
38 Evans, *Burden of Black Religion*.
39 Hentz, *Planter's Northern Bride*, 407.
40 Hentz, *Planter's Northern Bride*, 415.
41 Hentz, *Planter's Northern Bride*, 445.
42 Johnson, *African American Religions*.
43 Cowdin, *Ellen*, 56.
44 Cowdin, *Ellen*, 56.
45 Cowdin, *Ellen*, 82.
46 Cowdin, *Ellen*, 74.
47 Butt, *Antifanaticism*, 268.
48 Hentz, *Planter's Northern Bride*, 166.
49 Hentz, *Planter's Northern Bride*, 498–99.
50 Hentz, *Planter's Northern Bride*, 485.
51 Hentz, *Planter's Northern Bride*, 238.
52 Blum, *Reforging the White Republic*.
53 Smith, *Emma Bartlett*, 887.
54 *United States Magazine and Democratic Review*, "Conspiracy of Fanaticism."
55 A Southerner, *Fanaticism and Its Results*, 12.

CHAPTER 4. THE FANATIC MIND

1 "A Great Tragedy Ended: The World Rid of a Wretched Assassin," *New York Times*, July 1, 1882.
2 *Report of the Proceedings*, 3:2207.
3 *Report of the Proceedings*, 3:2205.
4 Guiteau, *Truth, and the Removal*, 111.
5 See Dain, *Concepts of Insanity*, chap. 1; Grob, *Mental Illness and American Society*.
6 See Rosenberg, *Trial of the Assassin Guiteau*; Weisbrod, "Charles Guiteau and the Christian Nation."
7 Rosenberg, *Trial of the Assassin Guiteau*, chap. 2.

8 "The Wretch," *Chicago Daily Tribune*, July 8, 1881.
9 "A Great Tragedy Ended: The World Rid of a Wretched Assassin," *New York Times*, July 1, 1882.
10 Taubes, "Healthy Avenues of the Mind," 1003.
11 Kendler, "Philippe Pinel," 2670.
12 Pinel, *Treatise on Insanity*, 73.
13 Pinel, *Treatise on Insanity*, 63.
14 Rush, *Medical Inquiries and Observations*, 137–38.
15 Rush, *Medical Inquiries and Observations*, 138.
16 Brigham, *Observations on the Influence of Religion*, xxi.
17 Brigham, *Observations on the Influence of Religion*, 178.
18 Brigham, *Observations on the Influence of Religion*, 186.
19 Brigham, *Observations on the Influence of Religion*, 330.
20 Brigham, *Observations on the Influence of Religion*, 330–31.
21 Brigham, *Observations on the Influence of Religion*, 275.
22 Earle, *History, Description and Statistics*, 84–85.
23 Gray, "Insanity," 3.
24 Gray, "Insanity," 7–8.
25 Boyer, "Religion, 'Moral Insanity,' and Psychology."
26 Spitzka, "Historical Case of Impulsive Monomania."
27 Hammond, *Treatise on Insanity*, 11.
28 Rosenberg, *Trial of the Assassin Guiteau*, 63.
29 *Report of the Proceedings*, 3:1248.
30 *Report of the Proceedings*, 1:281.
31 *Report of the Proceedings*, 1:283.
32 *Report of the Proceedings*, 1:286.
33 *Report of the Proceedings*, 1:289.
34 *Report of the Proceedings*, 1:291.
35 Spitzka, "Monomania, or Primaere Verruecktheit," 269.
36 *Report of the Proceedings*, 1:293.
37 *Report of the Proceedings*, 1:318.
38 *Report of the Proceedings*, 1:331.
39 *Report of the Proceedings*, 2:1265.
40 *Report of the Proceedings*, 2:967.
41 *Report of the Proceedings*, 2:987.
42 Channing, *Mental Status of Guiteau*, 8–9.
43 *Report of the Proceedings*, 1:305.
44 *Report of the Proceedings*, 2:982.
45 *Report of the Proceedings*, 3:1908.
46 *Report of the Proceedings*, 1:308.
47 "Possessed of a Demon: Guiteau's Brother Damages the Insanity Claim," *New York Times*, November 29, 1881.
48 *Report of the Proceedings*, 3:1918.

49 *Report of the Proceedings*, 3:2216–17.
50 Gray, "United States vs. Charles J. Guiteau," 361.
51 *Report of the Proceedings*, 1:743, 755–56.
52 Alexander and Easton, *Report of the Proceedings*, 3:1855–56.
53 *Report of the Proceedings*, 3:2615.
54 Elwell, "A Rejoinder," 631–32.
55 Davies, *Troubled by Faith*, 1.
56 Weiss and Gupta, "America's First M'Naghten Defense."
57 Hall, *Trial of William Freeman*, 374.
58 Brigham, *Observations on the Influence of Religion*, xiii–xxvi.
59 Weisenfeld, *Black Religion in the Madhouse*.
60 Spitzka, *Insanity, Its Classification, Diagnosis, and Treatment*, 20–21.
61 Weisenfeld, *Black Religion in the Madhouse*, 117–24.
62 Johnson, "Rise of Black Ethnics."
63 Gray, "United States vs. Charles J. Guiteau," 309.
64 Richards, *Race, Racism and Psychology*, chap. 2.
65 Thielman, "Psychiatry and Social Values."
66 Spitzka, "Contributions to Nervous and Mental Pathology."
67 Grob, *Mental Illness and American Society*, 169.

CHAPTER 5. POLICING FANATICISM ABROAD

1 As this chapter shows, there is a reality (and an exaggerated American perception) of how these religious categories blur together. See also Schumacher, "Syncretism in Philippine Catholicism."
2 For more on these terms and their intersections, see Cullamar, *Babaylanism in Negros*; Bankoff, "Bandits, Banditry and Landscapes of Crime"; Rafael, *Figures of Criminality*.
3 US Bureau of Insular Affairs, *Reports of the Philippine Commission*, 613.
4 The US colonial administration consisted primarily of white men. Relevant influencers of US colonial policy changed their official administrative position frequently. On the civil side, these men included William McKinley, Dean Worcester, William Howard Taft, Jacob Schurman, Theodore Roosevelt, Elihu Root, and Luke Right. Within the military, they included General Douglas MacArthur, Admiral George Dewey, Chief of Constabulary Harry Hill Bandholtz, and Captain John R. M. Taylor, who oversaw the collection of the Philippine Insurgent Records.
5 Dean Worcester wrote in regard to the prevalence of superstitions that "the worst of it is that even the native press does not dare to combat such superstitions, if indeed those who control it do not still themselves hold to them." Worcester, *Philippines Past and Present*, 2:945.
6 Kramer, *Blood of Government*.
7 For critical analyses of these categories, see Johnson, *African American Religions*; Matory, *Fetish Revisited*; Chidester, *Empire of Religion*.

8. The legal status of island nations annexed in the wake of the Spanish-American War was decided formally in a series of US Supreme Court cases known as the Insular Cases. Collectively, in these cases the justices argued that Congress had the right to hold indefinitely a seized territory with no intention of incorporating it or granting full constitutional rights to the inhabitants of the territory. As a number of scholars have claimed, the plenary power invoked here had formal and informal precedent in the rulings on the legal status of a variety of racialized and/or colonized peoples, including African Americans and Native Americans. See Torruella, "Ruling America's Colonies," and Saito, "Asserting Plenary Power."
9. For a sweeping overview of the relationship between the United States and the Philippines that privileges the US perspective, see Karnow, *In Our Image*. A more critical and argument-driven book is Alfred McCoy's examination of the mechanisms of state policing and surveillance that the United States developed through its colonial possession of the Philippines. McCoy, *Policing America's Empire*. Employing perspectives of critical ethnic studies, Vicente Rafael and Dylan Rodríguez have centered Filipinos' experiences of the occupation and the fluid forms of identity and politics that have followed. See Rafael, *White Love and Other Events in Filipino History*, and Rodríguez, *Suspended Apocalypse*.
10. See Albert Beveridge, "Our Philippine Policy," in Schirmer and Shalom, *Philippines Reader*, 23–26.
11. For more on how discourse about the Philippines operated in US religious public spheres, see Harris, *God's Arbiters*, and McCullough, *Cross of War*.
12. Wolff, *Little Brown Brother*.
13. See Roth, *Muddy Glory*.
14. See Wenger, *Religious Freedom*, chaps. 2, 3.
15. Ngozi-Brown, "African-American Soldiers and Filipinos."
16. For a study of white Americans who made anti-imperial arguments on the basis of racism, see Love, *Race over Empire*.
17. US Bureau of Insular Affairs, *What Has Been Done in the Philippines*, 8.
18. See Kramer, *Blood of Government*, esp. 87–158.
19. For an overview of Worcester's career, see Sullivan, *Exemplar of Americanism*.
20. "Taft's Opinion of Dean C. Worcester," *Springfield Union*, January 12, 1914.
21. See Rice, "Dean Worcester's Photographs." For the value and limits of Worcester's photograph collection, see Salvador-Amores, "Afterlives of Dean C. Worcester's Colonial Photographs."
22. See Sullivan, *Exemplar of Americanism*, 52–53.
23. Josephson-Storm, *Invention of Religion in Japan*, esp. 252–54.
24. Worcester, *Philippine Islands and Their People*, 429; Worcester, *Philippines Past and Present*, 2:945.
25. Worcester, *Philippine Islands and Their People*, 57. See also Sullivan, *Exemplar of Americanism*, 45–46.
26. Of course, how a colonial official or institution parsed the archipelago's human geography depended on the mission at hand. There were various levels. At times

the primary distinction was between Christian and non-Christian territories. In some reports the main distinction was between cities, countrysides, and mountainous regions. But in terms of how colonial officials assessed the social, economic, and political possibilities of different populations, the distinction between animist, Catholic, and Moro—though at times blurred (Moros and Catholics were believed to have animistic tendencies)—was key.

27 Racialization was never a singular or rationalized system of description and evaluation. Americans had competing and contradictory theories of how race operated on the Philippine archipelago. This is not surprising considering that racial difference is a social construct haphazardly created for the purposes of racial governance. Though nearly all white Americans involved in the colonial administration racialized Filipino/as, some used the term "Filipino" to describe all inhabitants of the archipelago. Others utilized different racialized categories, such as Malayan, Negroid, Negrito, Australoid, Japanese, Chinese, Papuan, and so on. Worcester, for one, went back and forth in his descriptions. He used different theories of race or race mixing to the extent that they were useful for his argument in the moment. Somewhat surprising considering his social Darwinist and zoological background, Worcester was not particularly interested in pseudo-scientific anatomical study of racial difference that emphasized a clean and neat difference in populations by various physical measurements (head size, nose, ears, etc.). His studies were more like to racialize Filipino/as through the means of cultural anthropology—descriptions of culture and religion, collections of stories, and evaluations of the level of civilizational development. For an example of US racial science popular at the time, see Bean, *Racial Anatomy of the Philippine Islanders*. Bean utilized photographs from Worcester's collection in his research.
28 Villegas, *You Shall Be as Gods*.
29 Worcester, *Philippine Islands and Their People*, 429.
30 Worcester, *Philippine Islands and Their People*, 432.
31 Worcester, *Philippine Islands and Their People*, 473.
32 Sullivan, *Exemplar of Americanism*, 47–52; Dees, "Equation of Language and Spirit."
33 Sullivan, *Exemplar of Americanism*, 52–53.
34 Kidd, *Social Evolution*, 123–24.
35 Gardener, "Life in the Philippines."
36 Taft and Roosevelt, *The Philippines*, 105.
37 Chidester, *Empire of Religion*, 91–123.
38 Keane, *Christian Moderns*, 6.
39 Hesse, "Racialized Modernity," 659.
40 For unmodern religions, see Orsi, "Afterword."
41 Crosson, "Impossibility of Liberal Secularism"; Weheliye, *Habeas Viscus*.
42 Though focusing on the nineteenth century and the era of Spanish rule, Greg Bankoff provides a portrait of the *tulisan* in historical context. See Bankoff, "Bandits, Banditry and Landscapes of Crime."

43 "Fanatics: May Give Us Deal of Trouble in the Philippines," *Cincinnati Enquirer*, January 24, 1899. Tisa Wenger has explored the underside of religious freedom within the domestic and imperial United States, looking at how US Americans have utilized religious freedom to justify colonial and racial practices. In it, she examines the US occupation of the Philippines with a focus on US engagement with the Philippine Independent Church and Moros. Wenger, *Religious Freedom*, esp. 15–100.
44 Worcester, *Philippines Past and Present*, 1:380.
45 See Walther, *Sacred Interests*; Su, *Exporting Freedom*; Wenger, *Religious Freedom*.
46 Ileto, *Pasyon and Revolution*.
47 Hurley, *Jungle Patrol*, 128.
48 Scott, "Colonial Governmentality," 193.
49 Cullamar, *Babaylanism in Negros*, esp. 18.
50 Scott, *Art of Not Being Governed*.
51 William Mowbray, "The Brown Man's Graft," *Washington Post*, October 7, 1906.
52 White, *Bullets and Bolos*.
53 Taylor, *Philippine Insurrection Against the United States*, 2:416.
54 US War Department, *Annual Report of the War Department*, 411.
55 Leandro de la Rama, "Report of the Governor of Occidental Negros," Bacolod, December 19, 1901, container 316, file no. 3029, Records of the Bureau of Insular Affairs, record group 350, National Archives at College Park, 438–39.
56 Cullamar, "Babaylanism in Negros: 1896–1907."
57 Taylor, *Philippine Insurrection Against the United States*, 5:625.
58 Taylor, *Philippine Insurrection Against the United States*, 5:626.
59 Taylor, *Philippine Insurrection Against the United States*, 5:625.
60 Dionisio Papa to Rufo Oyos, March 8, 1901, file 970.7, microcopy no. 254, Philippine Insurgent Records, National Archives Building, Washington, D.C.
61 *El Tiempo*, September 23, 1907, 2, quoted in McCoy, "Baylan," 172.
62 US War Department, *Annual Report of the Secretary of War*, 926.
63 Rev. Harry Maxwell, "The Bandits of Negros: Returned Missionary Tells of Their Crimes and Superstitions," *Washington Post*, July 5, 1908, sec. Editorial.
64 US Philippine Commission, *Report of the Philippine Commission*, 3:100.
65 US War Department, *Annual Report of the Secretary of War*, 926.
66 "Peace in Philippines: Favorable Outlook for Its Continuance—General Allen's Report American Troops Still Needed Disturbances of the Year," *New York Tribune*, November 1, 1903.
67 US Philippine Commission, *Report of the Philippine Commission*, 3:101.
68 US War Department, *Annual Report of the Secretary of War*, 926.
69 US War Department, *Annual Report of the Secretary of War*, 926.
70 Worcester, *Philippines Past and Present*, 2:949.
71 Worcester, *Philippines Past and Present*, 2:950–51.
72 Worcester, *Philippines Past and Present*, 2:960.
73 Sullivan, *Exemplar of Americanism*, 165–90.

74 US War Department, *Annual Report of the War Department*, 380.
75 Worcester, *Philippines Past and Present*, 1:399.
76 "Colonial Army Needed: Gen. Allen Gives Reasons Why the Force Now in the Philippines Must Not Be Reduced," *New York Times*, November 2, 1903.
77 US Philippine Commission, *Report of the Philippine Commission*, 3:39.
78 Worcester, *Philippines Past and Present*, 2:738. Taylor, *Philippine Insurrection Against the United States*, 5:625.
79 US War Department, *Annual Report of the Secretary of War*, 926.
80 *Manual for the Philippines Constabulary* (Bureau of Printing, 1911), container 174, General Classified Files, 1898–1945, record group 350, Bureau of Insular Affairs, National Archives at College Park.
81 White, *Bullets and Bolos*, 84.
82 US Bureau of the Census, *Census of the Philippine Islands*, 1:39.
83 For a socioecological explanation for the rise of banditry, see Bankoff, "Bandits, Banditry and Landscapes of Crime."
84 US War Department, *Annual Report of the Secretary of War*, 34.
85 Harry H. Bandholtz, "Report of the Second District, Philippines Constabulary," June 25, 1904, in US Philippine Commission, *Report of the Philippine Commission*, 3:88.
86 US War Department, *Annual Report of the War Department*, 411.
87 Condos, "'Fanaticism' and the Politics of Resistance."
88 White, *Bullets and Bolos*, 85.
89 A. C. Allen, "Charmed Shirts: Garments Worn by Filipinos to Ward Off the Bullets of American Soldiers—Character of Insurgent Soldiers," *Los Angeles Times*, April 1, 1901.
90 Special Dispatch to the *Baltimore Sun*, "Killed Moro Prophet: American Soldiers Showed Charms Did Not Protect Natives," *Baltimore Sun*, July 19, 1905.
91 William H. Taft, "Extracts from Personal Letter from Governor Taft to the Secretary of War," April 14, 1903, entry 5, box 393, record group 350, Bureau of Insular Affairs, National Archives at College Park.
92 "They Posed as Saints Filipino Constables Capture Two Women Who Imposed on Natives," *Salt Lake Telegram*, September 24, 1902.
93 See Camagay, "Salud Algabre."
94 *Official Catalogue Philippine Exhibits* (St. Louis: Official Catalogue Company, 1904), 295.
95 US Philippine Commission, *Report of the Philippine Commission*, 3:100.
96 McCoy, "Baylan," 181.
97 Evelyn Tan Cullamar's research provides localized richness and narrates the politicization of babaylanism in the context of shifting economic measures. She argues that the religious aspect of Papa Isio's movement in particular was a sign of the futility of the movement. Babaylans' "unrealistic, naïve and blundering efforts at revitalization have been amply demonstrated in their recourse to supernaturalistic devices such as the *anting-anting* and *oraciaiones* as well as

their fanatical tendencies. But it was the only way they knew of coping with the challenges that confronted them." Cullamar, "Babaylanism in Negros: 1896–1907," 6. Rather than seeing religion in this context as a sign of passivity and hardship, this chapter examines the active work that messianic and material practices did. Alfred McCoy offers a more culturally attuned analysis by examining the animist aspects of these peasant groups. But McCoy too sees the rituals and beliefs of these groups as a type of regression. He writes that the "cultural retreat into animist ritual and a continuous recurrence of millenarian revolts among minority groups which had previously had little contact with Spanish colonialism." McCoy, "Baylan."

98 Ileto, *Pasyon and Revolution*, 23.
99 Orsi, *Between Heaven and Earth*.
100 See Ileto, *Pasyon and Revolution*, and Reyes, "Loób and Kapwa."
101 *El Tiempo*, September 23, 1907, 2, quoted in McCoy, "Baylan," 172.
102 White, *Bullets and Bolos*, 139.
103 Ileto, *Pasyon and Revolution*, 25.
104 Hurley, *Jungle Patrol*, 126.
105 Ileto, *Pasyon and Revolution*, 189.
106 Cullamar, *Babaylanism in Negros*, xi.
107 Hobsbawm, *Bandits*.
108 White, *Bullets and Bolos*, 52.
109 "Those Filipino 'Fanatics': Such Is the Latest Title Our 'New Subjects' Get for Daring to Wish to Be Free," *Irish World*, June 13, 1903.
110 Durkheim, *Elementary Forms of Religious Life*, 212–13.
111 Durkheim, *Elementary Forms of Religious Life*, 213.
112 Durkheim, *Elementary Forms of Religious Life*, 213.
113 Durkheim, *Elementary Forms of Religious Life*, 192.
114 Taylor, *Philippine Insurrection Against the United States*, 1:210.
115 White, *Bullets and Bolos*, 101.
116 Durkheim, *Elementary Forms of Religious Life*, 222.
117 Kramer, *Blood of Government*, 66–68.
118 US Philippine Commission, *Acts of the Philippine Commission*, 305–6.
119 "Civilize 'Em with a Krag," in Keenan, *Encyclopedia of the Spanish-American and Philippine-American Wars*, 82.
120 "The Flag Must Stay: Memory of Those Who Have Fallen in Philippines Demands That Old," *Wilkes-Barre Times*, August 30, 1900.
121 "'Ours Forever': Senator Beveridge's View on the Philippines," *Boston Daily Advertiser*, February 16, 1899.
122 Durkheim, *Moral Education*, 193.
123 "Takes Issue with Dean Worcester," *Detroit Free Press*, January 28, 1900.
124 For an extended Durkheimian analysis of the power of the flag to mobilize and conceal, see Marvin and Ingle, *Blood Sacrifice and the Nation*.
125 Smith, "Gold and Wood," 79–81.
126 Worcester, *Philippine Islands and Their People*, 268.

CHAPTER 6. ENTHUSIASM AGAINST FANATICISM

1. George Milton Hammell, "Religion and Fanaticism," *Methodist Review*, July 1888.
2. *A Religious Encyclopædia* (1883), "enthusiasm."
3. Abbott, *Dictionary of Religious Knowledge*, 343.
4. *Dictionary of Doctrinal and Historical Theology* (1872), "enthusiasm."
5. Baldwin, *Dictionary of Philosophy and Psychology*, vol. 1, "fanaticism."
6. Moody, "Courage and Enthusiasm," 37.
7. Moody, "Courage and Enthusiasm," 37.
8. Kilgore, *Mania for Freedom*, 14.
9. Preston, *Sword of the Spirit*, 207.
10. Preston, *Sword of the Spirit*, chap. 12.
11. Ahlstrom, *Religious History of the American People*.
12. Strong, *Next Great Awakening*, 40–47.
13. Strong, *Our Country*.
14. Strong, *New Era*, 347.
15. Strong, "Preacher in Relation to the New Expansion."
16. Reed, "American Foreign Policy."
17. Strong, "Preacher in Relation to the New Expansion."
18. Strong, *Expansion Under New World-Conditions*, 292.
19. Painter, *History of White People*, 247–48.
20. Wynter, "Unsettling the Coloniality of Being/Power/Truth/Freedom," 266.
21. Scott, *Conscripts of Modernity*.
22. Twain, *Mark Twain's War Prayer*.
23. W. E. B. Du Bois's account of reconstruction remains excellent. See Du Bois, *Black Reconstruction in America*.
24. Wilmore, *Black Religion and Black Radicalism*, ix.
25. Johnson, *African American Religions*, esp. 273–324.
26. Douglass, *Abolition Fanaticism in New York*, 4. The pamphlet does not make clear if Douglass himself used the language of fanaticism to describe his speech or if the publishers of the pamphlets decided to add this language to sell copies.
27. Alexander Crummell, "The Negro as a Source of Conservative Power," in Crummell, *Destiny and Race*, 238.
28. Savage, "W. E. B. Du Bois and 'The Negro Church.'"
29. Du Bois, *Souls of Black Folk*, 54.
30. Evans, *Burden of Black Religion*.
31. Du Bois's description in the fictional story of John was similar to his ethnographic description of his own visit to rural revival. For the ethnographic description, see Du Bois, *Souls of Black Folk*, 95–96.
32. Du Bois, *Souls of Black Folk*, 121.
33. William D. Hart, "Secular Coloniality: The Afterlife of Religious and Racial Tropes," in Kahn and Lloyd, *Race and Secularism in America*, 200.
34. Du Bois, "Will the Church Remove the Color Line?," 174.

CONCLUSION

1 *X-Files*, season 3, episode 11, "Revelations," written by Kim Newton, directed by David Nutter, aired December 15, 1995, on Fox.
2 Modern, *Secularism in Antebellum America*.
3 Gin Lum, *Heathen*.
4 The work of Walter Laqueur might serve as a middle point in the transition from fanaticism to the increased usage of terrorism in the 1990s. See Laqueur, *New Terrorism*.
5 Erlenbusch-Anderson, *Genealogies of Terrorism*.
6 Li, *Universal Enemy*, 25.
7 Niebuhr, *Moral Man and Immoral Society*, 277.

BIBLIOGRAPHY

Abbott, Lyman, ed. *A Dictionary of Religious Knowledge, for Popular and Professional Use.* Harper & Brothers, 1885.
Ahlstrom, Sydney E. *A Religious History of the American People.* Yale University Press, 2004.
Ahmed, Sara. "Affective Economies." *Social Text* 22, no. 2 (Summer 2004): 117–39.
Akinyela, Makungu M. "Battling the Serpent: Nat Turner, Africanized Christianity, and a Black Ethos." *Journal of Black Studies* 33, no. 3 (2003): 255–80.
Alexander, H. H., and Edward D. Easton. *Report of the Proceedings in the Case of the United States vs. Charles J. Guiteau.* 3 vols. Washington, D.C.: Government Printing Office, 1882.
Asad, Talal. *On Suicide Bombing.* Columbia University Press, 2007.
Baldwin, James. "Everybody's Protest Novel." In *Notes of a Native Son*, 13–25. Beacon, 1984.
Baldwin, James Mark, ed. *Dictionary of Philosophy and Psychology.* 3 vols. Macmillan, 1901.
Bankoff, Greg. "Bandits, Banditry and Landscapes of Crime in the Nineteenth-Century Philippines." *Journal of Southeast Asian Studies* 29, no. 2 (1998): 319–39.
Bean, Robert Bennett. *The Racial Anatomy of the Philippine Islanders: Introducing New Methods of Anthropology and Showing Their Application to the Filipinos with a Classification of Human Ears and a Scheme for the Heredity of Anatomical Characters in Man.* J. B. Lippincott, 1910.
Beliso-de Jesús, Aisha M. *Electric Santería: Racial and Sexual Assemblages of Transnational Religion.* Columbia University Press, 2015.
Belt, Rabia. "When God Demands Blood: Unusual Minds and the Troubled Juridical Ties of Religion, Madness, and Culpability." *University of Miami Law Review* 69, no. 3 (May 1, 2015): 755–94.
Berlant, Lauren. *The Female Complaint: The Unfinished Business of Sentimentality in American Culture.* Duke University Press, 2008.
Blum, Edward J. *Reforging the White Republic: Race, Religion, and American Nationalism, 1865–1898.* Louisiana State University Press, 2007.
Boyer, Jodie. "Religion, 'Moral Insanity,' and Psychology in Nineteenth-Century America." *Religion and American Culture* 24, no. 1 (2014): 70–99.
Breen, Patrick H. *The Land Shall Be Deluged in Blood: A New History of the Nat Turner Revolt.* Oxford University Press, 2016.

Brigham, Amariah. *Observations on the Influence of Religion upon the Health and Physical Welfare of Mankind.* Boston: Marsh, Capen & Lyon, 1835.

Brooks, David. "How to Roll Back Fanaticism." *New York Times*, August 15, 2017, sec. Opinion. www.nytimes.com.

Brown, Wendy. *Regulating Aversion: Tolerance in the Age of Identity and Empire.* Princeton University Press, 2006.

Burnett, Amy Nelson. "Luther and the Schwärmer." In *The Oxford Handbook of Martin Luther's Theology*, edited by Robert Kolb, Irene Dingel, and L'ubomír Batka, 511–24. Oxford University Press, 2014.

Butt, Martha Haines. *Antifanaticism: A Tale of the South.* Philadelphia: Lippincott, Grambo, 1853.

Camagay, Ma. Luisa T. "Salud Algabre: A Forgotten Member of the Philippine Sakdal." In *Women in Southeast Asian Nationalist Movements: A Biographical Approach*, edited by Susan Blackburn and Helen Ting, 124–46. National University of Singapore Press, 2013.

Carté, Katherine. *Religion and the American Revolution: An Imperial History.* University of North Carolina Press, 2021.

Casson, Douglas John. *Liberating Judgment: Fanatics, Skeptics, and John Locke's Politics of Probability.* Princeton University Press, 2011.

Channing, Walter. *The Mental Status of Guiteau, the Assassin of President Garfield.* Cambridge, Mass.: Riverside Press, 1882.

Chicago Daily Tribune. "Rios Sentenced to Hang: Fanatical Filipino Leader Must Suffer Death Penalty." June 1, 1903.

Chidester, David. *Empire of Religion: Imperialism and Comparative Religion.* University of Chicago Press, 2014.

Chireau, Yvonne Patricia. *Black Magic: Religion and the African American Conjuring Tradition.* University of California Press, 2003.

Colas, Dominique. *Civil Society and Fanaticism: Conjoined Histories.* Translated by Amy Jacobs. Stanford University Press, 1997.

Condos, Mark. "'Fanaticism' and the Politics of Resistance Along the North-West Frontier of British India." *Comparative Studies in Society and History* 58, no. 3 (2016): 717–45.

Conroy-Krutz, Emily. *Missionary Diplomacy: Religion and Nineteenth-Century American Foreign Relations.* Cornell University Press, 2024.

Corrigan, John. "Introduction: How Do We Study Religion and Emotion?" In *Feeling Religion*, edited by John Corrigan, 1–21. Duke University Press, 2017.

Cowdin, V. G. *Ellen; or, The Fanatic's Daughter.* Mobile: S. H. Goetzel & Company, 1860.

Crosson, J. Brent. "The Impossibility of Liberal Secularism: Religious (In)Tolerance, Spirituality, and Not-Religion." *Method & Theory in the Study of Religion* 30, no. 1 (2018): 37–55.

Crummell, Alexander. *Destiny and Race: Selected Writings, 1840–1898.* Edited by Wilson Jeremiah Moses. University of Massachusetts Press, 1992.

Cullamar, Evelyn Tan. "Babaylanism in Negros: 1896–1907." *Social Science Information* 9, no. 1 (June 1981): 3–7.
———. *Babaylanism in Negros, 1896–1907*. New Day Publishers, 1986.
Curtis, Finbarr. *The Production of American Religious Freedom*. New York University Press, 2016.
Dain, Norman. *Concepts of Insanity in the United States, 1789–1865*. Rutgers University Press, 1964.
Davies, Owen. *Troubled by Faith: Insanity and the Supernatural in the Age of the Asylum*. Oxford University Press, 2023.
Dees, Sarah. "An Equation of Language and Spirit: Comparative Philology and the Study of American Indian Religions." *Method & Theory in the Study of Religion* 27, no. 3 (August 25, 2015): 195–219.
Dew, Thomas Roderick. "Abolition of Slavery." *United States' Telegraph*, no. 226 (September 19, 1833).
———. *An Essay on Slavery*. 2nd ed. Richmond, Va.: J. W. Randolph, 1849.
Douglas, Ann. *The Feminization of American Culture*. Farrar, Straus and Giroux, 1998.
Douglass, Frederick. *Abolition Fanaticism in New York*. Baltimore, 1847.
Du Bois, W. E. B. *Black Reconstruction in America, 1860–1880*. Free Press, 1998.
———. *The Souls of Black Folk*. Penguin, 1995.
———. "Will the Church Remove the Color Line?" In *Du Bois on Religion*, edited by Phil Zuckerman, 173–80. AltaMira Press, 2000.
Durkheim, Émile. *The Elementary Forms of Religious Life*. Translated by Karen E. Fields. Free Press, 1995.
———. *Moral Education: A Study in the Theory and Application of the Sociology of Education*. Translated by Everett K. Wilson. Free Press, 1961.
Durrill, Wayne K. "Nat Turner and Signs of the Apocalypse." In *Varieties of Southern Religious History: Essays in Honor of Donald G. Mathews*, edited by Regina D. Sullivan and Monte Harrell Hampton, 77–93. University of South Carolina Press, 2015.
Earle, Pliny. *History, Description and Statistics of the Bloomingdale Asylum for the Insane*. New York: Egbert, Hovey & King, 1848.
Egerton, Douglas. "Nat Turner in a Hemispheric Context." In *Nat Turner: A Slave Rebellion in History and Memory*, edited by Kenneth S. Greenberg. Oxford University Press, 2003.
Elwell, J. J. "A Rejoinder, by J. J. Elwell, to Reply of E. C. Spitzka." *Alienist and Neurologist (1880–1920)* 4, no. 4 (October 1, 1883): 621–45.
Erlenbusch-Anderson, Verena. *Genealogies of Terrorism: Revolution, State Violence, Empire*. Columbia University Press, 2018.
Evans, Curtis J. *The Burden of Black Religion*. Oxford University Press, 2008.
Evans, Richard Kent. *Move: An American Religion*. Oxford University Press, 2020.
Feffer, Steve. "'Judas the Maccabeas': Samuel B. H. Judah and the Staging of Jewish Identity in Early American Melodrama." *Prooftexts* 27, no. 3 (2007): 474–99.
Ferreira da Silva, Denise. *Toward a Global Idea of Race*. University of Minnesota Press, 2007.

Fessenden, Tracy. *Culture and Redemption: Religion, the Secular, and American Literature*. Princeton University Press, 2007.

Findlay, James. *Dwight L. Moody: American Evangelist 1837–1899*. University of Chicago Press, 1969.

Finney, Charles. *Lectures on Revivals of Religion*. Edited by William McLouglin. Harvard University Press, 2013.

———. "Letters on Revivals No. 9." *Oberlin Evangelist*, May 21, 1845.

———. *Memoirs of Rev. Charles G. Finney*. New York: A. S. Barnes, 1876.

———. *Revival Fire: Letters on Revivals*. Waukesha, Wisc.: Metropolitan Church Association, n.d.

Fisher, Linford D. "Evangelicals and Unevangelicals: The Contested History of a Word." In *Evangelicals: Who They Have Been, Are Now, and Could Be*, edited by Mark A. Noll, David W. Bebbington, and George M. Marsden, 188–213. Eerdmans, 2019.

Fluhman, J. Spencer. *"A Peculiar People": Anti-Mormonism and the Making of Religion in Nineteenth-Century America*. University of North Carolina Press, 2012.

Free Enquirer. "A Death by Fanaticism." March 16, 1833.

Gardener, Cornelius. "Life in the Philippines: A Review of Present Conditions in Our Asiatic Possessions." *Detroit Free Press*, June 30, 1901, sec. 5.

Gin Lum, Kathryn. *Heathen: Religion and Race in American History*. Harvard University Press, 2022.

———. "The Historyless Heathen and the Stagnating Pagan: History as Non-Native Category?" *Religion and American Culture* 28, no. 1 (2018): 52–91.

Gonaver, Wendy. *The Peculiar Institution and the Making of Modern Psychiatry, 1840–1880*. University of North Carolina Press, 2019.

Goodwin, Megan. *Abusing Religion: Literary Persecution, Sex Scandals, and American Minority Religions*. Rutgers University Press, 2020.

Graham, Billy. *Christianity vs. Communism*. Billy Graham Evangelistic Association, 1951.

Gray, John. "Insanity: Its Dependence on Physical Disease." Paper, annual meeting of the Medical Society of the State of New York, 1871.

———. "The United States vs. Charles J. Guiteau." *American Journal of Insanity* 38 (January 1882): 303–448.

Gray, Thomas, and Nat Turner. *The Confessions of Nat Turner*. Baltimore: Lucas & Deaver, 1831.

Greyser, Naomi. *On Sympathetic Grounds: Race, Gender, and Affective Geographies in Nineteenth-Century North America*. Oxford University Press, 2017.

Grob, Gerald. *Mental Illness and American Society 1875–1940*. Princeton University Press, 2019.

Guiteau, Charles J. *The Truth, and the Removal*. Washington, D.C.: Published by the Author, 1882.

Hall, Benjamin F., ed. *The Trial of William Freeman*. Auburn, N.Y.: Derby, Miller & Co., 1848.

Hammell, George Milton. "Religion and Fanaticism." *Methodist Review*, July 1888.

Hammond, William Alexander. *A Treatise on Insanity in Its Medical Relations*. New York: D. Appleton, 1883.
Hamner, Gail. "Theorizing Religion and the Public Sphere: Affect, Technology, Valuation." *Journal of the American Academy of Religion* 87, no. 4 (2019): 1008–49.
Harding, Vincent. *There Is a River: The Black Struggle for Freedom in America*. Harcourt Brace Jovanovich, 1981.
Harris, Susan K. *God's Arbiters: Americans and the Philippines, 1898–1902*. Oxford University Press, 2013.
Hartman, Sadiya V. *Scenes of Subjection: Terror, Slavery, and Self-Making in Nineteenth-Century America*. Oxford University Press, 1997.
Hazard, Sonia. "Evangelical Encounters: The American Tract Society and the Rituals of Print Distribution in Antebellum America." *Journal of the American Academy of Religion* 88, no. 1 (March 2020): 200–234.
Hendler, Glenn. *Public Sentiments: Structures of Feeling in Nineteenth-Century American Literature*. University of North Carolina Press, 2001.
Hentz, Caroline Lee. *The Planter's Northern Bride*. Philadelphia: T. B. Peterson, 1854.
Hesse, Barnor. "Racialized Modernity: An Analytics of White Mythologies." *Ethnic and Racial Studies* 30, no. 4 (2007): 643–63.
Hobsbawm, Eric. *Bandits*. Pantheon, 1981.
Holden, Vanessa M. *Surviving Southampton: African American Women and Resistance in Nat Turner's Community*. University of Illinois Press, 2021.
Howard, George S., and Cody D. Christopherson. "Pluralism: An Antidote for Fanaticism, the Delusion of Our Age." *Journal of Mind and Behavior* 30, no. 3 (2009): 139–47.
Hurley, Vic. *Jungle Patrol, the Story of the Philippine Constabulary*. Cerberus, 2011.
Ileto, Reynaldo Clemeña. *Pasyon and Revolution: Popular Movements in the Philippines, 1840–1910*. Ateneo de Manila University Press, 1979.
Johnson, Sylvester. *African American Religions, 1500–2000: Colonialism, Democracy, and Freedom*. Cambridge University Press, 2015.
———. "The Rise of Black Ethnics: The Ethnic Turn in African American Religions, 1916–1945." *Religion and American Culture* 20, no. 2 (July 1, 2010): 125–63.
Jordan-Lake, Joy. *Whitewashing Uncle Tom's Cabin: Nineteenth-Century Women Novelists Respond to Stowe*. Vanderbilt University Press, 2005.
Jortner, Adam Joseph. *Blood from the Sky: Miracles and Politics in the Early American Republic*. University of Virginia Press, 2017.
Josephson-Storm, Jason Ānanda. *The Invention of Religion in Japan*. University of Chicago Press, 2012.
Judah, Samuel B. H. *Spirit of Fanaticism: A Poetical Rhapsody*. New York: Beacon Office, 1842.
Kahn, Jonathon S., and Vincent W. Lloyd, eds. *Race and Secularism in America*. Columbia University Press, 2016.
Kant, Immanuel. "Essay on the Maladies of the Head." In *Observations on the Feeling of the Beautiful and Sublime and Other Writings*, edited by Patrick Frierson and Paul Guyer. Cambridge University Press, 2011.

Karnow, Stanley. *In Our Image: America's Empire in the Philippines.* Ballantine Books, 2010.

Katsafanas, Paul, ed. *Fanaticism and the History of Philosophy.* Routledge, 2023.

———. "Fanaticism and Sacred Values." *Philosophers' Imprint* 19, no. 17 (May 2019): 1–20.

Keane, Webb. *Christian Moderns: Freedom and Fetish in the Mission Encounter.* University of California Press, 2007.

Keenan, Jerry, ed. *Encyclopedia of the Spanish-American and Philippine-American Wars.* ABC-CLIO, 2001.

Kendler, Kenneth S. "Philippe Pinel and the Foundations of Modern Psychiatric Nosology." *Psychological Medicine* 50, no. 16 (December 2020): 2667–72.

Kidd, Benjamin. *Social Evolution.* New York: Macmillan, 1894.

Kilgore, John Mac. *Mania for Freedom: American Literatures of Enthusiasm from the Revolution to the Civil War.* University of North Carolina Press, 2016.

Klassen, Pamela E. *The Story of Radio Mind: A Missionary's Journey on Indigenous Land.* University of Chicago Press, 2018.

Kramer, Paul A. *The Blood of Government: Race, Empire, the United States, and the Philippines.* University of North Carolina Press, 2006.

Lampley, Karl. *A Theological Account of Nat Turner: Christianity, Violence, and Theology.* Palgrave Macmillan, 2013.

Laqueur, Walter. *New Terrorism: Fanaticism and the Arms of Mass Destruction.* Oxford University Press, 1999.

Li, Darryl. *The Universal Enemy: Jihad, Empire, and the Challenge of Solidarity.* Stanford University Press, 2019.

Logan, Dana. "It Was Never About the Snakes: Synanon, Cult, and the Devil in Religious Studies." *Religion and American Culture* 33, no. 3 (2023): 283–319.

Love, Eric T. L. *Race over Empire: Racism and U.S. Imperialism, 1865–1900.* University of North Carolina Press, 2004.

Lovejoy, Owen. "The Fanaticism of the Democratic Party: Speech of Hon. Owen Lovejoy, Illinois, Delivered in the US House of Representatives." February 21, 1859.

Mahmood, Saba. *Religious Difference in a Secular Age: A Minority Report.* Princeton University Press, 2015.

Mamdani, Mahmood. *Good Muslim, Bad Muslim: America, the Cold War, and the Roots of Terror.* Pantheon, 2004.

Manseau, Peter. *The Jefferson Bible: A Biography.* Princeton University Press, 2020.

Marty, Martin E. *Righteous Empire: The Protestant Experience in America.* Harper & Row, 1977.

Marvin, Carolyn, and David W. Ingle. *Blood Sacrifice and the Nation: Totem Rituals and the American Flag.* Cambridge University Press, 1999.

Matory, J. Lorand. *The Fetish Revisited: Marx, Freud, and the Gods Black People Make.* Duke University Press, 2018.

Mazzarella, William. "Affect: What Is It Good For?" In *Enchantments of Modernity: Empire, Nation, Globalization,* edited by Saurabh Dube, 291–309. Routledge, 2010.

McCoy, Alfred W. "Baylan: Animist Religion and Philippine Peasant Ideology." *Philippine Quarterly of Culture and Society* 10, no. 3 (1982): 141–94.

———. *Policing America's Empire: The United States, the Philippines, and the Rise of the Surveillance State*. University of Wisconsin Press, 2009.

McCrary, Charles. *Sincerely Held: American Secularism and Its Believers*. University of Chicago Press, 2022.

McCrary, Charles, and Jeffrey Wheatley. "The Protestant Secular in the Study of American Religion: Reappraisal and Suggestions." *Religion* 47, no. 2 (April 3, 2017): 256–76.

McCullough, Matthew. *The Cross of War: Christian Nationalism and U.S. Expansion in the Spanish-American War*. University of Wisconsin Press, 2014.

McDowell, James, Jr. *Speech of James M'Dowell, Jr. of Rockbridge, in the House of Delegates of Virginia, on the Slave Question: Delivered Saturday*. Richmond, Va.: T. W. White, 1832.

Modern, John Lardas. *Secularism in Antebellum America*. University of Chicago Press, 2011.

Moody, Dwight Lyman. "Courage and Enthusiasm." In *Holding the Fort: Comprising Sermons and Addresses at the Great Revival Meetings Conducted by Moody and Sankey*, edited by Michael Laird Simons, 34–41. Philadelphia: Porter & Coates, 1877.

Ngozi-Brown, Scot. "African-American Soldiers and Filipinos: Racial Imperialism, Jim Crow and Social Relations." *Journal of Negro History* 82, no. 1 (1997): 42–53.

Niebuhr, Reinhold. *Moral Man and Immoral Society: A Study in Ethics and Politics*. 1932. Charles Scribner's Sons, 1949.

Noll, Mark A. *The Civil War as a Theological Crisis*. University of North Carolina Press, 2006.

Ogden, Emily. *Credulity: A Cultural History of US Mesmerism*. University of Chicago Press, 2018.

Orsi, Robert. "Afterword: Everyday Religion and the Contemporary World: The Un-Modern, or What Was Supposed to Have Disappeared but Did Not." In *Ordinary Lives and Grand Schemes: An Anthropology of Everyday Religion*, edited by Samuli Schielke and Liza Debevec. Berghahn Books, 2012.

———. *Between Heaven and Earth: The Religious Worlds People Make and the Scholars Who Study Them*. Princeton University Press, 2005.

———. *History and Presence*. Belknap, 2016.

Painter, Nell Irvin. *The History of White People*. Norton, 2011.

Parsons, Tyler, and Elder Freeman Nickerson. *Mormon Fanaticism Exposed: A Compendium of the Book of Mormon, or Joseph Smith's Golden Bible*. Boston, 1841.

Pellegrini, Ann, and Janet R. Jakobsen. *Secularisms*. Duke University Press, 2008.

Pinel, Philippe. *A Treatise on Insanity: In Which Are Contained the Principles of a New and More Practical Nosology of Maniacal Disorders*. Translated by D. D. Davis. Sheffield: W. Todd for Cadell and Davies, 1806.

Pocock, J. G. A. "Enthusiasm: The Antiself of the Enlightenment." *Huntington Library Quarterly* 60, no. 1/2 (1997): 7–28.

Porter, Theodore M. *Genetics in the Madhouse: The Unknown History of Human Heredity*. Princeton University Press, 2018.

Porterfield, Amanda. *Conceived in Doubt: Religion and Politics in the New American Nation*. University of Chicago Press, 2012.

Prasch, Thomas. "Which God for Africa: The Islamic-Christian Missionary Debate in Late-Victorian England." *Victorian Studies* 33, no. 1 (1989): 51–73.

Preston, Andrew. *Sword of the Spirit, Shield of Faith: Religion in American War and Diplomacy*. Knopf, 2012.

Raboteau, Albert J. *Slave Religion: The "Invisible Institution" in the Antebellum South*. Oxford University Press, 2004.

Rafael, Vicente L., ed. *Figures of Criminality in Indonesia, the Philippines, and Colonial Vietnam*. SEAP Publications, 1999.

———. *White Love and Other Events in Filipino History*. Duke University Press, 2000.

Ramsey, Kate. *The Spirits and the Law: Vodou and Power in Haiti*. University of Chicago Press, 2011.

Reed, James Eldin. "American Foreign Policy, the Politics of Missions and Josiah Strong, 1890–1900." *Church History* 41, no. 2 (1972): 230–45.

Report of the Proceedings in the Case of the United States vs. Charles J. Guiteau, Tried in the Supreme Court of the District of Columbia, Holding a Criminal. 3 vols. Washington, D.C.: Government Printing Office, 1882.

Reyes, Jeremiah. "Loób and Kapwa: An Introduction to a Filipino Virtue Ethics." *Asian Philosophy* 25, no. 2 (April 3, 2015): 148–71.

Rice, Mark. "Dean Worcester's Photographs, American National Identity, and 'National Geographic Magazine.'" *Australasian Journal of American Studies* 31, no. 2 (2012): 42–56.

Richards, Graham. *Race, Racism and Psychology: Towards a Reflexive History*. Routledge, 1997.

Roberts, J. D. "Insanity in the Colored Race." *North Carolina Medical Journal* 12, no. 5 (November 1883).

Rodríguez, Dylan. *Suspended Apocalypse: White Supremacy, Genocide, and the Filipino Condition*. University of Minnesota Press, 2009.

Rosenberg, Charles E. *The Trial of the Assassin Guiteau*. University of Chicago Press, 1968.

Roth, Russell. *Muddy Glory: America's Indian Wars in the Philippines, 1899 to 1935*. Christopher Publishing House, 1981.

Rush, Benjamin. *Medical Inquiries and Observations, Upon the Diseases of the Mind*. Philadelphia: Kimber & Richardson, 1812.

Saito, Natsu Taylor. "Asserting Plenary Power over the 'Other': Indians, Immigrants, Colonial Subjects, and Why U.S. Jurisprudence Needs to Incorporate International Law." *Yale Law & Policy Review* 20, no. 2 (2002): 427–80.

Salvador-Amores, Analyn. "Afterlives of Dean C. Worcester's Colonial Photographs: Visualizing Igorot Material Culture, from Archives to Anthropological Fieldwork in Northern Luzon." *Visual Anthropology* 29, no. 1 (January 1, 2016): 54–80.

Savage, Barbara Dianne. "W. E. B. Du Bois and 'The Negro Church.'" *Annals of the American Academy of Political and Social Science* 568 (2000): 235–49.
Schirmer, Daniel B., and Stephen Rosskamm Shalom, eds. *The Philippines Reader: A History of Colonialism, Neocolonialism, Dictatorship, and Resistance.* South End Press, 1999.
Schuller, Kyla. *The Biopolitics of Feeling: Race, Sex, and Science in the Nineteenth Century.* Duke University Press Books, 2017.
Schumacher, John. "Syncretism in Philippine Catholicism: Its Historical Causes." *Philippine Studies* 32, no. 3 (1984): 251–72.
Scott, David. "Colonial Governmentality." *Social Text*, no. 43 (October 1, 1995): 191–220.
———. *Conscripts of Modernity: The Tragedy of Colonial Enlightenment.* Duke University Press, 2004.
Scott, James C. *The Art of Not Being Governed: An Anarchist History of Upland Southeast Asia.* Yale University Press, 2009.
Seabrook, Whitemarsh Benjamin. *An Essay on the Management of Slaves, and Especially, on Their Religious Instruction.* Charleston: A. F. Miller, 1834.
Sehat, David. *The Myth of American Religious Freedom.* Oxford University Press, 2011.
Sinha, Manisha. *The Slave's Cause: A History of Abolition.* Yale University Press, 2017.
Smith, Madison C. "Gold and Wood: Material Culture and Ritual in Precolonial and Catholic Philippines." M.A. thesis, University of Hawai'i at Manoa, 2023.
Smith, Rebecca Harrington. *Emma Bartlett; or, Prejudice and Fanaticism.* Cincinnati: Moore, Wilstach, Keys & Overend, 1856.
A Southerner. *Fanaticism and Its Results; or, Facts Versus Fancies.* Joseph Robinson, 1860.
Spitzka, Edward Charles. "Contributions to Nervous and Mental Pathology: Race and Insanity." *Journal of Nervous and Mental Disease* 7 (1880): 613–30.
———. "A Historical Case of Impulsive Monomania." *Journal of Nervous and Mental Disease* 8, no. 1 (January 1881): 87–89.
———. *Insanity, Its Classification, Diagnosis, and Treatment: A Manual for Students and Practitioners of Medicine.* Bermingham & Company, 1883.
———. "Monomania, or Primaere Verruecktheit." *St. Louis Clinical Record* 7 (1880): 257–71.
Stanton, Elizabeth Cady. *Eighty Years and More (1815–1897): Reminiscences of Elizabeth Cady Stanton.* European Publishing Company, 1898.
Stokes, Claudia. *The Altar at Home: Sentimental Literature and Nineteenth-Century American Religion.* University of Pennsylvania Press, 2014.
Stone, William L. *Matthias and His Impostures: Or, the Progress of Fanaticism.* Harper & Brothers, 1835.
Stowe, Harriet Beecher. *Uncle Tom's Cabin: Or Life Among the Lowly.* Modern Library, 2001.
Strong, Josiah. *Expansion Under New World-Conditions.* Baker and Taylor, 1900.
———. *The New Era; or, The Coming Kingdom.* Baker and Taylor, 1893.
———. *The Next Great Awakening.* Doubleday, Page & Company, 1913.

———. *Our Country—Its Possible Future and Its Present Crisis.* American Home Missionary Society, 1885.

———. "The Preacher in Relation to the New Expansion." *Homiletic Review* 42 (March 1898): 488–94.

Su, Anna. *Exporting Freedom: Religious Liberty and American Power.* Harvard University Press, 2016.

Sullivan, Rodney J. *Exemplar of Americanism: The Philippine Career of Dean C. Worcester.* University of Michigan Press, 1991.

Supp-Montgomerie, Jenna. *When the Medium Was the Mission: The Atlantic Telegraph and the Religious Origins of Network Culture.* New York University Press, 2021.

Syrett, Harold C., ed. *The Papers of Alexander Hamilton.* Vol. 24, *November 1799–June 1800.* Columbia University Press, 1976.

Taft, William H., and Theodore Roosevelt. *The Philippines: The First Civil Governor.* Outlook, 1902.

Taubes, Tanaquil. "'Healthy Avenues of the Mind': Psychological Theory Building and the Influence of Religion During the Era of Moral Treatment." *American Journal of Psychiatry* 155, no. 8 (August 1998): 1001–8.

Taves, Ann. *Fits, Trances, and Visions: Experiencing Religion and Explaining Experience from Wesley to James.* Princeton University Press, 1999.

Taylor, Charles. *A Secular Age.* Belknap, 2007.

Taylor, Isaac. *Fanaticism.* Jonathan Leavitt, 1834.

———. *Four Lectures on Spiritual Christianity.* Jackson and Walford, 1841.

———. *Natural History of Enthusiasm.* Henry G. Bohn, 1842.

———. *New Model of Christian Missions to Popish, Mahometan, and Pagan Nations: Explained in Four Letters to a Friend.* Holdsworth and Ball, 1829.

———. *Ultimate Civilization, and Other Essays.* Bell and Daldy, 1860.

Taylor, John R. M., ed. *The Philippine Insurrection Against the United States: A Compilation of Documents with Notes and Introduction.* 5 vols. Eugenio Lopez Foundation, 1971.

Thielman, Samuel B. "Psychiatry and Social Values: The American Psychiatric Association and Immigration Restriction, 1880–1930." *Psychiatry* 48, no. 4 (November 1, 1985): 299–310.

Thomas, Jolyon Baraka. *Faking Liberties: Religious Freedom in American-Occupied Japan.* University of Chicago Press, 2019.

Tomlins, Christopher. *In the Matter of Nat Turner: A Speculative History.* Princeton University Press, 2020.

Tompkins, Jane. *Sensational Designs: The Cultural Work of American Fiction, 1790–1860.* Oxford University Press, 1986.

Torruella, Juan R. "Ruling America's Colonies: The 'Insular Cases.'" *Yale Law & Policy Review* 32, no. 1 (2013): 57–95.

Tragle, Henry Irving, ed. *The Southampton Slave Revolt of 1831: A Compilation of Source Material, Including the Full Text of the Confessions of Nat Turner.* Vintage Books, 1973.

Twain, Mark. *Mark Twain's War Prayer*. Fantagraphics, 2024.
Underhill, Samuel. *A Lecture on Mysterious Religious Emotions: Delivered at Bethlehem, Ohio*. Steubenville, Ohio: Printed for the Author, 1829.
United States Magazine and Democratic Review. "The Conspiracy of Fanaticism." May 1850.
US Bureau of the Census. *Census of the Philippine Islands*. 4 vols. US Bureau of the Census, 1905.
US Bureau of Insular Affairs. *Reports of the Philippine Commission, the Civil Governor and the Heads of the Executive Departments of the Civil Government of the Philippine Islands (1900–1903)*. Government Printing Office, 1904.
———. *What Has Been Done in the Philippines: A Record of Practical Accomplishments Under Civil Government*. Government Printing Office, 1904.
US Philippine Commission. *Acts of the Philippine Commission, No. 1–1800*. Government Printing Office, 1901.
———. *Report of the Philippine Commission to the Secretary of War*. 3 vols. US War Office, 1904.
US War Department. *Annual Report of the Secretary of War*. Government Printing Office, 1903.
———. *Annual Report of the War Department*. Government Printing Office, 1902.
Vale, Gilbert. *Fanaticism: Its Source and Influence*. G. Vale, 1835.
Villegas, Dennis Santos. *You Shall Be as Gods: Anting-Anting and the Filipino Quest for Mystical Power*. Vibal Foundation, 2017.
Voltaire. *Fanaticism, or Mahomet the Prophet by Voltaire*. Sacramento, Calif.: Litwin Books, 1881.
Walther, Karine. *Sacred Interests: The United States and the Islamic World, 1821–1921*. University of North Carolina Press, 2015.
Weheliye, Alexander G. *Habeas Viscus: Racializing Assemblages, Biopolitics, and Black Feminist Theories of the Human*. Duke University Press, 2014.
Weisbrod, Carol. "Charles Guiteau and the Christian Nation." *Journal of Law and Religion* 7, no. 1 (January 1989): 187–233.
Weisenfeld, Judith. *Black Religion in the Madhouse: Race and Psychiatry in Slavery's Wake*. New York University Press, 2025.
———. *New World A-Coming: Black Religion and Racial Identity During the Great Migration*. New York University Press, 2017.
Weiss, Kenneth J., and Neha Gupta. "America's First M'Naghten Defense and the Origin of the Black Rage Syndrome." *Journal of the American Academy of Psychiatry and the Law Online* 46, no. 4 (December 1, 2018): 503–12.
Wenger, Tisa. *Religious Freedom: The Contested History of an American Ideal*. University of North Carolina Press, 2017.
Wenger, Tisa, and Sylvester Johnson, eds. *Religion and US Empire: Critical New Histories*. New York University Press, 2022.
White, John R. *Bullets and Bolos: Fifteen Years in the Philippine Islands*. Century Company, 1928.

Wilmore, Gayraud S. *Black Religion and Black Radicalism: An Interpretation of the Religious History of African Americans*. 3rd ed. Orbis Books, 1998.

Wilson, Carol. *Freedom at Risk: The Kidnapping of Free Blacks in America, 1780–1865*. University Press of Kentucky, 2014.

Wolff, Leon. *Little Brown Brother: How the United States Purchased and Pacified the Philippine Islands at the Century's Turn*. History Book Club, 2006.

Worcester, Dean. *The Philippine Islands and Their People: A Record of Personal Observation and Experience, with a Short Summary of the More Important Facts in the History of the Archipelago*. Macmillan, 1899.

———. *The Philippines Past and Present*. 2 vols. Macmillan, 1914.

Wright, Stuart A. *Armageddon in Waco: Critical Perspectives on the Branch Davidian Conflict*. University of Chicago Press, 1995.

Wynter, Sylvia. "Unsettling the Coloniality of Being/Power/Truth/Freedom: Towards the Human, After Man, Its Overrepresentation—An Argument." *CR: The New Centennial Review* 3, no. 3 (2003): 257–337.

Zuckert, Rachel. "Kant's Account of Practical Fanaticism." In *Kant's Moral Metaphysics: God, Freedom, and Immortality*, edited by Benjamin Lipscomb and James Krueger, 292–318. De Gruyter, 2010.

INDEX

Abbott, Lyman, 156, 158
abolition: anti-Tom literature and, 79–80, 83–84; Christianity driving, 85; in Cincinnati, 82; "The Conspiracy of Fanaticism" and, 89; evils of, 20; fanaticism influence and, 71, 82–85; irrationality and dangers of, 82–83, 88; as religious excess, 80; Southampton Rebellion rejected and, 56; white northerners and, 80–82
Abolition Fanaticism in New York (1847), 163
affectability, 178n32; economies, 50; fanatics and, 170; geographies, 77; power in, 53–58; religio-racial, 169–70; of sentimentality, 75; social context for, 33; willpower compromised in, 16
African American Religions, 1500–2000 (Johnson, Sylvester), 15
Aguinaldo, Emilio, 129, 151
Ahlstrom, Sydney, 158
Ahmed, Sara, 39, 50
Allen, A. C., 142
Allen, Henry, 136, 139
amenomania, 96–97
American flag, 150–52
ancient Rome, 7
Anderson, Benedict, 145
Anglo-American Protestantism, 29
Anglo-Saxon Protestantism, 42
Anglo-Saxon race, 111
Anglo-Saxon superiority, 120
antebellum era, 75–82
antebellum revivals, 29

Antifanaticism (Butt), 73, 77, 87
anti-Islamic sentiment, 3
anting anting (sacred Indigenous objects), 1; Catholic similarities to, 132; charms as, 141, 144, 150; cultural studies of, 124; Ileto's insights on, 145–46; independencia box and, 146–48; insurrectionaries violent resistance with, 129; Isio dispensing, 141; language of, 144; in Philippines, 118, 144–45; potent symbols of, 148; prophetic religious ideals with, 150; Rios's collection of, 136–37; role of, 131; sacred objects as, 117; spiritually powerful material objects and, 118; supernatural powers of, 144–45; U.S. military on falsity of superstitions and, 143–44; U.S. targeting combatants wearing, 142–43; weaponization of, 153; women as producers of, 143; Worcester with powerful, 124–25
antislavery rebellion, 60–61, 64–65
anti-Tom literature, 72–73, 75–77, 82; abolition and, 79–80; abolitionists face off in, 83–84; religious slaves in, 84; slavery in, 86
Arminian theological framework, 36
Army song (U.S.), 151
Asad, Talal, 4

babaylanism, 131, 191n97
balete (parasitic tree species), 153
Bandholtz, Harry Hill, 137, 140, 142
bandit leader (*tulisan*), 124–25
bandolerismo, 141–42, 148

207

Beecher, Harriet, 4
Beecher, Henry Ward, 93
Berlant, Lauren, 75
Beveridge, Albert, 120, 152
Bible, 93, 107
biblical literacy, 67
black and white spirits, 54–55
Black people: degraded intellect of, 111; fanaticism engagement by, 163–64; as fetishists, 112–13; free agency, 81–82; genocide of, 60; higher education for, 164–65; intellectual theories, 164; liberation of, 62–63; Philippine Revolutionary Army defections by, 121; preachers, 67; radicalism of, 163–64; religion of, 20, 65; religious rebellion of, 67–68; slavery rebellion by, 84; white people's sentimental energy toward, 86; white people violence against, 66; white supremacy and, 162–63; Worcester's belief about extinction of, 126
Bloomingdale Asylum, 98
Blum, Barbara J., 88
Bonifacio, Andrés, 130
Book of Revelation, 55
Brigham, Amariah, 97–98, 111–12
Brooks, David, 7
Brown, James, 163
Brown, Wendy, 16, 62
Bunn, Annie, 104
Butt, Martha Haines, 73, 77, 87

Calvinism, 29–31, 172
Casson, Douglas John, 9
Catholic Church, 44–45, 132
Catholicism, 74, 80
Catholic Spanish colonial rule, 120
Channing, Walter, 105
charismatic authority, 35
charismatic leader, energy flow of, 148–49
charms, 141, 144, 150
Chauncy, Charles, 4, 30
Chidester, David, 127

Christ, blood of, 55
Christianity: abolitionism driven by, 85; in Antebellum era, 75–82; civilizational aspects of, 122; colonialism spreading, 48; defense as antagonistic to, 107–8; disciplined enthusiasm of, 126; enslaved peoples learning, 68–69; Guiteau's trial and, 100–108; imperialism spreading, 43; Islamic faith contrasted with, 8; love as essence of, 159; ministers for, 69; narrow view of, 112; neurologists ridiculing, 99; non-Christian territories and, 188n26; passionate violence and, 46; paternal tenderness of, 46–47; Protestant style of, 97–98, 126; Rios's messianic worldview of, 12–13; secularism and, 11; sentimentality in, 72–73; slavery and, 68–70; Taylor, I., on renewed mission for, 47; Turner's knowledge of, 62; universal secular reason and, 10; of white families, 73–74; white people governing, 78; white supremacy in, 57; zeal for, 42
Christian missions, 181n79
Christian white race, 120–21
Christopherson, Cody D., 8, 16
Church of Jesus Christ of Latter-day Saints, 49
civilizational aspects, of Christianity, 122
civil society, 28
Civil War, 74, 77
climate, role of, 78–79
Cobb, Jeremiah, 57, 64
Colas, Dominique, 9
Colmenares, M., 143
colonial government, 141–42, 151
colonialism, 6, 48
Confessions (Gray and Turner), 182n20
"Confessions of an Abolitionist" (Omikron), 76
The Confessions of Nat Turner (Turner), 49, 51–59
Congress, Beveridge's speech to, 120

"The Conspiracy of Fanaticism," 89
contagion of sentiments, 41
Cooper, Thomas, 25
Corbin, H. C., 152
corruption, 9–10
Cowdin, V. G., 73, 78–80, 83, 85
Cox, Walter Smith, 100, 109–10
criminal responsibility, 100
criminal trial, 100–110
Crosson, J. Brent, 128
Crummell, Alexander, 164
Cullamar, Evelyn Tan, 147, 191n97
cultural studies, *of anting anting*, 124
cultures, racial inferiority and, 128
Curtis, Finbarr, 36

Davidge, Walter, 100, 105–8
Davies, Owen, 110
"A Death by Fanaticism" (Finney), 34
defense witness, 114–15
delusive thinking, 105
depravity, Guiteau with no record of, 105–6
Dew, Thomas Roderick, 57, 61, 69–70
Dickinson, Emily, 18, 173
The Dictionary of Doctrinal and Historical Theology (1872), 156
Dictionary of Philosophy and Psychology, 157
A Dictionary of Religious Knowledge, for Popular and Professional Use (Abbott), 156
Dimon, Thomas, 104–5
Dionisio. *See* Isio, Papa
discerning Eye, 18, 173
disciplined enthusiasm, 126
divine instrument, 133–34, 145–46, 150–52
divine plans, 65
divine power, individuals relationship with, 146–47
divine pressure, 107
divine providence, 91
divine revelations, 17
Douglass, Frederick, 163–64

Du Bois, W. E. B., 164–67, 193n31
Durham Test, 108
Durkheim, Émile, 145, 148–53

Earle, Pliny, 98
Edwards, Jonathan, 29
egalitarian, 37
Egerton, Douglas, 51
electricity, of religion, 178n6
Ellen (Cowdin), 73, 78–80, 83, 85
Elwell, J. J., 110
emancipation, 127
Emma Bartlett (Smith, R.), 73, 79, 87–88
emotions, flow of, 39–40
empire of liberty, 26
energy, revivalism generating, 30–31
enthusiasm: Christianity with disciplined, 126; evangelical imperial, 162; fanaticism and, 4, 27, 30, 155–57, 167, 169; fanaticism is inflamed hatred of, 157; global fanaticism against evangelical, 97, 157–61; for humanity, 160–61; revivalism with, 29–30
Eppes, Richard, 66
Esquirol, Jean-Étienne Dominique, 97
An Essay on Slavery (Dew), 57, 69
"Essay on the Maladies of the Head" (Kant), 9
An Essay on the Management of Slaves, and Especially, on Their Religious Instruction (Seabrook), 68
European Christians, 45–46
evangelicalism: enthusiasm in, 27; fanatical aspects of, 97, 157–61; imperial enthusiasm in, 162; Protestants and, 4–5, 23, 39, 179n8; revivalism with, 23, 28–37, 169; secularism with, 28; Taylor, I., on fanaticism with, 19; Taylor, I., on influence of white, 28; white supremacy and, 5–6
Evans, Curtis, 65, 84, 165
excited imagination, 83
exorcism, 70

Facts Versus Fancies, 89
family history, of Guiteau, 102
fanaticism, 70; abolitionism influenced by, 71, 82–85; affectability and, 170; anti-Tom literature and, 72–73; Black intellectual theories on, 164; Black writers engaging with, 163–64; concepts of, 7; critical analysis of, 7–8; dangers of, 94; Du Bois conveying sense of, 166–67; enthusiasm and, 4, 27, 30, 155–57, 167, 169; as enthusiasm inflamed by hatred, 157; evangelicalism with, 97, 157–61; gloomy, 59–60; human nature corruption in, 9–10; language of, 3, 18, 26, 147–48; line of no return crossed in, 41–42; nature and, 86–87; as overflowing signifier, 170; in Philippines, 2–3, 138–42; physiological disorder resulting in, 101; in *The Planter's Northern Bride*, 78–81; policing of, 128–44; political, 179n7; popularization of, 19; Protestants explaining causes of, 171; Protestant's revivalism in, 13–14; realistic approach to, 173; reductionism in, 171; in religion, 157, 173; religio-racial governance in, 14–15; revenge with, 63–64; revivalism with, 29–30; revivalism with dangerous energies of, 33; secularism with role of, 6–13; secular racial governance of, 15–16; sentimentality in, 75–76; southern climate threatened by, 78–79; sports fandom in, 172; Taylor, I., on, 19, 34, 39–41, 155–56; Taylor, J., on power of, 150; terrorism and, 172; threatening clouds of, 25–26; Turner and, 57–65, 171; in U.S., 5, 13, 161–67; violence in, 4–5, 129, 172; white supremacy challenged by, 166–67; Worcester beliefs on theory of, 171. *See also* religious fanatics
Fanaticism (Taylor, I.), 19, 23, 26, 49, 76, 156
Fanaticism, or Mahomet the Prophet (Voltaire), 180n64

Fanaticism and Its Results, 89
The Fanatic's Daughter (Cowdin), 73, 78, 83
Father Divine's Peace Mission, 14
Fessenden, Tracy, 10, 74
fetishists, Black people as, 112–13
Finney, Charles, 4, 19, 26, 97; Calvinism moved away from by, 30–31; "A Death by Fanaticism" by, 34; on evangelical revivalism, 28–37; performative power of, 31–32; revival argument by, 35, 48; slavery as moral abomination from, 37; Stanton influenced by, 31–32; unintelligent excitement disgusting, 36
First Great Awakening, 3, 41
Fisher, Linford, 179n8
Flag Law (1907), 151
Floyd, John, 65, 67
foreign occupation, 132–33
Four Lectures on Spiritual Christianity (Taylor, I.), 47
free agency, Black people, 81–82
freedom fighter, 171
free will, 36

Gardener, Cornelius, 126
Garfield, James, 20, 91, 93–94
Garrison, William Lloyd, 67
genocide, of Black people, 60
Gladden, Washington, 158
God: communing with, 134; disobedience to, 106; Kingdom of, 56; power of, 35; supernatural dealings with men of, 112; supernatural powers of, 98, 112; Taylor, I., view of only one, 90
government, 10–11; colonial, 141–42, 151; self, 21–22, 120, 127, 160
Graham, Billy, 22
Gray, John, 4, 98–100
Gray, Thomas, 49, 51, 53–54, 58–59
Greyser, Naomi, 77
guerrilla fighters, 131

Guiteau, Charles, 20; background of, 103–4; brother's testimony for, 106; Davidge stating sinfulness of, 107; divine providence beliefs of, 91; family history of, 102; Garfield assassinated by, 93–94; Jesus Christ & Co. employment of, 104; no record of depravity argument by, 105–6; popular hero imagining by, 94; prosecution claims against, 106; religious affections of, 110–11; religious insanity inherited by, 102–4; Spitzka arguing moral monstrosity of, 105; trial and Christianity of, 100–108; trial transcript of, 91–92

Haiti, 22
Haitian Revolution, 60
Halter v. Nebraska (1907), 151
Hamilton, Alexander, 179n7
Hammell, George Milton, 155
Hammond, William, 99
Harding, Vincent, 51, 56
Hart, William D., 166
head-hunters, of Mountain Province, 139
heathenism, 74, 181n79
Hendler, Glenn, 75
Hentz, Caroline Lee, 73, 78, 83–84, 88
hereditary disposition, 92–93, 113–14
heroism, superhuman, 149
Hesse, Barnor, 127–28
higher education, 164–65
Hobbs, H. P., 142
Hobsbawm, Eric, 147
Holy Spirit, 28, 37, 55
Howard, George S., 8, 16
human beings, 46, 160–61, 172–73
human bodies, emotions flowing between, 39–40
humanity, fallenness of, 34
human mind, study of, 114–15
human nature, 107
Hume, David, 126
Hurley, Vic, 2, 130, 146

Iglesia. Santa, 2
Ileto, Reynaldo Clemeña, 129, 145–46
imagination, 33; contagion of sentiments and, 41; excited, 83; fertility of, 54; race shaping, 42–43; religious fanatic's heated, 50; superstition and, 45
imperialism, 5–6, 21, 43, 161–62
impulsive monomania, 99
independence movements, 137
independencia box, 1–2, 146–48
Indigenous nations, 116
Ingersoll, Robert, 93
inner being (*loób* as state of), 146
insanity, 98–99, 104–5, 107, 112–14
insanity defense, 20–21, 92, 100–102; jury instructed on, 108; in *People v. William Freeman*, 111
insanity dodge theory, 101
Insular cases, 188n8
insurrectionaries, 117, 129, 140–41, 147–48
insurrections, 63; slavery demonization in, 68; of Southampton Rebellion, 51–52, 64, 66, 69–70, 85
In the Matter of Nat Turner (Tomlins), 52
Irresistible Impulse Test, 108
Isio, Papa, 2, 119; *anting anting* dispensed by, 141; divine instrument posing by, 133–34, 146; foreign occupation rejected by, 132–33; guerrilla fighters of, 131; Kennon views on, 142; movement futility of, 191n97; as religious rebel, 130–31; strategic violence used by, 133–34; supernatural power claims by, 131, 134; U.S. ally decapitated by, 140; various names of, 130
Islamic faith, 8, 22, 44–45, 181n75

Jakobsen, Janet R., 7
James (1:14–15), 107
James, William, 8
Japan, 22
Jefferson, Thomas, 19, 23, 25–26, 112
Jesus Christ & Co., 104

Jocelyn, Charles, 106
John, fictional story of, 165, 193n31
Johnson, Samuel, 99
Johnson, Sylvester, 15, 43, 113
Jones Bill, 138
Josephson-Storm, Jason, 11, 123
Judah, Samuel B. H., 32–33
jury instructions, 109–10

Kant, Immanuel, 9
Keane, Webb, 17, 127
Kennon, L. W. V., 132, 142
Kidd, Benjamin, 126
Kiernan, James, 107–8, 114–15
Kilgore, John Mac, 158
Kingdom of God, 56
Krag-Jørgensen rifle, 151
Kramer, Paul, 118, 151

Lampley, Karl, 52
language, 3, 18, 144
Laqueur, Walter, 194n4
leadership, of Rios, 137
Li, Darryl, 172
liberation, of Black people, 62–63
liberty, empire of, 26
literature, 73–77, 80–81
Lloyd, Vincent, 15
Locke, John, 9, 126
Locsin, Leandro de la Rama, 132–33
Logan, Dana, 17
loób (state of inner being), 146
love, as Christianity essence, 159
Lovejoy, Owen, 82
Lum, Kathryn Gin, 171
Luther, Martin, 9

Manual for the Philippines Constabulary, 140
materiality, 117–19
Matthew 20:16, 55
Matthews, Robert, 49
Maxfield, Harry, 135

Mazzarella, William, 39
McCoy, Alfred, 134, 191n97
McCrary, Charles, 10, 16
McDowell, James, Jr., 60
McKinley, William, 21, 23, 119, 121
mental disease, 92, 95–97, 103, 112
messianic revolutionary movements, 137
Mexican-American War, 82
militant groups, 116–17
militant messianic figures, 2
military strategies, 2–3
Miller, William, 19
ministers, for Christianity, 69
M'Naghten, Daniel, 108
M'Naghten Test, 108–9
Modern, John, 13, 28, 171
modernity, moral narrative of, 17
monomania, 99, 103
Moody, Dwight, 93, 104–6, 157–59
moral abomination, 37
moral depravity, 99
morally culpable theory, 101
Moral Man and Immoral Society (Niebuhr), 172
moral religion, 46
moral sentiments, 83
moral treatment, 96–97
Morgan, Lewis Henry, 126
Mormonism, 114–15
Moro territories, 124, 188n26
Moro troops, 143
Mountain Province, 139
"Much Madness is divinest Sense" (Dickinson), 173
Muhammad (prophet), 45, 48, 180n64
Murphy, Captain, 144, 146
Mysterious Religious Emotions (Underhill), 33

National Geographic Magazine, 122
national unity, 88
Nation of Islam, 14
Native American Ghost Dance, 120

INDEX | 213

Natural History of Enthusiasm (Taylor, I.), 38
Natural Religion, 46
nature, fanaticism and, 86–87
neurology, 99
New Jerusalem, 1, 135–36, 147
New Model of Christian Missions (Taylor, I.), 46
New Testament, 25, 97
New World A-Coming (Weisenfeld), 14
The Next Great Awakening (Strong), 159
Niebuhr, Reinhold, 172–73
Noll, Mark, 74
Noyes, John Humphrey, 19, 93, 103

Observations on the Influence of Religion (Brigham), 111
Ogden, Emily, 41
Omikron (pseudonym), 76–77
Oneida Community, 103–4
oriental faith, 44
Orsi, Robert, 16–17, 128, 145
Osborn, Sarah, 29
overflowing signifier, 170
Oyos, Rufo, 134

Pablo, Papa, 130
parasitic tree species (*balete*), 153
paternal tenderness, 46–47
patient treatment, 96
Pellegrini, Ann, 7
People v. William Freeman (1847), 111
performative power, 31–32
Philippine-American War, 118, 140, 162
Philippine Commissions, 117, 121, 123–24
Philippine Constabulary, 117, 129–30, 137, 139–40
The Philippine Islands and Their People (Worcester), 124–25
Philippine Revolutionary Army, 121, 135
Philippines: *anting anting* in, 118, 144–45; fanaticism in, 2–3, 138–42; independence movements in, 137; materiality of, 117–19; New Jerusalem in, 1, 135–36, 147; racial inferiority in, 128–29; religion in, 122; religiously inspired rebellions in, 145; Republic of, 116–17; Rios's future vision for, 14; self-government incapability in, 21–22, 120, 127, 160; superstitions in, 141; U.S. colonial governance of, 21; U.S. occupation of, 123; U.S. racial categorization on, 189n27; U.S. relationship with, 119–20; Worcester on civilizing, 137–38; Worcester on material culture of, 144; Worcester's unpopularity in, 138; Worcester visiting, 121
physical impairment, 98
physiological disorder, 101
Pinel, Philippe, 95
The Planter's Northern Bride (Hentz), 73, 78–81, 83–84, 88
"Pluralism" (Howard and Christopherson), 8
politics, 79–80, 179n7
polytheistic religions, 42
Porterfield, Amanda, 25
Powell, John Wesley, 126
"The Preacher in Relation to the New Expansion" (Strong), 159
preachers, Black, 67
Prejudice and Fanaticism (Smith, R.), 73, 79, 88
Preston, Andrew, 158
prophetic powers, 54
Prophet Matthias. *See* Matthews, Robert
Protestantism: Anglo-American, 29; Anglo-Saxon, 42; Catholic Spanish colonial rule and, 120; Christianity's style of, 97–98, 126; evangelicalism and, 4–5, 23, 39, 179n8; fanatical revivalism of, 13–14; fanaticism causes explained by, 171; religion, 13, 43; revivalism needed by, 33–34; state violence and, 22; theology of, 92; U.S. and norms of, 27–28; of white families, 4–5, 75, 85–89

Protestant Reformation, 9
Proverbs 19:2, 157
psychiatric illnesses, 114
psychiatry, 92, 94–95, 100
Puritanical morality, 89

Raboteau, Al, 68
race: Anglo-Saxon, 111; cultures and inferiority of, 128; heredity of, 113–14; imaginations shaped by, 42–43; Philippines inferiority of, 128–29; religio-racial affectability and, 169–70; religio-racial governance and, 14–15; religio-racial human social evolution and, 160; religio-racial theory and, 38–47; secular racial governance and, 15–16; skin color in, 15; U.S. categorizing Filipino/as by, 189n27; U.S. Christian white, 120–21; whiteness in Western philosophy and, 127–28
Rational Self of Man, 161
Rauschenbusch, Walter, 158
reason, 25
religion: abolition as excess in, 80; affections in, 38–39, 110–11; amenomania with elements of, 96–97; *anting anting* with prophetic, 150; anti-Tom literature with slaves and, 84; of Black people, 20, 65; Black people's rebellion in, 67–68; delusions in, 20–21; divine plans in, 65; electricity of, 178n6; fanaticism in, 157, 173; fanatic's heated imagination in, 50; freedom talk, 3; Guiteau's affections for, 110–11; Guiteau's inherited insanity for, 102–4; insanity and, 98–99, 113–14; insanity theory, 101; insurrectionary groups with aspects of, 147; Isio as rebel with, 130–31; leaders of, 130; material culture of, 119; mental health's role with, 95, 97; moral and natural, 46; in Philippines, 122; Philippine's rebellions inspired by, 145; politics mixed with, 79–80; polytheistic, 42; Protestant, 13, 43; psychology of, 41; revivalism generating feelings for, 36–37; Scoville emphasizing ambitions in, 104; sentiments in, 111; Shinto, 22; in slavery, 65–70; Spitzka's views on, 112; supernatural beings and rituals in, 11–12; superstitions and, 123–24; true and false, 113–15; Turner's journey in, 53–54; unmodern, 128; in U.S., 18; U.S. freedom of, 190n43
"Religion and Fanaticism" (Hammell), 155
religio-racial affectability, 169–70
religio-racial governance, 14–15
religio-racial human social evolution, 160
religio-racial theory, 38–47
A Religious Encyclopædia (Schaff), 156
religious fanatics, 12, 89, 173; agitation loved by, 76; Guiteau influenced by excitements of, 104; heated imagination in, 50; insanity similar to, 104–5; military strategies influenced by, 2–3; patient treatment and, 96; radical actions based on divine revelations of, 17; as ungovernable, 76
religious insanity, 29, 110; Guiteau inheriting, 102–4; hereditary disposition and, 92–93; psychological theories of, 115
Revelation 21, 1
revenge, with fanaticism, 63–64
revivalism, 112–13; in antebellum era, 29; dangerous fanatical energies in, 33; energy generated in, 30–31; enthusiastic and fanatical, 29–30; evangelical, 23, 28–37, 169; Finney's argument for, 35, 48; Holy Spirit in, 37; Protestantism needing, 33–34; Protestant's fanaticism in, 13–14; religious feelings in, 36–37; Taylor, I., defending, 169
Reynolds, George, 109
Reynolds v. United States (1879), 109
rhetoric, demonizing, 15
rhetorical strategy, 63–64
rights of conscience, 114

Rios, Ruperto, 1, 116, 119, 130; *anting anting* collection of, 136–37; barrio people superstitions and, 136; capture and execution of, 144; chain of command built by, 138; as charismatic leader, 135; Christian messianic worldview of, 12–13; leadership of, 137; Philippines future vision by, 14; supernatural claims of, 2–3
"Rios Sentenced to Hang" (headline), 2
rituals, 11–12
Roman Catholic Church, 44
Root, Elihu, 132, 152
Rush, Benjamin, 96

sacred Indigenous objects. *See anting anting*
sacred objects, 117
Salem Witchcraft, 80
Salvador, Felipe, 2, 130
Satan, power of, 106
Savage, Barbara Dianne, 164
Schaff, Philip, 156
schwärmer, 9
Scott, David, 130
Scoville, George, 100–104
Seabrook, Whitemarsh B., 68–69
secularism, 6–13, 15, 173
secularizing methodology, 170–71
secular racial governance, 15–16
Sehat, David, 27, 75
self-government, 21–22, 120, 127, 160
sentimentality, 72–77
Seward, William, 111
Shinto religion, 22
Silva, Denise Ferreira da, 16, 178n32
sin, affective power of, 115
sinfulness, 172–73
Sinha, Manisha, 56
skin color, in race, 15
slaveowners, 68
slavery, 6; antislavery rebellion in, 60–61, 64–65; in anti-Tom literature, 86; Black figures rebelling against, 84; Catholic style of domination in, 80; Christianity and, 68–70; insurrections demonization of, 68; in literature, 74–75; as moral abomination, 37; moral sentiments in fight against, 83; religion in, 65–70; as social system, 62; southern climate and, 78–79; Turner on morality of, 58; white northerners against, 72; white people and bonds in, 72, 81–82; white supremacy and, 63
Smith, Joseph, 18, 19
Smith, Rebecca Harrington, 4, 73, 87–88
social effervescence, 149
social equality, 37
social evolution, 160
Social Evolution (Kidd), 126
social movement, 89
social system, 62
The Souls of Black Folk (Du Bois), 164–66
Southampton Rebellion (1831), 50, 56, 60; insurrection of, 51–52, 64, 66, 69–70, 85; Turner mobilizing, 19–20, 85
southern climate, 78–79
sovereignty claims, of U.S., 158
Spanish-American War, 158–59, 188n8
speculative history, 52
Spirit, Turner and appearance of, 55–56
"The Spirit of Fanaticism" (Judah), 32
spiritual beings, 145
spiritually powerful material objects, 118
Spitzka, Charles, 99–100, 105, 112, 114
sports fandom, 172
Stanton, Elizabeth Cady, 31–32
state violence, 22
Stokes, Claudia, 74
Stowe, Harriet Beecher, 20, 72, 75–78, 82, 85
Strong, Josiah, 4, 126, 158–61, 164
suicide bomber, 16
Sullivan, Rodney, 126, 138
superhuman heroism, 149
supernatural beings, 11–12, 25, 150

supernatural powers, 94, 109–10; *of anting anting* objects, 144–45; of God, 98, 112; insurrectionary groups appealing to, 117; Isio claims of, 131, 134; mental disease explained by, 95–96; Rios claims of, 2–3; superstitions and, 127

superstitions: barrio people, 136; of Catholic Church, 44; colonial government targeting, 141–42; imagination and, 45; in Philippines, 141; religion and, 123–24; religious material culture and, 119; supernatural powers and, 127; U.S. military on falsity of, 143–44; Worcester on mentality of, 123–24, 187n5

Supreme Court cases, 100–109, 151, 188n8

Taft, William H., 121–22, 153
Taubes, Tanaquil, 95
Taves, Ann, 3, 26, 29
Taylor, Isaac, 4, 126, 164, 181n75; Catholicism and Islam condemned by, 44–45; Christianity and passionate violence from, 46; Christianity's paternal tenderness from, 46–47; evangelicalism and, 19, 28; on fanaticism, 19, 34, 39–41, 155–56; *Fanaticism* by, 19, 23, 26, 49, 76, 156; *Four Lectures on Spiritual Christianity* by, 47; *Natural History of Enthusiasm* by, 38; *New Model of Christian Missions* by, 46; only one God, 90; on religio-racial theory, 38–47; religious affections books by, 38–39; on renewed Christian mission, 47; revivalism defended by, 169; *Ultimate Civilization* by, 42; white evangelicalism influence shown by, 28; white-supremacists terms used by, 42–43

Taylor, John, 133, 150
terrorism, 172
Theological Account of Nat Turner (Lampley), 52
theological crisis, 74
theology, of Protestantism, 92

Thomas Jefferson's Letter to the Danbury Baptists (1802), 109
Tomlins, Christopher, 52
Toscano, Alberto, 47
Treatise on Insanity (Pinel), 95
Treaty of Paris (1898), 119
trial transcript, of Guiteau, 91–92
tulisan (bandit leader), 124–25
Turner, Nat, 4; biblical literacy of, 67; black and white spirits vision of, 54–55; blood of Christ and, 55; Christianity knowledge of, 62; Cobb presiding over trial of, 64; *The Confessions of Nat Turner* by, 49, 51–53; fanaticism and, 57–65, 171; as freedom fighter, 171; insurrection centering, 63; religious journey of, 53–54; slavery's morality from, 58; Southampton Rebellion mobilized by, 19–20, 85; Spirit appearing to, 55–56; terror and awe provoked by, 58–59; violent actions of, 71

Twain, Mark, 162

Ultimate Civilization (Taylor, I.), 42
Uncle Tom's Cabin (Stowe), 20, 72, 75–76
Underground Railroad, 82
Underhill, Samuel, 33
unintelligent excitement, 36
United States (U.S.): *anting anting* object wearers targeted by, 142–43; Army song of, 151; Christian white race in, 120–21; fanaticism in, 5, 13, 161–67; global imperialism of, 161–62; Indigenous nation expansion of, 116; insurrectionaries battle with, 140–41; insurrectionaries resisting colonial rule of, 148; Isio's decapitation of allies of, 140; militant messianic figures against rule by, 2; military on falsity of superstition, 143–44; Philippines categorization of race by, 189n27; Philippines' colonial governance by, 21; Philippines occupied by, 123; Philippines' relation-

ship with, 119–20; Protestant norms in, 27–28; religions in, 18; religious freedom in, 190n43; sovereignty claims made by, 158; white colonial administration of, 187n4

United States v. Charles J. Guiteau, 20, 91, 99–101

universal secular reason, 10

unmodern religion, 128

unregulated self, 9

violence: against Black people, 66; Christianity and passionate, 46; in fanaticism, 4–5, 129, 172; Isio using strategic, 133–34; Protestantism and state, 22; Turner's actions using, 71; in white supremacy, 48

Voltaire, 180n64

War on Terror, 3

"War Prayer" (Twain), 162

Washington, George, 88, 148

weaponization, *of anting anting* objects, 153

Webster, Noah, 59

Weisenfeld, Judith, 14–15, 112–13

Wenger, Tisa, 3, 120, 190n43

Western Christendom, 9

Western philosophy, 127–28

Western psychiatry, 94–95

Wheatley, Phillis, 29

White, John, 141–42, 146–47

white and black spirits, 54–55

white Christian supremacy, 57

Whitefield, George, 29

white-nationalist propaganda, 50

whiteness, of Western philosophy, 127–28

white northerners, 72, 80–82

white people: anti-Black violence by, 66; Black people getting sentimental energy of, 86; Christianity governed by, 78; Christianity in families of, 73–74; legislators, 66; slavery and bonds with, 72, 81–82; unity, 88; U.S. colonial administration made up of, 187n4

white Protestants, 4–5, 75, 85–89

white supremacy: Black people and, 162–63; evangelicalism and, 5–6; fanaticism challenging, 166–67; slavery and, 63; Taylor, I., using terminology of, 42–43; violence in, 48; Worcester using theories of, 125–26

willpower, 16

Wilmore, Gayraud S., 162

Wilson, Woodrow, 138

women, 2, 143

Worcester, Dean, 4, 119; administrative positions of, 122; American flag toast by, 152; Black people doomed to extinction from, 126; fanaticism theory beliefs of, 171; on Filipino material culture, 144; on insurrectionaries, 140; *The Philippine Islands and Their People* by, 124–25; on Philippines being civilized, 137–38; on Philippines' material culture, 144; Philippines unpopularity of, 138; Philippines visited by, 121; powerful *anting anting* of, 124–25; superstitious mentality of, 123–24, 187n5; white-supremacist theories used by, 125–26

Wright, Luke, 117, 130

Wynter, Sylvia, 160–61

ABOUT THE AUTHOR

JEFFREY WHEATLEY is Assistant Professor in the Department of Philosophy and Religious Studies at Iowa State University. He teaches courses on American religious history, popular culture, and game design. He received his M.A. from Florida State University and his Ph.D. from Northwestern University. He was a member of the Young Scholars of American Religion cohort for 2023–2025. To support research in this book, he received an American Academy of Religion Grant in 2024. That year he was also awarded the LAS Cassling Family Faculty Award for Early Achievement in Teaching. In 2025 he was a founding faculty member for the Game Design Major at Iowa State University.

www.ingramcontent.com/pod-product-compliance
Ingram Content Group UK Ltd.
Pitfield, Milton Keynes, MK11 3LW, UK
UKHW040610060326
468667UK00008B/268